Translation and Technology

C.K. Quah

palgrave
macmillan

First published 2006 by
PALGRAVE MACMILLAN
Houndmills, Basingstoke, Hampshire RG21 6XS and
175 Fifth Avenue, New York, N.Y. 10010
Companies and representatives throughout the world

PALGRAVE MACMILLAN is the global academic imprint of the Palgrave
Macmillan division of St. Martin's Press, LLC and of Palgrave Macmillan Ltd.
Macmillan® is a registered trademark in the United States, United Kingdom
and other countries. Palgrave is a registered trademark in the European
Union and other countries. /O 06543938

ISBN-13: 978-1-4039-1831-4 hardback
ISBN-10: 1-4039-1831-7 hardback
ISBN-13: 978-1-4039-1832-1 paperback
ISBN-10: 1-4039-1832-5 paperback

This book is printed on paper suitable for recycling and made from fully
managed and sustained forest sources. Logging, pulping and manufacturing
processes are expected to conform to the environmental regulations of the
country of origin.

A catalogue record for this book is available from the British Library.

A catalog record for this book is available from the Library of Congress.

Printed and bound in Great Britain by
CPI Antony Rowe, Chippenham and Eastbourne

For Paul

Contents

List of Figures, Tables and Boxes

Figures

Tables

Boxes

Series Editors' Preface

Recent years have witnessed momentous changes in the study of Modern Languages, globally as well as nationally. On the one hand, the rapid growth of English as a universal *lingua franca* has rendered the command of other languages a less compelling commodity. On the other hand, the demand for intercultural mediators including translators and interpreters has grown as a result of many recent social, political and economic developments; these include legislative changes, the emergence of supranational organisations, the ease of travel, telecommunications, commercial pressures raising awareness of local needs, migration and employment mobility, and a heightened awareness of linguistic and human rights. Today, linguistically oriented students wishing to pursue a career in which they are able to further their interest in languages and cultures would be more inclined to choose vocationally relevant courses in which translation and interpreting play an important part rather than traditional Modern Language degrees.

Thus the possibilities for professional work in translation and interpreting have been extended, particularly as a result of developments in technology, whether as facilitating the translation process or as a means of dissemination and broadening access to communications in a range of media. The role of translation is, for example, becoming increasingly important in the context of modern media such as television and cinema, whether for documentary or entertainment purposes. And the technological possibilities for providing interpreting services, whether to the police officer on the beat or to the businessperson on a different continent, have extended the previously physically confined nature of mediating the spoken word.

Not only do these new vistas open up opportunities for the professional linguist, they also point to expanding areas of research in Translation and Interpreting Studies. Practice and theory are of mutual benefit, especially in the case of a relatively young discipline such as Translation Studies. As a result, the first aim of this series, written primarily for the MA and advanced undergraduate student, is to highlight contemporary issues and concerns in order to provide informed, theoretically based, accounts of developments in translation and interpretation. The second aim is to provide ready access for students interested in the study and pursuit of Modern Languages to vocational issues which are of relevance to the contemporary world of translating and interpreting. The final aim is to offer informed updates to practising professionals on recent developments in the field impacting on their discipline.

Linguistic, Culture and Translation Studies Gunilla Anderman
University of Surrey Margaret Rogers
Guildford
UK

Acknowledgements

I am indebted to three individuals for their contributions. This book would have taken more time to complete if it had not been for Chooi Tsien Yeo who researched background information for me. Words cannot express my gratitude to Stephen Moore, in between translation deadlines, for putting his experiences as a professional translator into writing. I am extremely indebted to Paul Marriott for his comments and suggestions, particularly on helping to visualize a new way to depict the multidimensional classification of translation types in Chapter 7.

I would like to acknowledge especially the Duke University Libraries and Institute of Statistics and Decision Science at Duke University in providing me with the environment and research facilities where most of this book was written. Also my thanks to the National University of Singapore Libraries, George Edward Library at the University of Surrey, and the Department of Statistics and Actuarial Science at the University of Waterloo for their help.

I would also like to acknowledge the following authors, publishers and organizations for allowing the use of copyright material in this book: John Hutchins, Harold Somers and Elsevier (Academic Press Ltd) for the classification of translation types in Chapter 1; Eugene Nida and the Linguistic Society of America for the translation process in Chapter 2; John Smart and Smart Communications, Inc. for the controlled and simplified English samples in Chapter 2; Francis Bond and Takefumi Yamazaki for the KAMI Malay–English dictionary entry in Chapter 3; Paolo Dongilli and Johann Gamper for the building of a parallel corpus in Chapter 4; Tony Jewtushenko and Peter Reynolds of OASIS for XLIFF in Chapter 4; Enrique de Argaez at Internet World Stats for the statistical figure on the Internet population in Chapter 6; Michael Carl, Reinhard Schäler, Andy Way, Springer Science and Business Media, and Kluwer Academic Publishers for the model of the future use of translation technology in Chapter 6. To António Ribeiro, Tessadit Lagab, Margaret Rogers and Chooi Tsien Yeo, my most sincere thanks for translating from English into Portuguese, French, German and Chinese respectively. I am solely responsible for any translation errors that occurred. A special thank you goes to Elsie Lee, Shaun Yeo, Angeliki Petrits, Mirko Plitt and Ken Seng Tan for answering some of my queries.

To Caroline, Elizabeth, Gillian and Lyndsay, thank you for helping out with keying in corrections on the earlier drafts. Lastly, to my '*sifu*' and friend Peter Newmark, a big thank-you for all the translation discussions we had during our coffee–biscuit sessions years ago.

If it had not been for the series editors, Gunilla Anderman and Margaret Rogers, this book would not have been written. I am forever grateful to both of them for their feedback and comments. Thanks to Jill Lake of Palgrave Macmillan for her patience and understanding due to my 'country-hopping' from Southeast Asia to North America during the writing of this book.

Waterloo, Canada CHIEW KIN QUAH

List of Abbreviations

ACRoTERMITE	Terminology of Telecommunications
AECMA	European Association of Aerospace Industries
AIA	Aerospace Industries Association of America
ALPAC	Automatic Language Processing Advisory Committee
ALPS	Automatic Language Processing System
ALT-J/C	Automatic Language Translator Japanese to Chinese
ALT-J/E	Automatic Language Translator Japanese to English
ALT-J/M	Automatic Language Translator Japanese to Malay
AMTA	Association of Machine Translation in the Americas
ASCC	Automatic Spelling Checker Checker
ASD	AeroSpace and Defence
ATA	American Translators Association
BASIC	British American Scientific International, Commercial
BLEU	Bilingual Evaluation Understudy
BSO	Buro voor Systeemontwikkeling
CAT	Computer-Aided Translation
CAT2	Constructors, Atoms and Translators
CESTA	Campagne d'Evaluation de Systèmes de Traduction Automatique
CFE	Caterpillar Fundamental English
CIA	Central Intelligence Agency
CICC	Center of International Cooperation for Computerization
CRATER	Corpus Resources and Terminology Extraction
CTE	Caterpillar Technical English
CULT	Chinese University Language Translator
DARPA	Defense Advanced Research Projects Agency
DBMT	Dialogue-based Machine Translation
DIPLOMAT	Distributed Intelligent Processing of Language for Operational Machine Aided Translation
DLT	Distributed Language Translation
DTS	Descriptive Translation Studies
EAGLES	Expert Advisory Group on Language Engineering Standards
EARS	Effective, Affordable Reusable Speech-to-Text
EDIG	European Defence Industries Group

ELDA	Evaluations and Language resources Distribution Agency
ELRA	European Language Resources Association
ENGSPAN	English Spanish Machine Translation System
ENIAC	Electronic Numerical Integrator and Computer
EURODICAUTUM	European Terminology Database
EUROSPACE	Aerospace and Defence Industries Association of Europe
EUROTRA	European Translation
EVALDA	Infrastructure d'EVALuation à ELDA
EWG	Evaluation Working Group
FAHQT/FAHQMT	Fully Automatic High Quality (Machine) Translation
FEMTI	A Framework for the Evaluation of Machine Translation in ISLE
GENETER	Generic Model for Terminology
GETA	Groupe d'Étude pour la Traduction Automatique
HAMT	Human-Aided/Assisted Machine Translation
HICATS	Hitachi Computer Aided Translation System
HT	Human Translation
HTML	HyperText Markup Language
IAMT	International Association of Machine Translation
IATE	Inter-Agency Terminology Exchange
INTERSECT	International Sample of English Contrastive Texts
ISI	International Statistical Institute
ISLE	International Standards for Language Engineering
ISO	International Organization for Standardization
JEIDA	Japan Electronic Industry Development Association
JEITA	Japan Electronics and Information Technology Association
JICST-E	Japan Information Center of Science and Technology
KAMI	Kamus Melayu-Inggeris (Malay-English Dictionary)
KANT	Knowledge-based Accurate Translation
KGB	Komitet Gosudarstvennoi Bezopasnosti
LDC	Linguistic Data Consortium
LISA	Localisation Industry and Standards Association
LMT	Logic-based Machine Translation
LTC	Language Technology Centre
LTRAC	Language Translation Resources Automatic Console
MAHT	Machine-Aided/Assisted Human Translation
MANTRA	Machine Assisted Translation
MARTIF	Machine Readable Terminology Interchange Format

MASTOR	Multilingual Automatic Speech-to-Speech Translator
MAT	Machine-Aided/Assisted Translation
METAL	Mechanical Translation and Analysis of Language
METU	Middle East Technical University
MLIR	MultiLingual Information Retrieval
MT	Machine Translation
NAATI	National Accreditation Authority for Translators and Interpreters Ltd.
NIST	National Institute of Standards and Technology
OASIS	Organization for the Advancement of Structured Information Standards
OCP	Oxford Concordance Programme
OCR	Optical Character Recognition
OLIF	Open Lexicon Interchange Format
OS	Operating System
OSCAR	Open Standards for Container/Content Allowing Re-use
PaTrans	Patent Translation
PAHO	Pan-American Health Organization
PDA	Personal Digital Assistant
PESA	Portuguese-English Sentence Alignment
RDF	Resource Description Framework
RFC	Request for Comments
SALT	Standards-based Access to Lexicographical & Terminological Multilingual Resources
SGML	Standard Generalised Markup Language
SPANAM	Spanish American Machine Translation System
SUSY	Saarbrücker ÜbersetzungsSYstem
SYSTRAN	System Translation
TAP	Think-Aloud Protocols
TAUM	Traduction automatique à l'Université de Montréal
TBX	TermBase eXchange
TEMAA	Testbed Study of Evaluation Methodologies: Authoring Aids
TGT-1	Text-into-Gesture Translator
THETOS	Text into Sign Language Automatic Translator for Polish
TMF	Terminological Markup Framework
TMX	Translation Memory eXchange
TOLL	Thai On-Line Library
TONGUES	Act II Audio Voice Translation Guide Systems
TS	Translation Studies
TTS	Theoretical Translation Studies

WebDIPLOMAT	Web Distributed Intelligent Processing of Language for Operational Machine Aided Translation
WebOnt	Web Ontology
WWW	World Wide Web
W3C	WWW Consortium
XLIFF	XML Localisation Interchange File Format
XLT	XML Representation of Lexicons and Terminologies
XML	Extensible or Extensive Markup Language

Introduction

For over half a century, the demand for a variety of translations by different groups of end-users has enabled many types of translation tools to be developed. This is reflected in the systems that will be discussed in this book, ranging from machine translation systems, computer-aided translation tools and translation resources. The majority of books and articles on translation technology focusing on the development of these systems and tools have been written from the point of view of researchers and developers. More recent publications written with translators in mind have focused on the use of particular tools.

This book is intended as an introduction to translation technology for students of translation. It can also be useful to professional translators and those interested in knowing about translation technology. A different approach is taken in that descriptions of particular tools are not provided, and the development of different machine translation and computer-aided translation tools and their uses are discussed. Programming details and mathematical equations are not considered, except in the discussion of the statistical approach to machine translation where minimal essential formulae are included. Descriptions are given to allow readers to further investigate specific approaches or issues that might interest them, using references cited throughout the book. It is also important to note that no particular approach or design is deemed to be better than any other. Each and every one has their strengths and weaknesses. In many cases, readers will find that examples of systems and tools are given but this does not suggest that they are the best; they are simply examples to illustrate the points made.

While researching this book, I discovered that the majority of publications from the literature on translation technology are about the development of machine translation systems, primarily involving experimental systems developed or being developed at a number of universities and large commercial corporations across the globe. The book will show that many of these systems never achieved their commercial potential and remained as experimental tools, while some others served as tools for other natural-language processing applications. By contrast, not much literature seems to be available on computer-aided tools such as translation memory systems. As we shall see in this book, most computer-aided translation tools are developed by commercial companies and, as a result, progress reports on these tools are rarely published in the public domain. Furthermore, to cater to different needs and demands, a tool like a translation memory system comes in many versions from the most basic to the most advanced. Insights into the use of these tools can be found in translator magazines and occasionally also posted on the World Wide Web (WWW).

The evaluation of translation tools falls into a field that is well-researched. Again we will see that most of the literature focuses on the evaluation of machine translation systems. Furthermore, the extensive use of translation tools and translation processes involved in the localization industry tend to be discussed separately, giving the impression that they are not related to translation. These two areas are, however, directly relevant to translation technology. Hence they are also included in this book.

Essentially, the book contains what is felt should be included in order to provide an overview of translation technology. In order to keep the book at the given length, the topics have been carefully selected with some described in greater detail than others. In some chapters, an abbreviated historical background has been deemed necessary in order to provide a better understanding of the topics discussed, especially in the description of the development of machine translation systems and their evaluation. However, in all cases, references have been provided which readers may choose to pursue at a later time. Suggestions for further reading are provided at the end of every chapter (Chapters 1 to 6).

The first chapter discusses the definitions of terms referring to the use of computers in translation activities. Some of the terms can be confusing to anyone who is unfamiliar with translation tools. In some cases, the same translation tools are given different names depending on what they are used for; in other cases, a tool may be differently classified depending on the perspective of those who have developed that tool.

The aim in this chapter is therefore to clarify these terminological and related matters. An alternative perspective to the four basic translation types – fully automated high-quality machine translation, human-aided machine translation, machine-aided human translation, and human translation – first proposed by Hutchins and Somers (1992) is introduced to reflect current developments in translation technology. This will be explored in more detail in the final chapter where the four translation types are reviewed in relation to topics described in the book.

The second chapter discusses technology within the larger framework of Translation Studies as a discipline, focusing on the relationship between the engineering of translation technology, on the one hand, and Translation Studies including translation theory, on the other hand. The relationship between academic and professional groups involved in translation is also examined. This in turn leads to a discussion of the involvement of a particular approach in linguistic theories – known as 'formalisms' in natural-language processing – especially in the design of machine translation systems. A different perspective on the translation process involving pre- and post-editing tasks using a special variety of language called 'controlled language' is also presented. This translation process is described using the translation model proposed by Jakobson (1959/2000), a translation model that differs significantly from the one proposed by Nida (1969).

The third chapter gives detailed descriptions of different machine translation system designs also known as 'architectures'. The development of machine translation over several decades, its capabilities and the different types of machine translation systems, past and present, are also included. Both experimental and commercial systems are discussed, although the focus is on the experimental systems. Even though machine translation has been well-documented elsewhere, a discussion is deemed to be important for this book. It is felt that modern-day professional translators should be informed about machine translation systems because there is every reason to believe, as we shall discover in Chapter 6, that future trends in translation technology are moving towards integrated systems where at least one translation tool is combined with another, as is already the case in the integration of machine translation with translation memory.

The fourth chapter describes the architectures and uses of several computer-aided translation tools, such as translation memory systems, as well as resources such as parallel corpora. Unlike machine translation systems, which are largely developed by universities, most computer-aided translation tools are developed by commercial companies. Thus, information about such tools is harder to obtain. This chapter will also show that computer-aided translation tools are becoming more advanced and using different operating systems, and so 'standards for data interchange' have been created. Three different standards are described. Currently available commercial translation tools are also discussed. In addition, this chapter presents an overview of other commercially available tools such as those used in the localization industry.

The fifth chapter touches on the evaluation of translation technology. The discussion focuses on different groups of stakeholders from research sponsors to end-users. Also included in the discussion are the different methods of evaluation: human, machine, and a combination of human and machine as evaluator. The choice of method used depends on who the evaluation is for and its purpose. It also depends on whether an entire tool or only some components are evaluated. Also described in this chapter is the general framework of evaluation offered by various research groups in the USA and Europe. The literature on evaluation concentrates on the evaluation of machine translation systems either during the developmental stage or after the process of development is completed. Less information is available on the evaluation of computer-aided translation tools. What is available is found mainly in translation journals, magazines and newsletters.

The sixth chapter presents some recent developments and shows the direction in which translation technology is heading, in particular regarding the future of machine translation systems that are now incorporating speech technology features. The integration of speech technology and traditional machine translation systems allows translation not only between texts or between stretches of speech, but also between text and speech. This integration is proving to be useful in many specific situations around the globe especially in international relations and trade. This chapter also looks at research projects in countries that are involved in the development of translation tools for minority languages and discusses the problems encountered in developing machine translation systems for languages that are less well-known and not widely spoken. Another form of technology called the 'Semantic Web' that has the potential to improve the performance of certain machine translation systems is also described. Included in this chapter, too, are issues such as linguistic dominance and translation demands on the WWW that are already shaping parts of the translation industry.

The book concludes by presenting an expanded version of the four basic classifications of translation types as suggested by Hutchins and Somers (1992) and introduced in Chapter 1. It is concluded that the one-dimensional linear continuum originally proposed is no longer able to accurately reflect current developments in translation technology. Translation tools today come in different versions and types depending on the purposes for which they are built. Some are multifunctional while others remain monofunctional. An alternative way must therefore be found to depict the complexities and multidimensional relationships between the four translation types and the topics discussed in this book. It is not possible to put every single subject discussed here into one diagram or figure, and so, in order to gain a better understanding of how the issues are related to one another, they are divided into groups. Topics or issues in each group have a common theme that links them together, and are presented in a series of tables. However, it is important to bear in mind that not all topics can be presented neatly and easily even in this way. This clearly shows the complexity and multidimensionality of translation activities in the modern technological world.

At the end of the book, several Appendices provide information on the various Internet sites for many different translation tools and translation support tools such as monolingual, bilingual, trilingual and multilingual dictionaries, glossaries, thesauri and encyclopaedia. Only a selected few are listed here, and as a result the lists are not exhaustive. It is also important to note that some Internet sites may not be permanent; at the time of the writing, every effort has been made to ensure that all sites are accessible.

1
Definition of Terms

In translation technology, terms commonly used to describe translation
tools are as follows:

- machine translation (MT);
- machine-aided/assisted human translation (MAHT);
- human-aided/assisted machine translation (HAMT);
- computer-aided/assisted translation (CAT);
- machine-aided/assisted translation (MAT);
- fully automatic high-quality (machine) translation (FAHQT/FAHQMT).

Distinctions between some of these terms are not always clear. For
example, computer-aided translation (CAT) is often the term used in
Translation Studies (TS) and the localization industry (see the second
part of this chapter), while the software community which develops
this type of tool prefers to call it 'machine-aided translation' (MAT). As
the more familiar term among professional translators and in the field
of Translation Studies, 'computer-aided translation' is used throughout
the book to represent both computer-aided translation and machine-aided
translation tools, and the term 'aided' is chosen instead of 'assisted', as
also in 'human-aided machine translation' and 'machine-aided human
translation'.

Figure 1.1 distinguishes four types of translation relating human and
machine involvement in a classification along a linear continuum
introduced by Hutchins and Somers (1992: 148). This classification,
now more than a decade old, will become harder to sustain as more
tools become multifunctional, as we shall see in Chapters 3, 4 and 6.
Nevertheless, the concept in Figure 1.1 remains useful as a point of
reference for classifying translation in relation to technology.

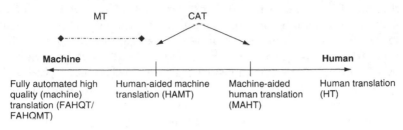

MT = machine translation; CAT = computer-aided translation

Figure 1.1 Classification of translation types
Source: Hutchins and Somers (1992): 148.

The initial goal of machine translation was to build a fully automatic high-quality machine translation that did not require any human intervention. At a 1952 conference, however, Bar-Hillel reported that building a fully automatic translation system was unrealistic and years later still remained convinced that a fully automatic high-quality machine translation system was essentially unattainable (Bar-Hillel 1960/2003: 45). Instead, what has emerged in its place is machine translation, placed between FAHQT and HAMT on the continuum of Figure 1.1. The main aim of machine translation is still to generate translation automatically, but it is no longer required that the output quality is high, rather that it is fit-for-purpose (see Chapters 2 and 3).

As for human-aided machine translation and machine-aided human translation, the boundary between these two areas is especially unclear. Both classes are considered to be computer-aided translation as indicated in Figure 1.1 (Tong 1994: 4,730; see also Slocum 1988; Hutchins and Somers 1992). However, in Schadek and Moses (2001), a different classification has been proposed where only machine-aided human translation is viewed as synonymous with computer-aided translation. Human-aided machine translation is considered as a separate category. The reasoning behind the view offered by Schadek and Moses is not difficult to understand. At least theoretically, the difference between the two is obvious. For human-aided machine translation, the machine is the principal translator, while in machine-aided human translation it is a human. In practice, however, it may be less easy today to draw a distinguishable boundary between them. The blurring of boundaries is further complicated when human-aided machine translation is considered as a subclass of machine translation, an approach chosen by Chellamuthu (2002). Since human-aided machine translation has the machine as the principal translator – a feature that is closer to machine translation than to machine-aided human translation – it makes little sense to include it under the category of computer-aided translation. Consequently, this book adopts the distinction suggested by Schadek and Moses (2001) in which machine-aided human translation is synonymous with computer-aided translation and human-aided machine translation is a class on its own.

A decade ago most tools could have been placed in these individual classes. A linear continuum, however, is no longer suitable for describing many integrated systems of today as they contain features from more than one class (see Chapter 6). An alternative way of presenting the current state of translation technology is now required. As implied by the linear continuum, these four translation types are not entirely separate and distinct, and they now share many more similarities than when they were first presented by Hutchins and Somers.

Table 1.1 An example of a table for describing translation types

	MT	HAMT	CAT	HT
Topic A				
Topic B				

MT = machine translation; HAMT = human-aided machine translation; CAT = computer-aided translation HT = human translation;

One way of presenting these changes is to use a series of tables in order to show the relationship of these four translation types with the topics discussed in this book, as illustrated in principle in Table 1.1, where the four translation types are reviewed in relation to selected groups of topics. The series of tables will be described in detail in Chapter 7 when all relevant topics have been discussed. Each table adopts a different perspective in order to show different kinds of relationship with respect to translation and technology.

Machine translation

The term 'machine translation' itself can be misleading. It has a long history and, as a result, many interpretations. The term originally referred only to automatic systems with no human involvement (Sager 1994: 326). The European Association of Machine Translation defines it as 'the application of computers to the task of translating texts from one natural language to another' (http://www.eamt.org/mt.html) while the International Association of Machine Translation (IAMT) defines machine translation as taking 'input in the form of full sentences at a time [*sic*] and generating corresponding full sentences (not necessarily of good quality)' (Hutchins 2000a). These definitions are essentially variants of the same concept focusing on source or 'input-language' texts and target or 'output-language' texts.

Neither of the definitions above includes human intervention. Others, such as Arnold *et al.* (1994: 1), mention some form of human intervention: 'the attempt to automate all *or part of* the process of translating from one human language to another' (my italics). When some form of human intervention is mentioned in a definition, it often becomes 'murky' (Balkan 1992: 408). This view is echoed by Archer (2002: 100), according to whom scholars and researchers still disagree on the definition of machine translation with respect to the involvement of humans. However, since no other term has been forthcoming, it continues to be used to refer to systems that are fully automated as well as those with human involvement (Somers 2003b: 1). Figure 1.2 shows how a source-language text can be processed by a machine translation system. If the target text is produced automatically there is no human intervention; however, human intervention may be employed before, during and/or after machine translation (see also Arnold *et al.* 1994).

Further distinctions are also made. A machine translation system, according to Hutchins (2000a), can be classified as operating on one of

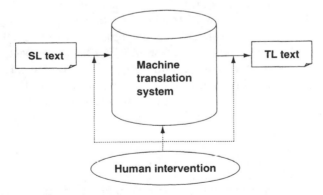

SL = source language; TL = target language

Figure 1.2 Machine translation model

three levels: basic, standard or advanced, each level having its own detailed technical definition given by the IAMT based on the size of the dictionaries and the syntactic analysis used.

A basic-level system typically has the following characteristics. It

- has less than 50,000 entries in its largest dictionary,
- has restricted dictionary expansion,
- is restricted to single-clause/basic sentence translations, and
- is suitable for home use.

A standard level system typically has the following characteristics. It

- has more than 50,000 entries in its largest dictionary,
- allows dictionary expansion,
- allows more than single-clause/basic sentence translations, and
- is suitable for home use and stand-alone office use.

An advanced level system typically has the following characteristics. It

- has more than 75,000 entries in its smallest dictionary,
- allows dictionary expansion,
- allows more than single-clause/basic sentence translations, and
- is suitable for offices with networked facilities.

Dictionaries as well as syntactic analysis and synthesis components are important parts of a machine translation system (see Chapter 3). The size of the dictionaries and the capabilities of the syntactic analysis and synthesis components generally indicate how good a system is. However, the levels indicated above may not necessarily be reflected in commercial systems (Hutchins 2000a). An alternative perspective based on usage is offered in the compendium compiled by Hutchins, Hartmann and Ito (2004) and shown in Figure 1.3. The type labelled 'Home' refers to machine translation systems for home users who have few or no translation skills. The second type of machine translation labelled

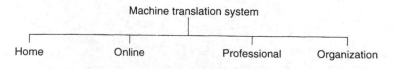

Figure 1.3 Machine translation system based on usage

'Online' is designed specifically for the translation of electronic documents obtained from the Web. The third type is designed for professional translators, and the last for employees of large companies.

Examples of successful commercial machine translation systems include SPANAM (Spanish American) and ENGSPAN (English Spanish), which were developed by the Pan American Health Organization (PAHO). Since 1980, both systems have processed over 70 million words (see http://www.paho.org/english/AGS/MT/Machine_Trans.htm). These two systems are licensed to public and commercial organizations in North America, Latin America and Europe. In contrast, examples of experimental machine translation systems include the ALT-J/E (Automatic Language Translator Japanese to English), and ALT-J/C (Automatic Language Translator Japanese to Chinese) systems, both developed by Nippon Telegraph and Telephone Corporation (NTT).

Human-aided machine translation

A generally accepted view of human-aided machine translation is 'a system wherein the computer is responsible for producing the translation *per se*, but may interact with a human monitor at many stages along the way' (Slocum 1988: 5). In other words, the machine carries out most of the work but it might need human assistance either at the text-preparation stage or the output stage. The former process is known as 'pre-editing' and the latter 'post-editing'. The main task of pre-editing is to discover any elements such as odd phrases or idioms and typographical errors that may create problems for the machine translation system during the translation process. The human editor or translator amends the source-language text accordingly. Post-editing involves correcting the translation output generated by the machine translation system, a task performed by the human editor or translator in order to bring the text to a certain pre-determined standard in terms of language style and appropriate use of terms. These processes will be described in further detail in Chapter 2. Human intervention is also possible during the translation stage – when prompted by the system – to provide appropriate equivalents for ambiguous or unknown terms. Figure 1.4 shows where human intervention [H] is possible.

Many human-aided machine translation systems are designed to operate on a limited number of types of source-language texts, for example, those written with a restricted grammar and vocabulary in a so-called 'controlled language' (see Chapter 2). This limitation on the types of text used as input to the system is similar to that on inputs to

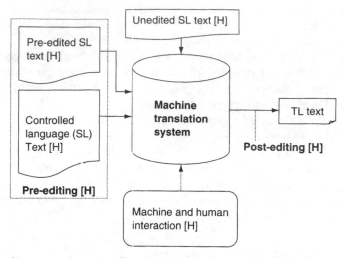

SL = source language; TL = target language; H = human

Figure 1.4   Human-aided machine translation model

machine translation, for example, technical texts such as legal briefs, manuals and laboratory reports are particularly suitable. A source-language text may come in different forms: pre-edited, controlled or unedited (see Figure 1.4). As we have seen, a pre-edited text is one that has been edited by a human, in most cases by someone other than the author, prior to the translation process, whereas a controlled-language text is usually written following certain strict linguistic rules. Sometimes, a source-language text can also be edited using the controlled-language vocabulary and linguistic rules. Ideally, pre-edited and controlled-language texts are free from ambiguity and complex sentences. Unedited text, on the other hand, has had no editing prior to translation. For systems that have an interactive mode, a human is allowed to correct or select appropriate equivalents during the automatic translation process (see Chapter 3). Otherwise, corrections can only be performed at the post-editing stage, which is after the machine translation system has produced the translation.

The literature on human-aided machine translation is very limited. The reason for this is that the difference between this category and full machine translation is blurred since some definitions of machine translation also allow for human translators to carry out pre- and post-editing, as indicated earlier. Examples of human-aided machine translation systems are MaTra Pro and Litc developed at the National Centre for Software Technology based in Mumbai, India, that translate from English into Hindi. Human-aided machine translation systems have been implemented at Schreiber Translations, Inc., Foreign Language Services, Inc. and Ralph McElroy Translation Company, all companies that are employed to translate patents for the United States (US) Patent and Trademark Office.

Machine-aided human translation

Machine-aided human translation has been described as the use of computer software by translators 'to perform part of the process of translation' (Sager 1994: 326). Integrated machine-aided human translation systems are sometimes known as 'workbenches' or 'work-stations', as they combine a number of tools. These are described in Chapter 4. Below, Figure 1.5 shows that the focus in this type of translation is on the human translator, who uses an assortment of tools such as spell-checkers, electronic glossaries, electronic diction-aries, terminology databases and collections of previously translated texts and their originals, that is translation 'memory', to support the translation process.

Some examples of commercial machine-aided human translation systems are the Translator's Workbench by Trados GmbH, Transit by Star AG, SDLX Translation Suite by SDL International and Déjà Vu by Atril.

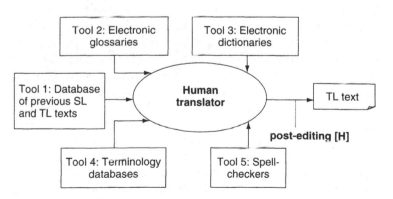

SL = source language; TL = target language; H = human

Figure 1.5 Machine-aided human translation model

Human translation

Nowadays, it is common to find professional translators using some kind of computer-aided translation tool in their work. A description of such a modern-day human translator at work is presented here, written specifically for this book by a professional translator based in Singapore and Sydney, Stephen Moore, who translates between English and Japanese. With Moore's permission, his piece was edited; explanations have been added in square brackets for further clarification. His description of a modern-day translator at work is as shown in Box 1.1.

The account is from a translator who is highly computer literate and willing to learn to use new tools in order to improve his translation service. His attitude guarantees that he is not being left behind in the competitive environment of securing translation jobs. This may not necessarily be the case for every translator. Researchers such as Gaspari (2001), Yuste Rodrigo (2001) and Bowker (2002) have discussed resistance

---

Box 1.1 A translator at work

I have registered with a number of agencies for the language pair of Japanese and English specializing in the chemical-related field. Various companies and organizations in the chemical industry also know my capabilities due to my work as a journalist in this area and have been working with me on a regular basis for some time. Part of my regular work involves translation of newspaper articles on a daily basis. I receive Word documents via email in the late afternoon, and generally I am committed to returning the translations within two days.

The first thing I do is to ascertain whether the material is based on a press release. If so, there is a likelihood that an English language version of the press release can be found on the Internet. The next best scenario would be that the Japanese language press release is posted on the Internet. This can help as background material.

Whilst working I always maintain a broadband connection to an online dictionary to look up technical words and the search engine Google for words that cannot be found in the online and the bilingual (Japanese–English) dictionaries. Other dictionaries that I use include one for chemical-specific terms and one for the names of organizations.

For words that cannot be sourced using online or conventional dictionaries, I may employ a variety of search engines. There is a technique, however, to finding English equivalents of Japanese

---

Box 1.1 (Continued)

words through the Google search engine that comes with experience. Sometimes some ingenuity is required. Just typing in the Japanese word and the word 'English' into the search field [where a query word or phrase is entered for Google to perform the search] is unlikely to produce any useful results. A good first attempt for a difficult technical term is to guess one of the component words found in the term. As an example, I would type in the Japanese term 異方導電性フィルム in the search field and then add the English word 'film'. This may lead me to the English equivalent, which is 'anisotropic conductive film' (a type of material used in the electronics industry).

One point I might add is that even with transliterations from English to Japanese I have to be careful. One example is 'shiito' [based on 'sheet'] as in 'polarization shiito', which can appear in English technical material but the proper English term is really 'polarization film'. Sometimes there is no English equivalent but enough examples of its use in the source language can be found to pinpoint the meaning. However, I would never use this method to 'hazard a guess'. If unsure, I have to seek help either in a mailing list I subscribe to or go back to my client. It may turn out to be a term that only my client's company uses.

With the growth of the chemical industry's interest in China, it is advantageous to have the knowledge of the Chinese language and capability on my computer to assist me with tracking down names of places and organizations. Although the Japanese pronunciation and character style are slightly different when compared to the Chinese characters, I sometimes have to revert to a Chinese dictionary to look up the relevant characters and pronunciation, and then input the Chinese characters into a search engine such as Google. As Japanese characters are derived from old Chinese characters, there are many similarities, even with the simplified characters that Mainland China [the People's Republic of China] now uses. [Simplified Chinese script has fewer strokes per character than Traditional Chinese, for example 马 compared to 馬 for 'horse' 宝 and compared to 寶 for 'treasure']. For example, I tried to look up the name of an obscure Chinese company (written in Simplified Chinese: 宁波连合投资控股有限公司) found in a Japanese language press release. Hence the search was unsuccessful. So I took out my Chinese dictionary, and systematically looked up each character

Box 1.1　(Continued)

from its radical. [A radical is a semantic classifier. It categorizes words based on their meanings rather than spelling since Chinese is logographic in nature – written from left to right or top to bottom – where each character stands for a single word or a single syllabic morpheme (Boltz 1996: 191, 199), for example, the character 月 'moon' is the radical of the word 股, which means 'shares' in a company.]

The Pinyin romanization of the obscure Chinese company name is 'Ningbo Lianhe Touzhi Konggu Youxian Gongsi'. [Pinyin romanization is a form of spelling based on sound in Mandarin. It is also known as Hanyu Pinyin, which literally means 'Han language pinyin'. Romanization refers to the phonetic notation and transliteration to Roman script. This is not anglicization.] Thus I typed the Pinyin romanization letters into my Chinese-capable Apple Macintosh computer and converted them to the appropriate characters in Chinese. I then conducted an Internet search using the Chinese Yahoo! search engine, but alas, I could still not find an English equivalent. I ended up having to go to the Japanese company that had issued the press release to ask.

Another useful link while translating is company websites. They contain proper nouns such as specific company departments and product names, which are useful as background material. When all else fails, I consult my peers on the Japanese translators mailing list for help. This has never failed me so far. At the end of the day, the less I trouble my clients with requests for assistance, the more likely I am to receive more work.

I was using the offline version of the online dictionary software when I was using OS 9.2 [operating system for Apple Macintosh computers] on my Mac, but when I upgraded to OS X [read as OS 'ten']. I found the software to be too unstable when running in the Classic mode [a choice of operating setting for Apple Macintosh computers]. However, now that OS X has been refined to a higher version (10.2.6), the software is working fine. This allows me to build up a custom dictionary, and it is particularly useful when I am on the road, where Internet dial-up connections can be slow and costly, thus precluding extensive use of the Web. For some clients who are version (10.2.6), the software is working fine. This allows me to build up a custom dictionary, and it is particularly useful when I am on the road, where Internet dial-up connections can be slow and costly, thus

Box 1.1   (Continued)

precluding extensive use of the Web. For some clients who are Microsoft Office savvy, I use tags [hidden comments or remarks which are inserted in the translated text by the translator] when I am unsure of my translation or want to clarify it. The client or the client's proof reader will similarly use tags for questions and clarifications.

I have also started to experiment with a translation memory tool called WordFast. The shareware program is a Microsoft macro that can be used on any version of Office and on any operating system. [A macro in Microsoft is a saved sequence of commands or keyboard strokes that can be stored and recalled with a single command or keyboard stroke]. Initial tests with my laptop (processing speed at 400 MHz) indicated that the software runs excessively slow to the point of being impractical. Once I have my desktop computer configured to 750 MHz, I plan to retest the software before deciding whether to purchase a license. An interesting point with this program is that translation memories [see Chapter 4] can be set up for each client and shared with them. Memories can also be imported/exported to/from Trados Translator's Workbench and other similar software.

One thing I am slightly concerned about is how applicable a translation memory will be to my line of work. For manuals or other repetitive work, memories are great, but for translating newspaper articles and other creative work, overreliance could result in boring news items! I might also lose a bit of my creativity. Therefore, it is good to exercise the mind a bit and think about what English word to use for a given Japanese source word. In my experience, Japanese news stories can be a bit mundane in that they tend to follow a fixed style and repeatedly use the same words. One example is the word 'kyoka' which literally means, 'make strong'. However, in English, I could use 'augment', 'enhance', 'enrich', 'reinforce', 'strengthen' or 'build up'. Sometimes the best choice is found in the context and sometimes the context might allow me to use a word I would never have thought of. My point is: I feel that overreliance on spell-checkers, grammar checkers, and thesauri would adversely affect my capability here. The same may be said for translation aids in certain cases of creative translations. It could dull our creativity as well. I feel that in order to remain a creative translator, I have to continue to exercise my brain. Note that for a lot of translation work, particularly manuals, this technology is great.

towards embracing translation technology and why in their view this attitude needs changing. The absence of input from translators in the development of machine translation and computer-aided translation tools, whether due to the lack of knowledge or interest, is probably the main reason for this resistance.

The tension between humans and machines developed as a corollary to new technology entering the translation process. According to Yuste Rodrigo (2001), a high proportion of translators-to-be are concerned about the impact of machine translation on their profession and have admitted that they do not know much about translation technology. The main fear of some professional translators was 'not to be seized by a machine' (Yuste Rodrigo 2001: 1). This fear is yet to be completely eliminated since, historically, many machine translation systems have been presented as a means to dispense with human translators (Bennett and Gerber 2003: 185, 189; see also Tsujii 1991). It is, however, unfounded and results from high expectations with respect to the potential of machine translation systems (Tsujii 1991: 3). Nevertheless, some professional translators still find technology that demands changes in their translation routine, and performance within a very brief time-span distressing. Others, who have been using translation tools in their work, acknowledge that the quality of their translations and the level of productivity have increased. What they still find difficult is to articulate and quantify the benefits that they have gained from using translation tools.

Through translation technology training, perhaps the negative mindset held by some professional translators may change (Robichaud and L'Homme 2003). It is difficult to imagine a translator who could not usefully employ some form of technology, be it online dictionaries or search engines, regardless of the type of text s/he works with. Moore's account illustrates that even for non-technical texts, resources such as online dictionaries, are extremely helpful. With increasing demands for rapid translation and the new working methods of many translation companies and clients, human translators today are more or less forced to use computer-aided translation tools; in rare cases, machine translation systems are also used. And whenever a machine translation system is used, professional translators need long-term commitment and positive attitudes, innovative responses and creative problem-solving ability (Koby 2001: 16).

Lack of information has also played a part in forming negative attitudes: 'Many professional translators, and their organisations, have proved to be remarkably ignorant about the progress made in machine translation technology' (Haynes 1998: viii). Similar preconceived notions are said to have spread even to the use of computer-aided translation tools (Gaspari 2001). These reactions may have originated from a lack of understanding or desire to learn the use of other tools apart from word-processing software, or from conflicting stories of the success and failure of different research and commercial machine translation systems. The lack of success by developers of translation technology may have been caused by not adhering to a set of simples rules: identify what technology can do best and what humans can do best, keep the technology simple to use and adapt the technology to meet the needs of professional translators (Hunt 2002).

Professional translators today are required to have 'professional and linguistic skills in connection with the increasing use of new technologies' (Archer 2002: 87). With extended exposure and further education in translation technology, translators are increasingly becoming familiar with the necessary technology. In recent years, many universities have started to offer courses in the use of translation tools to trainee translators. For example, the Chinese University of Hong Kong, Dublin City University in Ireland, Kent State University in the USA, Rand Afrikaans University in South Africa, the University of Surrey in the UK, the University of Joensuu in Finland and the University of Ottawa in Canada (see also Robichaud and L'Homme 2003).

The localization industry

In any discussion of translation technology, the significant role played by the localization industry cannot be ignored. Traditionally, the localization industry has consisted of two sectors: the manufacturers of hardware and software, and the localization service providers (see the website of the Localisation Industry and Standards Association or LISA at http://www.lisa.org/). Today, however, other sectors such as telecommunications, language service providers and even universities are involved in the localization industry as businesses try to reach out to a wider audience. Much has been written about this industry, and therefore, only a brief description will be given in this book. Detailed discussions of the localization industry can be found in Esselink (2000 and 2003) and Pym (2004).

Localization is the process of changing the documentation of a product, a product itself or the delivery of services so that they are appropriate and acceptable to the target society and culture. It concerns the changes required to cater to the needs of a particular 'locale' (Esselink 2000: 3), that is a group of people tied through a shared language and culture. An example of the process is the translation and adaptation of *Time* magazine into Portuguese and Spanish for Latin American readers (Sprung and Vourvoulias-Bush 2000). The Latin Portuguese and Spanish readers form two locales, both different from the European Portuguese and Spanish locales. A different locale is also likely to require changes to a number of items, including the currency and the way in which the date and time are written, all of which may vary according to the particular country (Esselink 2002).

From a translation point of view, localization is mainly but not entirely a linguistic task that involves transferring the text as naturally as possible into the target language, to make the translation 'linguistically and culturally appropriate' for a specific market (Esselink 1998: 2). However, localization goes beyond the mere linguistic and adjustments to measurements: target audiences may perceive colours, icons and symbols differently. Thus organizations have to tailor their products to match the language and culture of the countries they intend to do business in, including countries with different varieties of the same language. Sometimes the same word or symbol may have different meanings for different groups. Indonesia and Malaysia, for instance, use different varieties of Malay, resulting in possible misunderstandings. Hence, in Indonesian Malay, the verb 'butuh' is common and means 'need', 'necessity' or 'want'. In Malaysian Malay, however, the word falls under the noun class and is a vulgarism referring to human male genitalia. Moreover, the long colonization period of Indonesia by the Dutch and of Malaysia by the English has also resulted in different loan words being assimilated into the vocabulary such as 'karcis' from 'kaartje' by Indonesian Malay from Dutch, while Malaysian Malay uses 'tiket' from the English 'ticket'. Borrowed international terms from English also differ such as 'situs web' in Indonesian Malay and 'laman web' in Malaysian Malay for 'website'.

Conclusion

Until the early 1990s, the time when the Internet began to be used worldwide, the translation types given in Hutchins and Somers (1992) were certainly applicable. More than a decade later, the boundaries of these four translation types have become more blurred. Although many writers in the field still make clear distinctions, these have become harder to maintain as technology becomes increasingly multifunctional and more multitasking. The pace of change in the development of translation technology is extremely rapid; what is current today may become outdated tomorrow. With this development in mind, only two chapters of this book are loosely based on the classification proposed by Hutchins and Somers (1992); machine translation is discussed in Chapter 3 and computer-aided translation tools in Chapter 4, while the remaining chapters will cover other topics relevant to translation technology.

Suggested reading

Austermühl, F. (2001) *Electronic Tools for Translators*. Manchester: St Jerome Publishing. See chapter 1.

Hutchins, W.J. and H.L. Somers (1992) *An Introduction to Machine Translation*. London: Academic Press Limited.

O'Hagan, M. and D. Ashworth (2002) *Translation-Mediated Communication in A Digital World: Facing the Challenges of Globalization and Localization*. Cleveden: Multilingual Matters.

Pym, A. (2004) *The Moving Text: Localization, Translation and Distribution*. Amsterdam: John Benjamins.

Somers, H.L. (ed.) (2003a) *Computers and Translation: A Translator's Guide*. Amsterdam: John Benjamins.

2
Translation Studies and Translation Technology

This chapter is concerned with the relationship between Translation Studies and translation technology. We begin by discussing translation theory and describing the professional and academic groups who are involved in translation. In addition, the schema of the applied branch of Translation Studies proposed by John S. Holmes (1988/2000) is explored to show the areas of Translation Studies that have direct relevance to natural-language processing applications. A description of several stages in the translation process follows, involving pre- and post-editing tasks. We also consider the idea of a 'controlled language', frequently used to author texts as input for machine translation systems. The semiotic classification of translation models introduced by Roman Jakobson (1959/2000) is used to illustrate a different perspective on the translation process, involving editing tasks and controlled language.

Translation theory

According to Chesterman (2003), the notion of translation theory is 'fuzzy'. It is also said to be 'a misnomer, a blanket term' (Newmark 1981: 19). A translation theory may refer to many different things such as hypotheses, models, assumptions, beliefs, concepts and doctrines. It has numerous interpretations but only one aim: to increase the understanding of translation phenomena. Even the notion of translation itself is not entirely clear. However, the core notion of translation is generally accepted to be the transfer of a message written in one language into another. Translation theory is, therefore, in one view an attempt to create a model of how messages are transferred from a source-language text into a target-language text by giving 'some insight into the relation between thought, meaning and language' (Newmark 1981: 19). It is concerned with what is transferred and why.

Figure 2.1 shows the approximate chronological continuum of translation theories (see also Gentzler 1993; Munday 2001) ranging from 'word-for-word versus sense-for-sense' prior to the early twentieth century to a number of different approaches emerging in the 1970s. We see here that translation theories evolved from simple word-for-word versus sense-for-sense or 'literal versus free' approaches into something considerably more complex. The debate can be traced back to Cicero (first century BC) and St Jerome (fourth/fifth centuries AD). For centuries, until the second half of the twentieth century, the word-for-word approach, which refers to the replacement of one word in the source-language text with another in the target-language text, was pitched against the sense-for-sense approach, more concerned with preserving the meaning of the source-language text rather than its precise wording, but without being completely 'free'. The translations of Greek texts and the Holy Bible into Latin, the translations of Greek scientific and philosophical texts into Arabic and the Chinese translations of Buddhist sutras from Sanskrit influenced these early writings on translation theory (Munday 2001: 19–20; see also Delisle and Woodsworth 1995).

In the first half of the twentieth century, translation theory was heavily influenced by the German literary and philosophical traditions that can be seen in the works of philosophers such as Walter Benjamin and Ezra Pound (Venuti 2000: 11). The period between the 1950s and the 1960s saw the dominance of linguistic theories that focused on the description and analysis of translation procedures, for example Vinay and Darbelnet (1958/2000), and typologies of equivalence, for example Catford (1965). Vinay and Darbelnet's work identifies a number of different strategies and procedures of translation. Although their analysis was restricted to English and French, the seven procedures that they introduced, ranging from simple borrowing of a source-language word

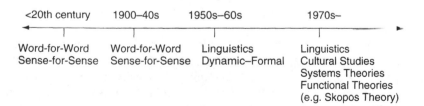

<20th century	1900–40s	1950s–60s	1970s–
Word-for-Word Sense-for-Sense	Word-for-Word Sense-for-Sense	Linguistics Dynamic–Formal	Linguistics Cultural Studies Systems Theories Functional Theories (e.g. Skopos Theory)

Figure 2.1 Chronology of translation theories

into the target language to the more complex procedure of adapting cultural references that do not exist in the target-language culture, have had a wider impact.

The same period also saw the return of the dichotomy of oppositions similar to that of word-for-word versus sense-for-sense such as 'formal versus dynamic' as proposed by Eugene Nida (1964), where the former leans toward the source-language text structures while the latter adapts the translation more closely to the target language in order to achieve naturalness. In the late 1970s, another similar dichotomy was introduced by Juliane House in the form of 'overt versus covert'. While in 'overt' translation, it is clear that the target-language text is a translation from another language, 'covert' translation does not show that the target text originates in another language. In the early 1980s, Peter Newmark introduced the dichotomy of 'semantic translation', which follows as closely as possible the semantic and syntactic structures of the source-language text, and 'communicative translation', which is focused on the reader and 'attempts to produce...an effect as close as possible to that obtained on the readers of the original' (Newmark 1981: 39), recalling Nida's well-known 'dynamic equivalence'. All these dichotomies are in a way reminiscent of the word-for-word versus sense-for-sense debate, documented earlier in the history of translation theory; however, they are not identical since these new dichotomies were often influenced by linguistics (Venuti 2000: 122).

With *Syntactic Structures* and *Aspects of the Theory of Syntax* – published in 1957 and 1965 respectively – Noam Chomsky introduced 'transformational grammar' or more specifically 'transformational-generative grammar' and, as a result, changed the way language could be studied. Here, the grammar attempts to define linguistic rules that can produce an infinite number of grammatical sentences in a language from a set of finite rules and a lexicon. With his original transformational-generative grammar, Chomsky proposed that a sentence has two levels of representation in the form of an underlying deep structure and a surface form which can be mapped onto the semantic deep structure via 'transformations', such as passivization, pronominalization and topicalization.

In the early days of translation theory, Nida's idea of the translation process as working from the source text to the target text by reaching down to an underlying level of meaning as the means of 'transfer' between the languages resonates with Chomsky's model, as we shall see below in Figure 2.2. The phrase structure rules used in some rule-based machine translation systems are also derivative (see, for instance, the transfer approach in Chapter 3). However, since Chomsky's transformational generative grammar was first introduced, notions such as deep and surface structures have been abandoned and newer aspects of the transformational grammar were introduced in the 1980s and the 1990s.

Although linguistic theories remained influential, by the late 1970s other theories had begun to emerge in order to explain phenomena in translation that had not been addressed in linguistics. One such example is 'Skopos' theory, one of a number of so-called 'functional approaches' to translation that had developed in Germany. The emergence of Skopos theory is seen as part of a general shift from predominantly linguistic-based translation theories to a theory that has an orientation towards the way a translation functions in the target society and culture. In Greek, *skopos* means aim, purpose, goal, objective and intention. It is a technical term used by Hans Vermeer (1996) to refer to the purpose of a translation, which determines the strategy to be used during the translation process (Munday 2001:79). Skopos theory also allows a source-language text to be translated into a number of different target-language texts depending on the purpose specified in the so-called 'translation commission' or brief.

Vermeer's Skopos theory draws heavily on the 'translational action theory' developed by Justa Holz-Mänttäri, which represents a function-oriented approach to the theory and practice of translation. A source-language text is an 'offer of information' ('*Informationsangebot*') made by the source-language author to his/her recipients. The translation of the source text is then characterized as an 'offering' of that same information to another culture in its own language. The way the translation is performed is determined by many factors such as the needs, expectations and culture of the target-language text recipients. Thus, translation is seen as a process of intercultural communication where the translated text is capable of functioning according to specific target situations and uses (Mason 1998: 33). With respect to machine translation, the intended use of the target-language text will decide, for example, whether the source-language text gets pre-edited and/or the target-language text gets post-edited in line with quality expectations. In other words, translation is guided by how the target-language text will be used by its intended readers.

Common ground between Translation Studies and translation technology – and machine translation in particular – may be found within functional approaches to translation. According to Trujillo (1999: 3), the Skopos theory of translation strategy, for example, 'arose as a response to the growing need for non-literary translation'. The focus on the purpose of the target text in relation to its translation setting resonates with a common definition of translation quality as 'fitness for purpose'. In addition to influencing whether a text submitted to machine translation is pre- and/or post-edited depending on its intended use, it is also appropriate to consider how the purpose may influence the decision to choose human or machine translation in the first place. As we shall see, a 'dirty' machine translation output may be perfectly adequate for information on the topic of a text, but not for the annual speech by the chairman of the board.

Owing to 'the very nature of translation as a complex human (and machine) activity', Chesterman (2000) has argued that there is a need to explore different translation theories in order 'to build a general empirical theory of translation that is both rich and robust'. Thus far, no single theory is able to explain every translation phenomenon. Instead theories of translation have been influenced by different disciplines and the philosophical backgrounds of translation scholars. Consequently, the definition of a 'translation theory' depends on the ideology subscribed to by the translation scholar (Chesterman 2000). Perhaps for scholars who are involved in developing natural-language processing applications, in particular machine translation, a translation theory that could guide computer programming to enable the translations of controlled language texts in restricted subject fields may be needed (Melby and Warner 1995: 157, 165).

Academic and professional groups in translation

The next few sections will discuss the often uneasy relationships between four professional and academic groups: linguists, professional translators, translation theorists and scientists, and how each group approaches the phenomenon of translation.

Translators and linguists

According to Halliday (2001: 13), linguists have introduced nearly all known translation theories. To most linguists, translation theory is about 'the study of how things are' including 'the nature of the translation process and the relation between texts in translation' (Halliday 2001: 13) and 'why translations are the way they are' (Mossop 2000: 44). The perspective is descriptive in nature (Mossop 2000: 44). The goal is to provide explanations by describing linguistic usage as it actually is (Crystal 1993: 100; see also Shreve 2002). This is a departure from the prescriptive perspective propagated by earlier generations of scholars whereby linguists sought to prescribe norms of usage (Crystal 1993: 275; see also Riccardi 2002b). The change in linguistics has also influenced the way translation is viewed by linguists. As viewed by many, translation is an extension of language studies (Neubert 1996: 88) or a sub-field of applied linguistics (Baker 2001: 47); hence the dependence on linguistics as a descriptive and explanatory discipline is inevitable.

To most professional translators, on the other hand, translation theory is about 'how things ought to be: what constitutes good or effective translation and what can help to achieve a better or more effective product' (Halliday 2001: 13). For translators, translation theory is a 'solution provider' to problems they encounter during translation (Chesterman 2000). Professional translators continue to view translation theory from a prescriptive perspective expecting theory to take on a problem-solving role. Thus the two groups have very different ideas as to what embodies translation theory.

Translators and translation theorists

The 'antagonism between "practicing" [sic][professional] translators and "theorists of translation"' (Lefevere 1996: 46–50) runs deep because each camp has its own traditions and holds the firm opinion that their method is best. Newmark (1981: 23–36) states that translation theorists are concerned primarily with meaning and the varieties of meaning. They are also concerned with the appropriate general method of translation, every type of translation procedure, specific linguistic problems such as cultural terms and metaphor, and with ensuring that no linguistic or cultural factor is ignored during the translation process. For translation theorists, solving the problems of professional translators is a matter of interest only when the approaches they have suggested are involved.

It has been said that professional translators do not always produce convincing theoretical explanations for their translation decisions. They are also said to be only interested in 'workplace procedures...in order to help them improve' their translations (Mossop 2000: 46). However, translation theorists as well as linguists often have little interest in providing specific guidelines to professional translators and to translation trainees, with a few exceptions such as Malone (1988) and Vinay and Darbelnet (1958/1995). Their research focus is to describe and explain the processes and products of translation (Fawcett 1997; Chesterman 2000).

One professional translator (Moore 2002: personal communication) finds that his lack of knowledge of translation theory considerably reduces his ability to explain to his clients the reason why he translates in a particular way (see also Ulrych 2002). Noguiera (2002), also a professional translator, captures this sentiment when he states that there are many bright and brilliant translators who could but do not contribute to translation theory. Since they are practising translators they can ill-afford to spend the time or effort working on theory. Thus most of what they write is usually found in the form of short e-mails in discussion lists for professional translators. As a result, the majority of written contributions come from the theorists. The existence of two groups among professional translators, the translators of creative texts on the one hand, and of specialists including the translators of technical texts on the other hand, complicates the matter further, with the former subscribing to literary- and/or cultural studies-based theories, and the latter favouring linguistic-based theories, according to Lefevere (1996: 45–55).

Given the contradictory functions of translation theorists and professional translators with respect to translation theory, Newmark (1981: 36) offers a suggestion about what translation theory can do for professional translators: it can show what is or what may be involved in the translation process, offer general principles and guidelines, and stop translators from making mistakes. He cautions, however, that no translation theory can turn a bad translator into a good one.

Linguists and translation theorists

In its concern with the study of language, linguistics has produced numerous theories about how language works. As a language activity, translation can be seen as part of linguistics. Thus a theory of translation drawn from linguistic theory must be viewed as a logical outcome (see also Catford 1965). For example, by studying linguistics it can be shown how language varies in relation to social status, age, gender and so on, and this can help to inform translation decisions. The relationship between linguistics and translation theory could, however, be more mutually beneficial, something that has continued to be reflected in the literature (Fawcett 1997: 1–2). This was anticipated by Bell (1991: xv, 21) when he pointed out that translation theorists had made limited use of the techniques and insights of contemporary linguistics and, at times, have demonstrated their lack of understanding of the principles of linguistics and its methods of investigation. Linguists, on the other hand, have been either neutral or, at times, even hostile to the notion of a theory of translation because they have failed to fully understand its objectives and methods.

The concept of translation as a 'science' and at the same time, an 'art' or 'craft', may have something to do with the view held by some linguists. The notion that translation is a 'science', or perhaps a 'discipline', is acceptable to linguists, who strive to make objective observations and descriptions of linguistic phenomena. It is the notion of translation as an 'art' or 'craft', as influenced by literary theory and criticism, philosophy and rhetoric, with the creative aspect as the focal point in translation (see also Savory 1968; Biguenet and Schulte 1989) that is a notion less easily embraced by linguists, as it is not open to objective description and explanation. As a result of these contradictory views, a theory of translation is often not taken seriously (Bell 1991: 4).

Linguists and scientists

Another group that exists almost independently of the ones discussed above are the 'scientists', including computer scientists, language engineers and computational linguists, who write computer programs and use linguistic theories to develop the language component of machine translation systems. Computational scientists have applied linguistic theories to enhance the performance of machine translation systems because linguistics offers 'a range of observations, techniques and theories that may be adopted and extended within the MT [machine translation] enterprise' (Bennett 2003: 157). However, scientists do not in general contribute to the body of linguistic and/or translation literature. Acknowledgements or references to translation theory are also scarce even in relation to the architectures of rule-based machine translation systems, which contain linguistic applications (see Chapter 3). Although rule-based architectures rely on linguistic approaches, they also resemble the three-step translation process introduced by Nida (1969: 484) as illustrated in Figure 2.2.

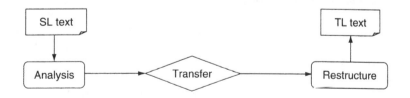

SL = source language; TL = target language

Figure 2.2 Translation process model
Source: Nida (1969): 484.

For the scientist, the main issue is not whether linguistics is prescriptive or descriptive; a more important criterion is that the particular approach applied must be computationally tractable (Bennett 2003: 144). This means that to be useful to the building of a machine translation system, the computer program implementing the linguistic approach must run at a practical or acceptable speed on a standard computer. Linguists, on the other hand, are more interested in language from a human perspective and since many obstacles are encountered in the process of studying and describing a single language, it is not in their interest to even consider studying and describing two languages involving translation. This is compounded by their misconception (like many others) of the real purpose of the development of machine translation systems (Hutchins 1979: 29), which is not to replace human translators.

In the absence of a real human brain which can provide immediate insights into the processing and generation of texts, to the scientist, machine translation is a good alternative that can be used to test linguistic theories through simulation. However, the reluctance of linguists to venture into experimenting with simulating brain processes via machines may be due to the fact that there are still many uncertainties as to what goes on in the brain. As speakers of a language, linguists can always rely on their own intuitions about what is correct or grammatical and what is not in order to conduct linguistic testing. This is based on the assumption that a language user must 'know' the 'rules' of his/her language system in order to use it. The user also 'knows' when mistakes are made. The same, however, does not apply to a machine translation system. The programming code is at best 'readable', that is the machine can read and execute it, but it is not capable of 'understanding' its purpose (see Chapter 6). Since the first attempt more than fifty years ago at building a machine translation system, translation problems such as lexical and syntactic ambiguities still have to be solved (see Chapter 4).

Linguistic theories in machine translation systems

Until the late 1960s, the method used to generate translations in nearly all machine translation systems was the 'direct translation' approach (see Chapter 3). This approach is based on the assumption that one target-language word can be generated from one source-language word. It also requires a minimal syntactic analysis, for example, recognition of word classes such as noun and verb (Hutchins 1979: 29; see also Chapter 3). One of the original systems built was the Georgetown University System. The poor quality of the translations produced by the system highlighted the complexities of language and the need for a better analysis and synthesis of texts (Hutchins 1979: 31; see Chapter 3). Hence, in the subsequent system known as Systran (System Translation), linguistic and computational components were divided into separate modules in order to resolve the problems encountered in the Georgetown University System. Even with Systran, the underlying linguistic component was not based on any specific linguistic theory (Hutchins 1979: 32).

In subsequent machine translation system designs, two linguistic approaches or grammars are considered useful: the formal and the functional. The formal approach puts emphasis on the description of morphological and syntactic structures. The functional approach, on the other hand, is concerned with the use of language and the ways words and sentences are combined to produce well-formed texts (Bennett 2003: 144). Of the two, the formal approach is easier to compute and therefore to incorporate into machine translation than the functional approach, which takes the pragmatic view that language is a form of social interaction (Crystal 1993: 146). Thus the formal approach has had more influence on machine translation research and development. However, it was not until the appearance of Chomsky's transformational-generative grammar that the formal approach became the mainstream method of describing language.

The focus of the formal approach is to establish rules for the formation of grammatical structures: how phrases, clauses and sentences are generated (Finch 2000: 99). The grammar is used 'to provide a rigorous and explicit framework that can produce (or generate) from a small number of general principles, or rules, all the well-formed sentences of a language' (Finch 2000: 99).

The representation method of formal linguistics involves the conversion of a sentence into a representation that consists of its structure and meaning. A simple example of a representation is illustrated in Figure 2.3

CS: The mechanic repaired the car.
 ∧ *mechanic* (noun), *repair* (verb), *car* (noun)
SR: predicate: *repair* (past)
  subject: *mechanic* (singular, definite)
  object: *car* (singular, definite)

CS = complete sentence; SR = sentence representation

Figure 2.3 Example of sentence representations

(see also Bennett 2003: 146) where what can be called the 'complete sentence' (CS) is stripped to show the syntactic structure that describes its actions and properties; one way of displaying a sentence representation (SR) of the sentence 'The mechanic repaired the car', is as shown in Figure 2.3.

However, according to Hutchins, transformational grammar was found to be unsuitable for machine translation purposes, as it required extensive and complex computer programming (Hutchins 1979: 33). Chomsky himself probably never intended for his transformational-generative grammar to be employed in translation, although others such as Nida modified deep structure analysis for the purpose of representing the translation process (Fawcett 1997: 65; see also Figure 2.2 above). An alternative approach – arguably better-suited to machine processing – was offered by so-called 'formalisms', some of which are linguistic formalisms while others are found in logic, mathematics and computer science, which can also be applied in machine translation systems. Some formalisms are syntax-based such as Chomsky's transformational generative grammar, while others are lexicon-based, as we will see below.

Formalisms – or 'formal grammars' – were developed as a departure from descriptive linguistics in the 1950s. However, since the formalisms of the early 1990s, several changes have been introduced whereby formal grammars have been combined with logic, computation and statistics to create stronger formalisms that would allow them to be written for computational programming (see also Hutchins and Somers 1992). According to Zaharin Yusuf (1989: 319), 'a formalism is a set of notations with well-defined semantics (namely for the interpretation of the symbols used and their manipulation), by means of which one formally expresses certain domain knowledge, which is to be utilised for specific purposes'. In other words, it is a specific rigorous mathematical method known as 'formal grammar' in which language, in this case, is treated as a mathematical object. A formal grammar is a set of rules that describes a formal language (a set of finite words) which is able to represent the syntax of a given sentence. The formal nature of the grammar enables the sentence to be completely analysed by the computer. Thus, after the direct translation approach, which had much in common with a word-for-word approach to translation owing to the central role of dictionaries in the system, the next generation of systems – known as 'rule-based' systems – make use of a number of formal grammars in the design of machine translation systems.

By the mid-1980s, a variant of formal grammar stemming from the 'lexicalist approach' – different from the syntax-based 'constraint-based grammar' or 'unification grammar' – was applied in most rule-based machine translation systems (see also Kay 1984). Unification or constraint-based grammar is the general name for a number of linguistic approaches or 'models': 'Tree Adjoining Grammar', a lexically-oriented grammar that imposes mathematical formalism to capture the syntactic properties of natural languages developed by Joshi, Levy and Takahashi (1975); 'Lexical Functional Grammar', a theory of grammar (syntax, morphology and semantics) by Kaplan and Bresnan (1982); 'Generalized Phrase Structure Grammar', a framework that describes syntax and semantics by Gazdar *et al.* (1985); and 'Head-driven Phrase Structure Grammar', theoretically influenced by other theories of syntax and semantics, and an immediate successor to Generalized Phrase Structure Grammar, developed by Pollard and Sag (1987). All four models rely heavily on logic and computations to encode human languages into mathematical codes. It is important to note that since their inception, many aspects of these models have undergone changes and refinement.

The aim of unification or constraint-based grammars is to reduce the transfer rules – in this case the computational processes of analysis, transfer and synthesis – to simple bilingual lexical equivalences. In Lexical Functional Grammar, a formal description of grammatical units via the 'constituent structure' and 'functional- or feature-structure' is provided (Hutchins and Somers 1992: 39). The constituent structure or 'c-structure' consists of groups of phrases analysed as hierarchies. In short, it represents a sentence structure. In c-structure, the rules that identify the grammatical functions are called phrase structure rules. An example of the English phrase structure rules for a simple sentence like 'Jane kicks David' would be:

$$S \rightarrow NP\ VP$$
$$NP \rightarrow N$$
$$VP \rightarrow V\ NP$$
$$NP \rightarrow N$$

The NP (noun phrase) and its 'lower hierarchy' (noun) represent 'Jane', while the VP (verb phrase) represents 'kicks David', which has a lower hierarchy of V (verb), that represents 'kicks', and the NP and its lower hierarchy of N that represents 'David'. The f-structure (feature structure), on the other hand, is used to represent the internal structure of a sentence; its properties can be encoded with sets of attributes and values in a matrix-like diagram: [*attribute value*], where 'attribute' refers to the grammatical category such as gender or a syntactic function, and 'value' is the corresponding feature possessed by the constituent, for example, feminine: [GEN fem]. The f-structure integrates the lexical and structural information from the c-structure.

Using the same sentence 'Jane kicks David', the f-structure below shows the hierarchical attribute-value matrix that represents underlying grammatical relations. In this example, the predicate – the present tense of the verb 'kicks' – is grammatically related to the subject ('Jane') and the object ('David'). The attribute-value matrix for the subject (SUB) relates the attribute or the grammatical function of the predicate (the verb 'kicks'), to the value, 'Jane'. The subject 'Jane' in turn has the attribute indicated here by NUM (number) that has the value of one or singular (sgl), which falls under the category of the third person (the attribute is person, the value is 3). The part of predicate that contains the object (OBJ) 'David' also has the same attributes as 'Jane' (see Kaplan and Bresnan 1982).

PRED   *kicks* <(_SUB) (_OBJ)>

SUB   ⎡ PRED   *Jane* ⎤
         ⎢ NUM   sgl   ⎥
         ⎣ PERS   3   ⎦

Present tense

OBJ   ⎡ PRED   *David* ⎤
         ⎢ NUM   sgl   ⎥
         ⎣ PERS   3   ⎦

SUB = subject	PRED = predicate	OBJ = object
NUM = number	PERS = person	sgl = singular

One of the major advantages of constraint-based grammars for machine translation systems is the reversibility principle, a feature that allows the same grammars, in theory, to be applied to both language directions. This has the potential to reduce the effort needed to construct a different grammar in the reverse direction for the same language pair. Clearly this is particularly desirable in developing bidirectional machine translation systems.

In formalisms, linguists and computational linguists address the same issues. However, their focus is different as the latter group are more interested in formalisms that are computationally viable. Formalisms exercise an important influence on the development of and progress in natural-language processing research. Since formalisms allow human languages to be mathematically coded, the computational features of these types of grammar are attractive to researchers in machine translation systems. As we have seen, the major contribution to rule-based machine translation systems has come from linguistics and different types of formalism, not from translation theory.

Although a number of early linguistic and translation procedures had seemed promising as the basis for machine translation rules, there is little evidence that these are computable for use in machine translation systems. Examples include Catford's (1965) translation shifts where a target-language text is reworded as a result of structural (grammatical or lexical) incompatibilities between a source and a target language (Shuttleworth and Cowie 1999: 152), and Vinay and Darbelnet's (1958/ 1995) taxonomy of seven comparative translation procedures mentioned earlier in this chapter (see also Fawcett 1997; Munday 2001). The machine translation literature does not seem to indicate that any of the translation procedures suggested by translation scholars have been implemented in the linguistic component of any machine translation system.

This almost non-existent contribution is unfortunate since linguists, scientists, translation theorists and professional translators all have similar concerns such as: 'how translation can be best performed' and 'what it means to translate' (Balkan 1996: 121). The statement by Rajapurohit (1994: 12) that 'there are in fact no theories in automatic translation' may contain some truth. The different paths chosen were largely due to the lack of early involvement of linguists, translation theorists and professional translators in the development of translation technology, especially machine translation systems. Linguistic researchers such as Peter Toma who founded Systran (System Translation) in 1968 are rare, machine translation research being 'initiated [mostly] by communications and information theoreticians, and not by linguists or TS [Translation Studies] scholars' (Wilss 1999: 141).

As for professional translators, there are two possible reasons why they have had little interest in machine translation development (Wilss 1999: 141). First, machine translation is seen as a distinct area of research. Second, there is a lack of knowledge among many professional translators of programming languages, artificial intelligence (computer programs that can solve problems creatively by making computers behave like humans) and neural networks (systems that simulate intelligence on the computer to imitate the way a human brain works) needed for the development of machine translation systems. The absence of translators' input in the development of machine translation may also be a reason for their resistance to using the technology (see also Chapter 1). In many cases, translators' contributions occur only at the end of the development process when a machine translation system is ready to generate outputs (Bédard 1993: 254). However, translators' experiences of translation processes and strategies have the potential to provide invaluable insights into the development of machine translation systems. A more translator-friendly machine translation system could be the outcome of a closer kind of collaboration, which in turn would make machine translation more acceptable to translators.

In a way resembling the tendency of the machine translation literature not to discuss translation theories, many accounts of translation have also been written without any mention of machine translation systems or computer-aided translation tools; for example, Gentzler (1993) and Riccardi (2002a). Brief mention of machine translation systems can be found in Bell (1991), Robinson (1997) and Munday (2001), while some attempts have been made to relate both human and machine translation within a narrow field of discourse such as those described in Hatim and Mason (1990) (Gentzler 1997: x; Matthiessen 2001: 42). These works give the impression that both machine translation and computer-aided translation tools belong to a separate field of studies, having very little to do with Translation Studies. These assumptions are not helpful to students of translation, since learning to translate specialist and in particular technical texts tends increasingly to involve the use of certain translation tools as part of the training.

Translation studies

In a seminal paper at the Third International Conference of Applied Linguistics in Copenhagen in 1972, John S. Holmes put forward a conceptual schema that described various elements of 'Translation Studies'. It is generally accepted that his paper turned Translation Studies into a distinct discipline (Gentzler 1993: 92), now acknowledged as an interdisciplinary field (Riccardi 2002b: 2), although it was Nida (1975) who is widely considered to be the founder of the field of Translation Studies as the first to lay down methods of translation in a systematic fashion (Robinson 2003: 13). A wide range of disciplines is involved, including linguistics, sociology, cultural studies, neuroscience, cognitive psychology and computer science (Wilss 1999: 133). In the following sections, we shall explore Holmes' (1988/2000) schematic description of Translation Studies, in order to place technology in this context.

The schema proposed by Holmes had simple categories, which were hierarchically arranged. The entire schema is shown in diagram format in Figure 2.4. There are two main branches: Pure Translation Studies and Applied Translation Studies. The Pure Translation Studies branch has a larger number of levels and sub-branches, consisting at the next level of Descriptive Translation Studies and Theoretical Translation Studies. The Applied Translation Studies branch of the schema has four sub-branches to do with training, 'aids', policy and translation criticism. Holmes' classification allows the areas of Translation Studies to be seen clearly but it should not be taken as 'unidirectional' as different areas can still influence one another (Holmes 1988/2000: 183). Descriptive Translation Studies, for example, encompasses a host of approaches and disciplines in translation research (see also Ulrych 2002). The schema is also flexible enough in our case to allow changes and developments to occur when technology is involved in both the Pure and Applied branches. The italicized branches in Figure 2.4 indicate where in Holmes' scheme we could locate a strong possibility of a relationship

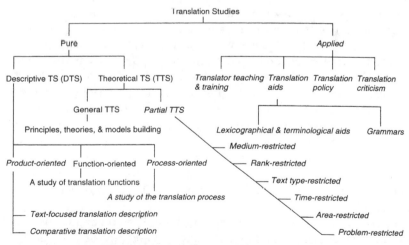

TS = translation studies; DTS = descriptive translation studies; TTS = theoretical translation studies

Figure 2.4 Holmes' schema of translation studies

between translation and technology, either during the development of various translation systems or at a later stage when they are in use.

Descriptive translation studies

The objective of pure research is to describe translation phenomena (Descriptive Translation Studies) and to establish the principles (Theoretical Translation Studies) that explain these phenomena. Describing phenomena and establishing principles increases the understanding of questions such as 'why are translations they way they are' and 'what effect do translations have on their readers'.

Three different types of research are found in Descriptive Translation Studies: product, function and process. Product-oriented research concentrates on the description of existing translations. Function-oriented research focuses on the description of the impact a translation has on the socio-culture of the target readers. Process-oriented research is concerned with the process of translation itself: what really goes on in the mind of a translator during the translation process? Think-aloud protocols (TAP), for example, are one technique used to investigate what comes into the mind of a translator and the actions performed in the creation of a target-language text (Shuttleworth and Cowie 1999: 171). Of the three, product- and process-oriented Descriptive Translation Studies have a higher possibility of technological involvement. The use of translation tools such as terminology databases and translation memory and/or linguistic tools such as spell-checkers during the translation process can provide much material for research. We shall return to the subject of translation memory, a kind of database of previously translated texts and their corresponding target texts, in Chapter 4.

Product-oriented research focuses on existing translations and comes in two forms, text-focused translation description and comparative translation description. Text-focused translation description involves describing individual translations of a source text, whereas comparative translation description involves comparing and analysing a number of translations of a single source text. Technological developments in the 1980s and 1990s mean that corpora of texts can now be stored and studied using techniques such as concordancing (see Chapter 4; see also Bowker 2002) in order to carry out linguistic analyses in this product-oriented research.

In Theoretical Translation Studies, the focus is on theoretical work to establish general or partial principles, theories and models. The concept of a 'partial' principle is based on the assumption that a translation theory is limited to researching only certain translation phenomena and can be restricted in more than one way. An example of this would be the analysis of novels and short stories written by Gabriel García Márquez, which is restricted to language and culture (Colombian Spanish into English), genre (novels and short stories) and time (1960s to the 1990s) (Munday 2001: 12, 192–5). While the ultimate goal of Translation Studies is to build 'a full inclusive theory accommodating so many elements that it can serve to explain and predict all phenomena falling within the terrain of translating and translation...' (Holmes 1988/2000: 178), Holmes' restricted research types allow translation problems and issues to be studied in a manageable way.

The first type is medium-restricted theories, referring to the medium that is used to present a text, that is oral (interpreting) and written (translation). When Holmes (1988/2000: 178) first described his schema, interpreting only involved humans, while translation involved humans as well as machines. Nowadays speech technology has developed to the point where it is possible to interpret automatically using machines (see Chapter 6), thereby opening up new research possibilities in the area of interpreting. It is also possible now for translations/interpretations to be made automatically between written and spoken media (see also Chapter 6). In addition, written texts, which used to be handwritten or typed on a manual typewriter, are now more commonly produced in electronic or digital format, facilitating the processing of such texts for research purposes.

The second type is rank-restricted theories, which is concerned with translation from the point of view of linguistic 'ranks' (a Hallidayan term) or levels of linguistic analysis: sentence, clause, group, word and morpheme (Shuttleworth and Cowie 1997: 138). Translations may be compared with their source texts at any level to establish correspondences, that is whether there is a correspondence at the lowest rank (morpheme); for example 'Freund' ('friend') as corresponding roots (here: words), and 'freund*lich*' ('friend*ly*') as affixes or bound morphemes. As Holmes points out (1988:179), '[t]raditionally, a great deal of writing on translation was concerned almost entirely with the rank of the word'; this is also reflected in the direct translation approach used in first-generation machine translation systems, where a word in the source text is matched to an equivalent word in the target text (see Chapter 3) in a kind of 'rank-restricted' way. Since Holmes first proposed his schema, his prediction that the upper rank limit of the sentence would give way to the text, has been realized. Further examples of analysing translation with respect to ranks are described in Matthiessen (2001).

The third type is text type-restricted theories. The study of text types such as those discussed by Reiss (1977/1989) shows the functional characteristics of three text types and how they can be linked to translation methods. The informative type of text ideally uses plain language to convey information, facts and so on in a logical way; examples of informative texts include operating instructions and reports. The expressive type of text uses creative language to express aesthetic form from the author's perspective; examples of expressive texts include poems and plays. The operative type of text uses a dialogic language to induce desired responses from readers; examples of operative texts include advertisements and sermons (Munday 2001: 73–4). The use of translation tools such as machine translation systems is currently mainly limited to translating technical texts, often falling into the category of informative texts. Text typology is therefore helpful in restricting the research object, that is the type of text which tends to be translated using electronic tools.

The fourth type concerns area-restricted theories, which Holmes interprets as restricted by language pair (e.g. translation between French and German) or language group (e.g. translation within the Slavic languages), on the one hand, and by culture (e.g. within the Swiss culture or between the Swiss and Belgian cultures), on the other hand (Holmes 1988/2000:179). Close proximity between the source and target language within a language group or 'family', for example between Romance languages (Spanish and Italian or Spanish and Catalan), usually means fewer problems for machine translation systems than if the language pair is not closely related genealogically, suggesting that the analysis of family-based similarities may generate better translation quality (Hajic, Hric and Kubon 2000; see also Altintas and Cicekli 2002). Holmes warns against the danger of cultural bias in so far as 'some aspects of theories that are presented as general in reality pertain only to the Western cultural area' (1988/2000:179). We can also observe cultural bias in the development of machine translation and other natural-language processing systems – often dictated by socio-economic or military reasons – so that languages such as Fongoro, for example, spoken near the Chad-Sudanese border, are unlikely to be explored from the point of view of translation technology, owing to a lack of commercial viability or demonstrated need.

The fifth type is problem-restricted theories. This sub-type is concerned with investigating specific linguistic phenomena such as grammatical errors. While translators use tools like spell and grammar-checkers, dictionaries and glossaries to produce their work, particular types of error may still occur and provide a fruitful area of research which could inform translation practice as well as translator training and the design of checking tools.

Finally, the sixth type, time-restricted theories – which may be focused, according to Holmes, on contemporary translations or on translations from an earlier period – could also be developed using electronic corpora and tools. However, older texts would need to be converted from paper into digital form, using, for example, an electronic scanner or optical character recognition (OCR). Issues of copyright may be relevant here, depending on the date and provenance of the texts chosen for analysis.

Applied translation studies

Let us now turn to Applied Translation Studies, as outlined in Holmes' schema. As we have seen, this second main branch has four subcategories in which the respective objectives of each category are: to improve the quality of translation by developing effective methods of translation teaching and training; to develop better translation tools (or 'aids'); to establish principles and regulations for professional translators (policy); and to critique translations. In the context of our theme of translation and technology, we can interpret this last subcategory as encompassing the evaluation of translation tools, products and processes.

Among Translation Studies researchers, opinions differ about the relevance of Applied Translation Studies and its relationship to Pure Translation Studies (Ulrych 2002: 200). The relationship between them is, however, important for today's translation needs, as I am attempting to show in this section. Pure Translation Studies research aims for a better understanding of languages, cultures and translation phenomena. Applied Translation Studies can use the information obtained by Pure Translation Studies to train translators, to enhance the use of translation tools and to critique translation works (Ulrych 2002: 200). Similarly, findings in Applied Translation Studies can help researchers of Pure Translation Studies to advance their own areas of research. The sub-branch translation criticism 'is an essential link between translation theory and its practice' (Newmark 1988: 184), which can contribute to the development of translation theories. Applied Translation Studies is also useful for the localization industry, discussed in Chapters 1 and 4.

With his interest in Pure Translation Studies, Holmes did not describe applied areas of research in great detail (Munday 2001: 13). However, our concern here is primarily with the applied areas, specifically what Holmes calls translation aids. A detailed description of this sub-branch is given in Figure 2.5, building on Holmes' original schema. It is important to remember that the four branches under Applied Translation Studies are not independent but feed material to one another. Consider, for example, the relationship between translation training and translation criticism where critiquing translations is one good way of learning. Note also that I have replaced the term 'translation aids' with 'translation technology' and suggested all the sub-branches below it in order to reflect contemporary developments; these are no longer confined to lexicographical and terminological aids as originally suggested by Holmes (1988/2000: 182).

In my updated and revised model of Holmes' schema, the sub-branches of 'translation technology' are automatic systems and computer-aided translation tools, which will be described in Chapters 3 and 4 respectively. The branch called computer-aided tools covers a wide range, which I have further divided into translation, linguistic and localization tools. The translation sub-branch includes tools such as translation memory and terminology management systems while localization tools are used to localize products including software and documentation. The linguistic tools sub-branch includes tools that are language-dependent, such as dictionaries and glossaries, and tools which are language-independent, such as optical character recognition (OCR) and concordancers. Although Figure 2.5 neatly divides the tools into their own classes, we need to be aware that many of these tools are now

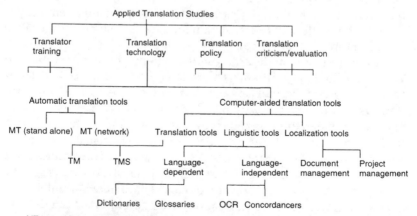

MT = machine translation; TM = translation memory; TMS = terminology management systems;
OCR = optical character recognition

Figure 2.5   A schema of applied translation studies

multifunctional. In other words, some tools may be integrated into a single system made up of several different applications as we shall discover in subsequent chapters.

The evaluation of translation tools – the fourth sub-branch of Applied Translation Studies as interpreted here – is discussed in Chapter 5. Translator training and policy are not dealt with in any detail in this book.

Having extended and interpreted Holmes' Applied Translation Studies schema in the modern idiom with a particular emphasis on technology, let us now turn to the translation process, classified by Holmes under Pure Translation Studies. Our perspective will, once again, be rather different.

The translation process

In his discussion of process-oriented Translation Studies, Holmes had in mind the investigation of mental processes. In the context of translation technology, we can interpret this rather differently as the stages in the automation of the translation process. The description of the translation process given below and illustrated in Figure 2.6 is also viewed from a perspective different from those commonly used, for example that of Nida (1969). Here, the tasks of pre- and post-editing texts as input to and output from machine translation systems, and a language variety known as controlled language are described. Pre-editing is carried out on a source-language text while post-editing is performed on an output (target-language text) generated by a translation tool. Pre- and post-editing are not always necessary but might be required owing to a number of

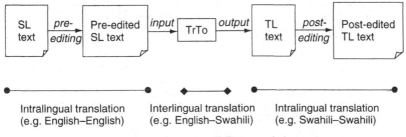

Intralingual translation   Interlingual translation   Intralingual translation
(e.g. English–English)   (e.g. English–Swahili)   (e.g. Swahili–Swahili)

SL = source language; TL = target language; TrTo = translation tool

Figure 2.6   A model of the translation process including pre- and post-editing tasks

factors such as the linguistic quality of a source-language text, the type of translation tool used and the required quality of the target-language text (fitness for purpose).

In Figure 2.6, Jakobson's (1959/2000: 114) semiotic categories of translation are used to characterize the pre- and post-editing tasks performed when using a translation tool. One of his categories is intralingual translation, which is 'an interpretation of verbal signs by means of other signs in the same language' or, in other words, 'rewording', for example, the translation of a poem into prose in the same language (Jakobson 1959/2000: 114). Here we understand intralingual translation as pre-editing or post-editing. The other is interlingual translation, which occurs when a source-language text undergoes a translation process, in this case carried out by a translation tool or a human translator using a tool, to generate a target text in another language. Interlingual translation is also known as 'translation proper' (Jakobson 1959/2000: 114).

Pre-editing

Pre-editing may entail restricting vocabulary and grammar before the translation process can take place. It can also simply mean checking the source-language text for errors and ambiguities (Gross 1992: 98). Based on the translation process shown in Figure 2.6, an English source-language text undergoes a pre-editing process to produce a pre-edited source-language text. This is still in the intralingual stage since the languages of both texts are still in English. As an example, Figure 2.7 shows an original English text and its pre-edited version, which is easier to read and understand than the original.

SL text in English	Pre-edited SL text in English
Let the water run hot at the sink and then pull the connector from the recess in the back of the dishwasher. Upon the completion of the above task, lift the connector to the faucet by pressing down the thumb release.	1 Turn on the faucet at the sink until the water runs hot. 2 Pull the connector from the recess in the back of the dishwasher. 3 Press down on the thumb release and lift the connector onto the faucet.

SL = source language

Figure 2.7   Example of an English SL text and its pre-edited version

Pre-editing of source-language texts is becoming more widespread as a form of cost and quality control, and is particularly frequent when the need arises to translate it into several target languages. This task becomes especially crucial when a product needs to be launched simultaneously or in quick succession over a short period of time in a number of countries with different languages. We can see this happening in the localization industry where documentation accompanying a product undergoes translation into several languages. For example, the source-language documentation of the N-Gage QD by Nokia, a gaming platform and mobile telephone set, had to be treated as a single product even though it appears in different languages after having undergone the localization process (see Chapter 4; see also Chapter 1).

Pre-editing a source-language text may reduce or eliminate the post-editing task. It is an unattainable goal to input a natural language text directly into a machine translation system and expect it to produce a high-quality output without pre-editing. Current machine translation systems have yet to produce acceptable quality translations of general and specialized texts even when source-language texts are well written (Koby 2001: 7, 12). Nevertheless, a machine translation system may be able to generate a good-quality output without much post-editing if the subject field of the source-language text is highly restricted, the system is built specifically to handle a particular subject field, and its source language is written in a 'controlled' manner (Koby 2001: 5).

A text written in a natural language may contain ambiguity, a word or a sentence having more than one meaning. Therefore, a language that only contains a restricted set of terms, all of which can in turn be processed by a computer efficiently and accurately can simplify the translation process. Such a language is called a sublanguage (see also Sager 1994). The best-known use of a sublanguage is in Météo, a machine translation system that translates weather forecasts, which are linguistically and textually highly formulaic, from English into French (Somers 2003e: 289). Another type of language known as controlled language is a carefully constructed variety of a language which is used to pre-edit a source-language text (Gross 1992: 98) or to author original texts. The critical difference between a sublanguage and a controlled language is that the terms, syntax and semantics of the former evolve naturally (within a specialist group), while in the case of the latter they are artificially constructed with certain restrictions imposed (Somers 2003e: 283). We shall return to controlled language in the last section of this chapter.

Post-editing

It is said that the post-editing task is not confined to machine translation output but also applies to translations produced by human translators. The term 'post-editing' is, however, normally reserved for outputs generated by machine translation systems (Allen 2001a: 26). Editing a human translation is more commonly referred to as 'revising' (Somers 1997: 199; Allen 2003; see also Chapter 7). Post-editing, according to Laurian (1984), is not a rewriting, revision or correction task but a method of considering a text and working on it for a new aim. Allen (2003: 297), on the other hand, defines post-editing as a task of editing, modifying and/or correcting translated text that a machine translation system has processed and generated. Post-editing is essentially a specialized skill, which tries 'to preserve as much of the machine's output as possible and "zapping" the text at strategic points rather than redoing it from scratch' (Vasconcellos and Bostad 1992: 68).

In order to follow the translation process (as in Figure 2.6) through its stages, the pre-edited controlled language text previously shown in Figure 2.7 is now shown in Figure 2.8 as the output of a machine translation system in Spanish. The machine translation output contains sentences which are more freely formulated and the choice of words is not suitable for a user's manual. Therefore, post-editing is required on

TL text generated by a machine translation system	TL text post-edited by a human translator
1 Dé vuelta encendido al grifo en el fregadero hasta el agua funciona caliente.	1 Abra la llave del agua del fregadero hasta que salga agua caliente. [Turn the faucet on at the sink until the water runs hot.]
2 Tire del conectador a partir de la hendidura en la parte posteriora del lavaplatos.	2 Jale el conector del hueco que se encuentra en la parte posteriora de la lavaplatos. [Pull the connector from the recess in the back of the dishwasher.]
3 Presione abajo en el lanzamiento del pulgar y levante el conectador sobre el grifo.	3 Oprima hacia abajo el liberador manual y levante el conector a la llave del agua. [Press down on the thumb release and lift the connector onto the faucet.]

TL = target language

Figure 2.8 Unedited and post-edited Spanish machine translation output

the Spanish output by a professional translator as shown in the right-hand column of Figure 2.8.

Post-editing is almost always required if the output from a machine translation is for publication purposes (Nirenburg *et al.* 1992: 11). Several techniques of post-editing, from rapid post-editing for information-only purposes, to polished post-editing may be applied to make a translation look like a professional translator has translated it. Rapid post-editing aims at producing a correct text by taking into account the content but not the style. A translated version of minutes of a meeting to be circulated to board members of a corporation is an example of an occasion when rapid post-editing might be called for. Where only obvious spelling, grammatical and stylistic errors are corrected to make the translation as comprehensible as possible, the amount of post-editing is minimal. The type of translated texts that undergo rapid post-editing are restricted in use to specific target readerships and times (Laurian 1984; see also Allen 2001b; Krings 2001). Polished post-editing, on the other hand, usually results in a high-quality translation. However, it is only applicable when a machine translation output is good enough to warrant it. In other words, the quality of the output cannot be so low as to make it necessary for a human translator to retranslate it from scratch. Even unedited output has its uses, especially for those interested only in the information provided by a source-language text (Newton 1992b: 4). This is evident in the use of free translations offered by online machine translation systems, often found in search engines.

Based on the current development of machine translation technology, post-editing is likely to be a fixture for the foreseeable future. As a result, in 1999, an initiative called the Post-Editing Special Interest Group was set up by a number of members of the Association of Machine Translation in the Americas (AMTA) to provide post-editing guidelines and training for the American Translators Association (ATA; see also Allen 2001b). The aims of this group are to develop specifications for an optimum post-editing environment, to educate relevant groups in the translation industry about post-editing, to organize and promote post-editing workshops and to develop post-editing courseware for translation programmes. Controlled languages have been developed for a range of text types by groups of users or organizations such as the European Commission Translation Services, General Motors and PAHO, all of whom have developed their own post-editing guidelines. As a result, no one governing body has ever been established that could standardize different versions of controlled languages (Allen 2000: 24–5, 44–5). In the future, it is possible that pre- and post-editing tasks may be included as part of a programme of translation training for those translating technical texts and using machine translation systems (Koby 2001: 11–12).

Controlled language

A controlled language can be defined as 'a subset of a natural language with an artificially restricted vocabulary, grammar and style' (Kaji 1999: 37); one of its goals is to improve the quality of translation output by humans or machines. It is also employed to restrict the inconsistent use of words and of odd sentences (Wojcik and Hoard 1997: 238). In other words, the maxim of a controlled language is to use simple vocabulary and sentence structures in order to convey complex ideas in writing to ensure rapid reading, understanding, and ease of translation.

A controlled language has three important elements: vocabulary, grammar and style (Kaji 1999: 38). The size of the permitted vocabulary is usually restricted to limit the occurrence of lexical ambiguity. The grammar restriction occurs at two levels: phrase and sentence. For example, a noun phrase should not consist of more than four nouns, a sentence should not exceed 20 words in length, a paragraph should not exceed six sentences, the passive voice must not be used and the future tense must be avoided (Nyberg, Mitamura and Huijsen 2003: 247). The sentences used as an illustration in Figure 2.9 are written in both natural and controlled language. The controlled language sentences are shorter and more precise than the natural language sentences, only one instruction occurring per sentence and in the proper order of sequence. As a result of the restrictions imposed on the controlled language sentences, the risk of errors in translation is reduced, thus reducing the burden of post-editing (Allen and Hogan 2000). Essentially, a controlled language is not expressive and requires some introductory training before a technical writer or professional translator is able to use it.

Natural language	Controlled language
Remove screws holding the blower and pull the blower from the cabinet. Before the screws are installed to the blower, a new blower is pushed back into the cabinet.	1 Remove screws from the blower. 2 Pull the blower from the cabinet. 3 Push a new blower into the cabinet. 4 Secure the blower with screws.

Figure 2.9 Example of natural and controlled languages

The concept of a controlled language itself is not new. In 1932, Charles Ogden introduced a form of English known as 'Simplified English' via the publication of BASIC English (British American Scientific International, Commercial). The Simplified English of BASIC had several hundred words; the aim was to promote a type of English suitable for use in science and commerce (Macklovitch 1999: 75). In the 1970s, based on Ogden's BASIC English, the Caterpillar Tractor Company introduced for commercial use a new version of English for technical writing known as the Caterpillar Fundamental English (CFE). In the 1990s, Caterpillar developed Caterpillar Technical English (CTE), the successor to CFE. Today, the aims of CTE are the standardization of English terminology, better comprehension of English documentation by native and non-native English readers, and easy translation into other languages (see also Nyberg, Mitamura and Huijsen 2003).

The best-known and most widely used controlled language, however, is AECMA (European Association of Aerospace Industries) Simplified English, a joint effort between AECMA and AIA (Aerospace Industries Association of America). An example of a text for the aerospace industry in AECMA Simple English and its original English text is shown in Figure 2.10. In 2004, when AECMA merged with EDIG (European Defence Industries Group) and EUROSPACE (Aerospace and Defence Industries Association of Europe), AECMA Simplified English was replaced by AeroSpace and Defence (ASD) Simplified Technical English. ASD Simplified Technical English contains a set of writing rules and a dictionary of several hundred basic words that can be expanded to express technical concepts in the aerospace industry in the English language.

The idea of Simplified English has also been adopted for the creation of Controlled English for non-aerospace industries such as automotive, healthcare, semiconductors and telecommunications. Controlled English is said to use only 1 per cent of the English language vocabulary to reach readers around the world (Smart Communications, Inc. 2005b: 1). It has many advantages including clarity and concision designed to prevent any confusion, as this may cause legal problems resulting from product liability legislation which in some jurisdictions includes packaging and documentation as part of the 'product'. As English is the common language in worldwide communication, short sentences are used to enhance the readability, comprehensibility and usability of a text for global readers. Training and development costs notwithstanding, the use of a controlled language also involves less writing time and lower costs. The most important advantage of using Controlled English is the clarity of the text, of obvious importance when the text needs to

Original English text	AECMA simplified English text
The Model ADI-999 Attitude Indicator (Photo 8) *provides* a *visual display* of pitch and roll attitude and both *enroute Course* Deviation Indicator (CDI)/*Very* High Frequency Omnirange (VOR)/*Distance* Measuring Equipment (DME)/*Flight* Management System (FMS) navigation aids and precision approach *Instrument* Landing System (ILS) *information.* The indicator *may be used as* a *long range standby attitude reference*, during a primary power failure, when *coupled with* an emergency power supply. After *complete loss* of power, nine minutes of *useful* attitude *information* is *presented*.	The model ADI-999 Attitude Indicator (see photo 8) has a display for pitch and roll. This display also includes these indicators: • Course Deviation Indicator (CDI) • Very-High Frequency Omnirange (VOR) • Distance Measuring Equipment (DME) • Flight Management System (FMS) • Instrument Landing System (ILS) When there is a power failure, the model ADI-999 can supply an attitude reference for the next nine minutes. After nine minutes, obey the emergency procedures.

Figure 2.10 Example of original English text and its AECMA simplified English version

Source: Smart Communications, Inc. (2005a).

be translated into many target languages and both commercial and safety reasons are uppermost.

Figure 2.11 shows a sample from a manual for a water desalinisation plant that was originally written by an engineer with English as his/her native language for other engineers in natural English. The original text may create problems of comprehension and translation including (as indicated by the underlined phrases in Figure 2.11), for example, understanding the meaning of a phrasal verb such as 'take up', the role of agent and object ('who does what to whom' in gerunds or words ending with '-ing') and loss of meaning in long sentences.

Before the product is exported, the manual is rewritten in Simplified English (a type of controlled language in English) for technicians who do not have English as their first language. The Simplified English version is easier to read and understand as a second language. The manual is later translated into the local language based on the Simplified English version, in this case into Simplified Arabic (a type of controlled language in Arabic) which is different from the natural Arabic language (Smart Communications, Inc. 2005c).

Original English text	Simplified English version	Simplified Arabic version
(q) The lime must be mixed into a solution before being added to the digester because dry lime would settle to the bottom in lumps, which is not only ineffective but the lumps take up digester capacity and are difficult to remove when cleaning the digester. Use all the mixing energy available while liming and thereafter in digester mixing. The easiest application point is through the scum box, if one is available. Add small quantities of lime daily until the pH and volatile acid/alkalinity relationship of the tank are restored to desired levels, and gas production is normal. (h) In any case, use lime only if recovery by natural methods cannot be accomplished within the time available.	(q) Mix the lime with the water into a solution before you put the solution into the digester. Add the solution to the digester through the scum box. Add a small amount of solution each day until the amount of pH (the balance between the acid and the alkaline) and the production of gas are normal. NEVER put lumps of dry lime into the digester. These lumps fall to the bottom of the digester and are difficult to remove (h) Use the lime only when there is not enough time to correct the liquid in the digester by other methods.	ج - أخلط الجير بالماء قبل وضع المحلول في الصهريج ثم امزج المحلول جيدا. أضف المحلول الى الرحال عن طريق صندوق الرغاوي. أضف كمية بسيطة من المحلول كل يوم حتى تصبح كل من كمية أيون الهيدروجين والتعادل بين الحامض والقلوي، وإنتاج الغاز.. طبيعية. لا تضع كتلا من الجير الجاف أبدا.. جميع هذه الكتل ترسب في القاع ويصعب من الصهريج ازالتها. د - استخدم الجير فقط اذا لم يكن لديك وقت كاف لتصحيح السائل في الصهريج بوسائل أخرى.

Figure 2.11 Example of natural English, simplified English and simplified Arabic texts
Source: Smart Communications, Inc. (2005c).

Controlled English for non-aerospace industries has a larger number of basic words and terms than Simplified English. It is important to remember, however, that a technical writer or professional translator who specializes in the Controlled English of one narrow subject field in the aerospace industry is not necessarily equally proficient in other subject fields within the same industry, let alone in other industries, as each subject field is highly specialized. For example, in the glossary for pilots and air-traffic personnel, the term 'interrogator' refers to a specific device known as 'a ground-based secondary surveillance system transmitter' and, not as we generally understand it, a person whose job is to ask questions. Similarly, 'under way' means specifically 'the state of being on the surface of the water but not moored to any fixed object on the land or in the water', it does not mean 'in progress' or 'in operation'.

Non-English-based controlled language can also be found in Chinese, German, Spanish and Swedish. For example, 'ScaniaSwedish' is the controlled language which is used by native Swedish-speaking technical writers to author truck-maintenance manuals for the company, Scania. The maintenance manuals written in ScaniaSwedish are then translated into other languages. Controlled languages such as these are designed to meet the authoring and communication needs of a particular subject field or organization (Hartley and Paris 2001: 309). Often a controlled language is used for technical documents such as procedures, descriptions and reports (Wojcik and Hoard 1997: 238).

As mentioned earlier, controlled languages – notably Controlled English – have been in existence for more than seven decades. However, use their has never been so extensive as it is now, with, for instance, different Controlled English versions each containing the vocabulary of an individual subject field. Controlled English or indeed any controlled language is created by a group of subject-field specialists to serve a specific purpose, such as Controlled English for the aerospace industry, a unique variety language which is used exclusively in that industry. With respect to vocabulary, instead of using the entire English language vocabulary, Controlled English merely selects a specific number of vocabulary items together with their meanings to ensure that polysemy and synonymy are eliminated; as a result, one word has only one sense and each sense is conveyed by only one word. Even though controlled language commonly occurs in the technical field, emotional and aesthetic qualities should not be excluded entirely because over-simplification may create other problems. In fact, controlled languages should be applied appropriately, pragmatically and sensibly (Janowski 1998).

In the near future, translators could find themselves working increasingly from controlled language sources regardless of the type of translation tool used. Some original documents are destined for translation because the decision to translate these documents was made even before the original documents were written. For such documents, authoring the original documentation in a controlled language could, to a very high degree, improve translatability. Examples of tools that help with implementing controlled language authoring include SIMPLUS: Controlled Language Editing Tool by Lingua Technology, and MAXit: Controlled English Checker by Smart Communications, Inc.

One of the objectives of controlled language is to predict translation choices and to provide the best equivalents in the target language. In some cases, more than one target-language text may be produced, as shown in Figure 2.12 where the controlled English language text has been translated into French and Spanish. From the translation perspective, the use of a controlled language presents both benefits and challenges. The benefits are numerous, including: the reduction of product support costs through better manuals and web pages; uniformity in the training of technicians, customer support and management staff; the prevention of common grammatical errors; and the improvement of reader comprehension through the 'one word one meaning' idea (Smart Communications, Inc. 2005b). Challenges for translators include having a syntactically and stylistically rigid text that may be hard to work with (Nyberg, Mitamura and Huijsen 2003: 272). To create a controlled

CL: English	*Translation*: French	*Translation*: Spanish
1 Remove the diffuser panels on the hood.	1 Retirez les panneaux du diffuseur de la hotte.	1 Retire los paneles de difusión de la campana.
2 Clip carbon filter onto the bracket of diffuser panels.	2 Agrafez le filter au charbon sur le support des panneaux du diffuseur.	2 Enganche los filtros de carbon a los soportes de los paneles de difusión.
3 Reinstall diffuser panels.	3 Réinstallez les panneaux du diffuseur.	3 Vuelva a instalar los paneles de difusión.

CL = controlled language

Figure 2.12   Example of an English controlled language text and its translations

language for a highly specialized subject field can be costly and can take several years of research (see for example The Scania Project at http://stp.ling.uu.se/~corpora/scania/) as vocabulary, grammar, punctuation and general writing conventions have to be redefined, and professional translators as well as writers have to be trained to use the syntactic rules and the terms.

To conclude this section, we present an example of the complete sequence of a translation process (see Figure 2.6) in Figure 2.13. Here

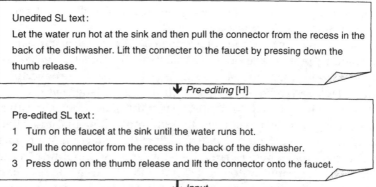

Unedited SL text:
Let the water run hot at the sink and then pull the connector from the recess in the back of the dishwasher. Lift the connecter to the faucet by pressing down the thumb release.

⬇ *Pre-editing* [H]

Pre-edited SL text:
1 Turn on the faucet at the sink until the water runs hot.
2 Pull the connector from the recess in the back of the dishwasher.
3 Press down on the thumb release and lift the connector onto the faucet.

⬇ *Input*

MACHINE TRANSLATION SYSTEM

⬇ *Output*

Unedited Spanish TL text:
1 Dé vuelta encendido al grifo en el fregadero hasta el agua funciona caliente.
2 Tire del conectador a partir de la hendidura en la parte posteriora del lavaplatos.
3 Presione abajo en el lanzamiento del pulgar y levante el conectador sobre el grifo.

⬇ *Post-editing* [H]

Post-edited Spanish TL text:
1 Abra la llave del agua del fregadero hasta que salga agua caliente.
2 Jale el conector del hueco que se encuentra en la parte posteriora de la lavaplatos.
3 Oprima hacia abajo el liberador manual y levante el conector a la llave delagua.

SL = source language; TL = target language; H = human

Figure 2.13 Illustration of the translation process using a machine translation system

the source-language text in English is pre-edited in order to ensure that the machine translation system will be able to generate a better quality output in the Spanish language than it could have done using an unedited version. The pre-edited text has been edited through the use of controlled language rules to ensure the elimination of ambiguity. The output generated by the system is then post-edited for publishing purposes by a professional translator. Humans (marked as [H]) are still required to perform pre- and post-editing tasks, although they now have the use of tools such as spell-checkers that can assist them in their editing process.

Conclusion

The discussion in this chapter has introduced a number of issues relating to translation and technology. It has been shown that translation theory has been overshadowed by linguistic theories and various formalisms in the development of rule-based machine translation systems. Taking a broader view, the evolution of translation theory over many centuries and the views on the subject by different groups of scholars has culminated in Translation Studies as an interdisciplinary field. We have also discussed the often shaky relationship between academic and professional groups involved with translation technology, owing to differences in research focus and interests. This discussion has provided us with an introduction to the major players in translation, while at the same time the relationship between Translation Studies as a discipline and translation technology has been explored. Where translation involves the use of translation tools – in particular machine translation systems – a particular approach needs to be taken in order to describe translation processes, including pre-editing and post-editing tasks. It has been shown that this translation process is more likely to be successful when a special man-made language variety is employed, such as a controlled language.

Suggested reading

Chesterman, A. and E. Wagner (2002) *Can Theory help Translators?* Manchester: St Jerome Publishing.

Melby, A. and C.T. Warner (1995) *The Possibility of Language: A Discussion of the Nature of Language with Implications for Human and Machine Translation.* Amsterdam: John Benjamins.

Munday, J. (2001) *Introducing Translation Studies: Theories and Applications.* London: Routledge.

Newton, J. (ed.) (1992a) *Computers in Translation: A Practical Appraisal*. London: Routledge.

Steiner, E. and C. Yallop (eds) (2001) *Exploring Translation and Multilingual Text Production: Beyond Context*. Berlin: Mouton de Gruyter.

Wilss, W. (1996) *Knowledge and Skills in Translator Behavior*. Amsterdam: John Benjamins.

Venuti, L. (ed.) (2000) *The Translation Studies Reader*. London: Routledge.

3
Machine Translation Systems

Machine translation is an important technology socio-politically, commercially and scientifically, despite many misconceptions about its success or lack of it over the decades. The emergence of the Internet as one of the main media of modern communication has turned translation into a bridge that connects speakers of different languages. The endless traffic of communication between different language groups requires translation, but when instant translations are needed, human translators are not able to supply them fast enough. A highly skilled profession like translation using human translators is expensive and also slow, especially when a large number of languages and subject fields are involved. In order to meet the growing translation demand, machine translation systems are seen as a cost-effective alternative to human translators in a variety of situations. Ever since the first system was built, machine translation has been presenting scientific challenges (see also Nirenburg 1996). It became the testing ground for many experiments and applications for natural-language processing, artificial intelligence and even linguistics (Arnold *et al.* 1994: 4–5).

Machine translation is an interdisciplinary enterprise that combines a number of fields of study such as lexicography, linguistics, computational linguistics, computer science and language engineering (Whitelock and Kilby 1995: 2; see also Wilss 1999). It is based on the hypothesis that natural languages can be fully described, controlled and mathematically coded (Wilss 1999: 140).

This chapter begins with a brief history of machine translation (see also Slocum 1988; Hutchins 2000b; Nirenburg, Somers and Wilks 2003), followed by a description of the components involved in a machine translation system. These components and their configurations are sometimes referred to as the machine translation architecture. Hybrid and interactive machine translation, online machine translation and commercial machine translation systems are also discussed. In addition, we also examine the different purposes for which machine translation systems are used.

Major historical developments

Machine translation is over five decades old, although the notion of 'mechanical translation' appeared nearly four hundred years ago. In 1629, Descartes may have been the first to propose the idea that a language could be represented by codes and that words of different languages with equivalent meaning could share the same code (Pugh 1992: 15). It was based on the hypothesis that a custom-designed machine might be able to manipulate codified rules of natural language. This may have been the precursor to modern machine technology (Wilss 1999: 140). In the early years of machine technology, the common term used was 'automatic translation' or 'mechanical translation' (Tong 1994: 4,731). However, it was only after the Second World War (1939–45) that the possibilities of language translation using stored-program computers, a recent invention at that time, were explored (Somers 2003b: 4).

Figure 3.1 shows the approximation on the time continuum of approaches used in machine translation system development since the second half of the twentieth century. Figure 3.1 will serve as a guide for the discussion in this chapter, and as an indicator of time periods when a particular approach was at its peak.

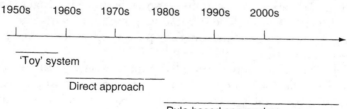

Figure 3.1   Chronology of machine translation development

Pioneer years

The pioneer years began in 1949 with the well-known memorandum from Warren Weaver that effectively marked the beginning of machine translation research. This memorandum focused on four issues: meaning and context, language and logic, translation and cryptography techniques, and language and invariants (Pugh 1992: 16). This memorandum, in which Weaver proposed the use of cryptographic techniques to mechanize translation, was rejected by many, who felt that it was too simplistic, naïve and perhaps presumptuous about the logical structures of language, its formalization and the complexity and subtleness of translation (see also Chapter 2). However, it struck researchers as sufficiently intriguing to begin experimenting although, at the same time, not everyone took the memorandum seriously (Tong 1994: 4,731; Somers 1998a: 140). In the memorandum, Weaver proposed cryptographic techniques to mechanize translation.

The idea of using cryptographic techniques was a direct consequence of two 'highly specific programmed machines'. One was called Colossus that was built in 1943 in London by Tommy Flowers, an engineer at the British General Post Office; the other was called ENIAC (Electronic Numerical Integrator and Computer). Designed by J. Presper Eckert and John William Mauchly of the University of Pennsylvania, ENIAC was built in 1945 by the US Army (http://en.wikipedia.org/wiki/). Unfortunately, the techniques of cryptography were not found to be useful, as deciphering coded messages and translating natural language texts proved to be rather different. This would come as no surprise to any translator, or even linguist, but most researchers who pioneered machine translation research were not linguists and, as a result, may have been naïve about the complexities and characteristics of natural language. As they discovered, words cannot be treated in isolation. However, their attempts seemed to generate serious interest in the process of mechanizing translation (Tong 1994: 4,731, Somers 1998b: 140).

While in the USA high-level funding came mostly from the military and the CIA (Central Intelligence Agency), in the Soviet Union the KGB (Komitet Gosudarstvennoi Bezopasnosti) provided most of the financial support for machine translation research. The goal at the time was to produce fully automated high-quality machine translation systems. In the early days of the Cold War, the purpose of machine translation research by both countries was to gather intelligence, in contrast to Weaver's original more altruistic motives of fostering peace through international communication. In recent years, military funding for more advanced machine translation systems has made a comeback due to security threats around the world, particularly in the USA (see Chapter 6). Research on machine translation was also undertaken in France, Germany, Japan, the Soviet Union and the UK.

First-generation systems

The first public demonstration of a machine translation system was the Russian–English Georgetown University System, a collaborative effort between IBM and Georgetown University, carried out in 1954 (Hutchins 1995: 434). Early machine translation systems, such as the Georgetown University system, often referred to as the 'first generation', employed word-for-word translation methods with no clear built-in linguistic component. Although the system was considered only a 'toy system' with 250 words, six grammar rules and 49 sentences, it prompted the US government to fund large-scale machine translation research projects (Goshawke, Kelly and Wigg 1987: 26). According to Somers (2003b: 4), in the early days, the US government invested between $12 and $20 million on machine translation research. The sponsors and the general public were optimistic that high-quality translations could be produced by fully automatic systems.

In 1966, a committee known as the Automatic Language Processing Advisory Committee (ALPAC) was established to investigate the feasibility of high-quality machine translation. The report concluded that the machine translation systems evaluated were slow, less accurate than human translations and expensive (see also ALPAC 1966). Thus machine translation systems were deemed a failure in meeting their objectives and ALPAC did not foresee any possibility of achieving useful results in the near future. However, the ALPAC report was considered biased due to the unrealistic expectation that machine translation is capable of producing perfect translations of the highest quality. It also did not include any study of the long-term needs and possibilities of machine translation systems. Even Chomsky's dominance in linguistic studies did not have much of an impact on machine translation during this period (Tong 1994: 4,731).

Instead, the report recommended the development of machine aids for translators and shifted its support to research in computational linguistics. It also brought about the realization that 'language is too complex and the task of translation therefore requires human capabilities, which...cannot be easily simulated in a computer program' (Somers 1997: 194). The after-effect of the report resulted in the demise of large-scale research funding from government agencies in the USA and across Europe, specifically France and Germany, although it flourished in Eastern European countries such as the Soviet Union, Hungary and Czechoslovakia which had little technological know-how, according to Pugh (1992: 17; see also Somers 1998b: 141). The general mood 'changed from enthusiastic optimism to fatalistic condemnation'

(Pugh 1992: 16). As a consequence, machine translation became the victim of its own unrealistic expectations.

In 1959, Bar-Hillel argued convincingly that FAHQMT (fully automatic high-quality machine translation) should not be the goal of machine translation researchers (Nirenburg 1996; see also Melby and Warner 1995). He was highly critical of the machine translation projects then in existence, which were mostly theory-based. We can recall that the original objective of machine translation was to build fully automatic systems that could translate as well as human translators, potentially replacing human translators with machines. It was arguably a grave error when, in their enthusiasm to build the perfect system, machine translation researchers failed to seek the views of translators. This later led to antagonism among translators towards machine translation systems, fearing that they would be 'phased out' by machines; as for their part, they also did not understand the limited or highly specific capabilities of such systems. This is a feeling that is still evident even today.

The quiet years

The ALPAC report brought machine translation research almost to a halt, and as a result the first half of the 1970s was a quiet period for machine translation, especially in the USA. Some groups continued machine translation research under different names such as 'computer-assisted translation', while others moved on and concentrated on research related to linguistics and artificial intelligence (Tong 1994: 4,731). Only a handful of research groups survived the aftermath of the report and continued on a much smaller scale. Logos, a privately funded company set up in 1969, produced its first English–Vietnamese machine translation system three years later in the context of the US military involvement in Vietnam. In 1977 and 1980, two machine translation systems called Weidner and ALPS (Automatic Language Processing System) were successfully developed by Brigham Young University. Neither Weidner nor ALPS, however, are machine translation systems in the real sense but more like multilingual terminological data manipulation systems (Ananiadou 1987: 176–80).

Outside the USA, the Traduction automatique à l'Université de Montréal (TAUM) in Canada was one of the few research groups to survive. In 1976, they successfully developed the TAUM-Météo machine translation system to translate meteorological bulletins between English and French. Météo continues to operate successfully to this day. Another survivor is the SUSY (Saarbrücker ÜbersetzungsSYstem) machine translation system developed in Germany involving English, German and

Russian (Freigang 2001: 20). Since 1995, SUSY can be accessed online for German–English and Russian–German translation. Research activities in the Soviet Union concentrated mainly on languages spoken within the Union itself (Goshawke, Kelly and Wigg 1987: 28). Some other European countries such as Hungary and Czechoslovakia continued their research but with limited technological expertise (Somers 1998a: 141). In Asia, the Chinese University of Hong Kong successfully developed a Chinese–English machine translation system called CULT (Chinese University Language Translator) in 1968. Initially, only a small amount of machine translation research was carried out in Japan, but by the 1970s machine translation activity had increased, particularly at the Kyoto University research laboratory headed by Makoto Nagao (see also Slocum 1988).

Second-generation systems

In the late 1970s, the USA saw a revival of machine translation research with the development of SPANAM (Spanish American), a Spanish–English machine translation system, and ENGSPAN (English Spanish), an English–Spanish system by PAHO as well as METAL (Mechanical Translation and Analysis of Language), a German-English machine translation system built by the US Air Force at the University of Texas in Austin with support from Siemens (Arnold *et al.* 1994: 14; see also Slocum 1988).

In Europe, between the 1970s and 1992, machine translation research reemerged with the EUROTRA (European Translation) project based on the work of the Groupe d'Étude pour la Traduction Automatique (GETA) in France and the University of Saarbrücken in Germany. This project covered all the languages spoken in the European Community at that time. Although it was not successful in building a 'working' machine translation system, several EUROTRA-inspired machine translation systems were developed, for example PaTrans (Patent Translation) in Denmark, a commercial machine translation system for translating patent texts from English into Danish, and an experimental machine translation system involving 13 languages called CAT2 (Constructors, Atoms and Translators) in Germany. This era lasted until the end of the 1980s, which saw the emergence of corpus-based approaches (the use of bilingual or parallel corpora based on statistical- and example-based approaches), and also the development of new rule-based approaches using constraint-based grammars (see also Chapter 2).

Machine translation research continued throughout the 1980s in an attempt to find better methods and techniques for translation. In the 1980s, the most active machine translation research took place in Japan, initiated by the Mu machine translation system developed at Kyoto University. Another well-known project was the joint research project between Japan's Center of International Cooperation for Computerization (CICC) and four Asian countries known as the Fifth Generation Multilingual Interlingua-based Machine Translation System Project (1987–95), which developed a system for translating in and out of Chinese, Indonesian, Japanese, Malay and Thai. At the same time, major Japanese electronic and telecommunication companies such as Fujitsu and Hitachi also began to develop machine translation systems for commercial use (Somers 1998a: 142).

In the 1980s, there were also advances in computational linguistics that allowed research into machine translation systems to develop more sophisticated approaches to translation. A number of machine translation systems adopted the 'indirect' approach to translation that was based on certain linguistic rules. An indirect approach enables the source-language text to be analysed and turned into abstract representations using programs that can identify word and sentence structures in an attempt to solve the problem of ambiguity. The abstract representations are also able to generate more than one target-language text. We shall return to this later in the chapter.

Most of the products developed at the time were software for computer-aided translation between Japanese and English specifically for the Japanese market. Most of the machine translation systems such as Pensee by OKI, HICATS (Hitachi Computer Aided Translation System) by Hitachi and Meltran-J/E (Japanese/English) by Mitsubishi Electric Corporation are based on the direct or transfer approach (see sections below). They all consist of only word and sentence structure analysis with much of the lexical ambiguities unresolved. Their domains are restricted to certain subject fields such as computer science and information technology. These machine translation systems require extensive pre-editing and post-editing by human translators (Hutchins 1995; see Chapter 2). Other commercial machine translation systems, which started out as basic research projects, such as METAL by Siemens and LMT (Logic-based Machine Translation) by IBM, were fully developed by the late 1980s (Somers 1998b: 142). Although they were simple in design with limited performance capacity, they showed that machine translation systems had potential for improvement.

Until the late 1980s, two approaches were used in machine translation systems, the indirect and the direct approaches. The indirect approach consisted of two basic systems, 'interlingua' and 'transfer'. These systems are described below. The best-known direct machine translation systems for mainframe computers (a term used to refer to a larger, expensive and more complex computer that processes massive amount of data such as censuses) are Systran, Logos and Atlas. The best-known transfer machine translation systems are Ariane developed by GETA, a machine translation project dating back to the 1960s, and EUTROTRA funded by the Commission of the European Communities. Neither Ariane nor EUTROTRA, nor the interlingua machine translation system developed by CICC of Japan with a number of Asian countries, performed as well as many had expected.

Most of the machine translation system research during this period focused on the rule-based transfer and interlingua approaches. The needs of professional translators were overlooked and commercial companies such as ALPNET, Inc. seized the opportunity to market a series of translation tools. One of them was an early generation of a translation memory system (see Chapter 4).

The modern years

The early 1990s saw another major event when IBM developed a machine translation system called Candide using 'statistical methods' (Brown *et al.* 1993; see also Berger *et al.* 1994). At the same time, methods based on corpora of translation examples were experimented with in Japan. This method was later known as the 'example-based' approach. Neither method, statistical- nor example-based, used any syntactic or semantic rules, relying instead on large electronic corpora of text to establish patterns of equivalence. Hence, they differ from earlier (prior to 1990) methods such as rule-based approaches that employed linguistic rules. The statistical-based machine translation system draws its idea from communication theory, which had been suggested nearly six decades earlier by Weaver in his memorandum. In contrast to the rule-based approaches, the new corpus-based approaches used aligned texts – pairs of source and target-language texts – meaning that the source and target-language texts are structurally matched often at sentence level. Statistical calculations are then performed on the aligned bilingual texts to establish the probabilities of various translation equivalents, or examples are extracted from the aligned bilingual texts by matching examples (strings of source-language and target-language words, phrases or sentences).

The older methods have continued even with the introduction of these two new methods. At the same time, a shift in machine translation research was seen moving from 'pure' to 'applied'. This trend has continued until today, along with the integration of machine translation systems with other translation tools, particularly in the area of software localization, from stand-alone to network systems and from offline to online.

By the early 1990s, the world also began to undergo dramatic changes with respect to international communication. Advanced telecommunication systems and the Internet gave rise to a variety of translation requirements for different groups of people. At the same time, affordable stand-alone personal computers (PC) became available for individuals, and small businesses began to replace earlier more expensive mainframe computers. In the late 1990s and the early years of the twenty first century, the use of machine translation and computer-aided translation tools began to increase rapidly. The impact of the Internet on machine translation research also had a significant effect as it created a new medium for translation. As a result, in recent years a number of machine translation systems have been designed to translate Web pages as well as other types of text such as e-mail and chat-room messages. The communities of machine translation research as well as commercial companies also began to realize that different types of machine translation systems were required in order to fulfil diversifying translation requirements. Some of these systems are:

- translation software for stand-alone and networked personal computers for professional translators;
- machine translation systems for professional translators or organizations;
- online machine translation systems for home users and non-translators; and
- portable hand-held audio-visual translation devices for non-translators.

Since the early 1990s, a significant development in machine translation research has been in speech translation where speech recognition technology, which deals with the interpretation of conversation and dialogue, has combined with machine translation to enable the conversion of speech to text, a topic discussed in Chapter 6.

Active machine translation research is also found in China, Taiwan, Korea, India and Southeast Asian countries, while machine translation research in Eastern Europe was greatly affected by the political changes and the lack of funding after 1989. While researchers from the former Soviet Union progressed at a much-reduced rate, their counterparts in the Czech Republic and Bulgaria adopted the approach of entering into collaborative projects with organizations in Western Europe.

In retrospect, the substantial military and government funding in the early years of machine translation research in the USA and Soviet Union contributed to its longevity (Pugh 1992: 16). The setbacks and obstacles experienced during machine translation development do not, however, indicate a lack of success. The achievements of today's machine translation systems are due not only to advances in computer engineering, but also to the realization that in developing such systems, there are limitations. The limitations include the size of general and specialized dictionaries, the type of text, the languages and the number of language pairs in a system. As a result, most systems today are built either for specific-purposes or general-purposes.

Subject field-specific machine translation systems are designed to translate source texts of restricted and well-defined subject fields with pre-established vocabulary and sentence structures; for example, the Météo weather forecast system (English into French) and the JICST-E system (Japan Information Center of Science and Technology – English) that translates Japanese scientific and technical abstracts into English (Vasconcellos 1995: 375–6). Wider subject fields are usually handled by general-purpose machine translation systems such as online machine translation systems, described later in this chapter. Atlas-II by Fujitsu and HICATS by Hitachi were arguably originally subject field-specific systems but have been adapted gradually to become general-purpose systems (Vasconcellos 1995: 375). It has to be made clear that general-purpose machine translation systems are still not suitable for certain types of text, especially creative texts such as advertisements (see also Allen 2000).

The evolution of machine translation from mainframe, through PC-based systems to free online systems has made automatic language support almost a necessity (O'Hagan and Ashworth 2002: 39). Current machine translation systems are considered to be the third generation of hybrid systems that combine the earlier rule-based approaches and the subsequent corpus-based approaches. However, the differences between rule-based, knowledge-based and corpus-based architectures are sometimes not easy to tell as a result of various methods of integration. Nevertheless, it is still useful to understand the individual architectures from the first generation to the current generation of machine translation systems, as we shall see in the next section.

Architectures

A machine translation system normally consists of several main components, and two of these particularly associated with rule-based systems are briefly described here. The first component consists of a set of monolingual and bilingual dictionaries, whilst the second is a parser, to which we return below. The function of a source-language monolingual dictionary is to present grammatical information (morphology, syntax and semantics). A bilingual dictionary is consulted by the system when a source-language word is subsequently matched to its target-language equivalent (Lewis 1992: 76).

As an example, the KAMI dictionary (Kamus Melayu–Inggeris; Malay–English dictionary) contains eight fields of grammatical information for Malay words. In Table 3.1, the word 'gajah' (elephant) is called the index word (1). If the index word is a derivative, the original word of the derivative is given in the root word entry (2). The index word 'gajah' is a kind of animal, and the word is classed accordingly as a noun in the field for part-of-speech (3). Field (4) gives information on any important syntactic features of the index word which is used in the source-language text. Semantic information is stored in field (5). The following two fields are the English translation (6) and the definition of the index word (7). Meta-tags (8) is a field for any additional information that is relevant to the index word, for example archaic, vernacular or a loan word, in which case the language of origin is indicated.

Table 3.1 Example of a word entry in KAMI

Field	Explanation	Example	Comment
(1)	Malay Index Word	*gajah*	required
(2)	Malay Root Word	—	if index is a derivative
(3)	Part-of-Speech	Noun	required
(4)	Syntactic Features	Classifier = *ekor* [tail]	list of features
(5)	Semantic Features	mammal	list of features
(6)	English Translation	*elephant*	translation equivalent
(7)	English Definition	a kind of animal	translation description
(8)	Meta-Tags	—	list of relevant meta-tags

Source: Quah, Bond and Yamazaki (2001): 202.

The second main component of the architecture is the parser. A parser assigns a structure to each string made up of a word or phrase in the source-language text based on the stored grammatical information already pre-determined for that language. The goal of the parser is to identify the relationships between source-language words and their structural representations. A structural representation provides grammatical information related to these words or phrases. The word 'supplies' in the sentence 'The instant hot air supplies the necessary heat to all laboratories' has the structural representations of a verb in the present tense and in the declarative mood (see Figure 3.2). The grammatical information is 'attached' to the words and phrases of the source-language text by means of the parsing process. The closer a source language is to its target language genealogically, for example Italian to Spanish, the less elaborate the parser tends to be (Lewis 1992: 77; see also Schwarzl 2001).

'The instant hot air supplies the necessary heat to all laboratories.'
(*a-supplies
   (tense present)
   (mood declarative)
   (punctuation period)
   (source (*o-hot air
         (reference definite)
         (number singular)
         (attribute (*p-instant))))
   (theme (*u-heat
         (reference definite)
         (number singular)
         (attribute (*p-necessary))))
   (goal_to (*o-all laboratories
         (reference indefinite)
         (number plural)))

Figure 3.2   Example of structural representations

The following sections deal with the architectures of different machine translation systems, and Figure 3.3 gives an overview. The systems from the second-generation onwards were designed differently from

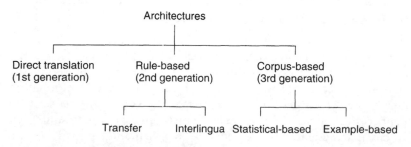

Figure 3.3   Machine translation architectures

the first-generation systems using what is known as a modular structure. Unlike the second-generation systems, the direct translation systems of the first-generation could not be modified without the danger of consequent unforeseen changes happening elsewhere in the system. A modular approach means that when grammar rules and dictionaries have to be updated or a new pair of languages added, this can be done without affecting the performance of the system as a whole, as the analysis, synthesis, grammar rules and dictionary are separated into different modules. Both later approaches, not only rule-based but also corpus-based machine translation systems, are modular. In all this, it is clear that a machine translation system is not really a machine in a physical sense but a complex software program (Nagao 1989: 70–1, 126).

Direct translation approach

Direct translation was the first approach employed in machine translation development and is considered to be the first generation of machine translation systems. Since the direct approach was the first to be developed, its system was rather primitive and required a long processing time. No linguistic analysis was carried out on the source-language text before its translation was generated. Also, this approach does not have the capability to resolve ambiguities, to deal with metaphorical expressions or to translate sentences between unrelated language pairs. This type of machine translation system is generally designed to translate between two closely related languages.

In direct translation systems, the source-language text is treated as a string of words, and a number of operations are performed by replacing source-language words with target-language words, re-ordering words until they end up with a string of symbols in the target language; for example, standard contrastive differences such as the order of adjectives and nouns in English (adjective + noun) and French (noun + adjective), for example 'the blue chair' → 'la chaise bleue' can be taken account of by the system (Jurafsky and Martin 2000: 817). A direct system is essentially a dictionary-based system that matches each source-language word to its target-language equivalent. The translation task is a single processing operation that stores all data in one bilingual dictionary with no separate grammar module (Lewis 1992: 79). The approach mirrors early translation approaches of word-for-word translation (see also Chapter 2). It is based on the principle of doing 'simple operations that can be done reliably' and was designed to deal with only one language pair at a time (Jurafsky and Martin 2000: 816). Sentences in the target language are constructed by directly replacing source-language strings with target-language strings (Jurafsky and Martin 2000: 817; see Figure 3.4). The operation consists of a matching of finite sets of lexical items from a source language with limited context onto target-language lexical items (Whitelock and Kilby 1995: 6).

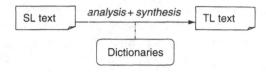

SL = source language; TL = target language

Figure 3.4   Direct translation model

A direct translation system depends on well-developed dictionaries, morphological analysis and text-processing software. This approach was simple and cheap but the output results were poor and mimic – for obvious reasons – the syntactic structures of the source language (Drakos and Moore 2001). Furthermore, as mentioned earlier it only works well with pairs of closely related languages that have similar grammatical structures. The syntactic analysis used is very basic while semantic analysis is rarely included. Input to the design of direct machine translation systems by linguists and translators was virtually nil since this type of system model was designed and built by mathematicians and engineers. A direct translation approach does not incorporate any application of translation theory, and only contains a minimal application of linguistic theory (Somers 1998c: 144; Jurafsky and Martin 2000: 818). As a result, the machine translation systems resulting from this approach as originally conceived proved to be unreliable and insufficiently powerful, yet it was adopted in almost all machine translation systems developed before 1966–67 (Jurafsky and Martin 2000: 817).

Early direct machine translation systems include Météo, Weidner, CULT and the old Systran. The current Systran, originally designed to translate from Russian into English, can now accommodate a larger number of language pairs. This has been made possible by reconfiguring Systran into a highly modular, modifiable and extendable system. In practice, however, most working machine translation systems tend to combine a number of different approaches as described below (Jurafsky and Martin 2000: 818).

Rule-based approaches

Ruled-based approaches involve the application of morphological, syntactic and/or semantic rules to the analysis of a source-language text and synthesis of a target-language text (Carl and Way 2003b: xviii). As noted earlier, there are two rule-based approaches: interlingua and transfer. Rule-based machine translation assumes that translation is a process consisting of analysis and representation of the source-language text 'meaning' to enable its equivalent to be generated in the target language. The representation must be precise and clear. On this assumption, interlingua and transfer systems were built to improve on and modularize earlier direct machine translation systems. As second generation systems (Somers 1998b: 144), both types of rule-based systems have abstract or intermediate representations. The interlingua machine translation systems had a language-independent or 'universal' abstract representation, reflecting the aims of theoretical linguists in the 1960s to identify features which all languages have in common at some level. Transfer systems, on the other hand, had separate representations for source-language and target-language texts, with the system moving from source-language text to source-language representation, which was then converted into the target-language representation before the target-language representation produced the target text. Let us look at each of these architectures in turn.

The interlingua approach

In the interlingua approach, a source language text is converted into a highly abstract representation that captures all the essential syntactic and semantic information that can then be converted into several target languages. An 'interlingua' represents 'all sentences that mean the "same" thing in the same way, regardless of the language they happen to be in' (Jurafsky and Martin 2000: 812). Thus it is designed to be language-independent. See Reeder (2000) and Bennett (2003) for examples of interlingua representations.

An interlingua is intended to function in stages as the intermediary between natural languages. During the analysis stage, a source-language text is analysed and transformed into its interlingua representation. Target-language sentences are produced from this interlingua representation with the help of target-language dictionaries and grammar rules during the synthesis stage (Lewis 1992: 78). Figure 3.5 illustrates this process.

Interlingua systems are highly modular in the sense that one part of the system does not affect other parts. Modularity also allows the addition of new modules without affecting existing modules in the system. The modularity ensures independence; for example, in a Dutch to Russian machine translation system, if the Dutch parser is being upgraded it does not affect the Russian sentence generator.

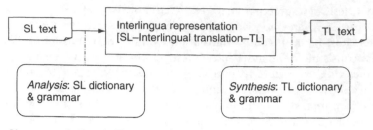

SL = source language; TL = target language

Figure 3.5   Interlingua model

Figure 3.6 illustrates a multilingual system using the interlingua approach, which started with Dutch as the source language and Russian as the target language. With modularity, it is possible to add three other source languages (French, Italian and Russian) and generate three other target languages (Dutch, Italian and French). In all, a total of 12 combinations of language pairs (from Dutch into Russian, French and Italian; from French into Dutch, Russian and Italian; from Italian into Russian, Dutch and French; and from Russian into Dutch, French and Italian) from four languages can be produced by such a system.

A more advanced approach, which displays extensive semantic and pragmatic knowledge and also includes, to some degree, the ability to reason about concepts, has been developed by Carnegie Mellon University. This so-called 'knowledge-based machine translation' evolved from interlingua-oriented systems which assume that translation goes beyond linguistic knowledge. The method emphasizes the importance of a

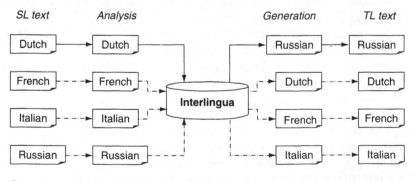

SL = source language; TL = target language

Figure 3.6   Interlingua multilingual machine translation system model

'complete understanding of the meaning of the source text' (Nirenburg *et al.* 1992: 27). It requires a parser to map a source-language text into a semantic representation, and also a generator to map this representation into a target-language text. The Carnegie Mellon University system, which uses lexical, grammatical and matching rules, is known as KANT (Knowledge-based Accurate Translation) and its newer version as KANTOO. Other similar types of systems are Mikrokosmos developed by New Mexico State University, Pivot by NEC and HICATS by Hitachi. Non-knowledge-based interlingua machine translation systems include DLT (Distributed Language Translation) developed by the BSO (Buro voor Systeemontwikkeling) Company in Utrecht, and Rosetta by Philips Research Laboratories in Eindhoven. The DLT machine translation system uses a modified form of the Esperanto language while the Rosetta system uses Montague grammar as the interlingua. The Montague grammar contains a syntactic and a semantic component in which a new expression and its grammatical category is generated by using existing expressions and their grammatical categories based on a set of syntactic rules (Crystal 1993: 222).

The main problem for an interlingua system to overcome is how to define a universal representation that can accommodate all languages. Various possibilities can be explored for the interlingua, including an artificial or a formal language; it could also be based on semantic or syntactic dictionary-type information (Lewis 1992: 78). In reality, however, it is difficult to build a truly language-neutral representation that represents 'all' possible aspects of syntax and semantics for 'all' known languages. Just as early machine translation systems were based on naïve assumptions about translation as a word-for-word process, interlingua systems were influenced by optimistic research in theoretical linguistics on language universals. Much has been written about this approach but to this day there is no definitive methodology that results in the building of a true language-neutral representation. The advantage of an interlingua approach is that it requires less work and is cheaper when a new language is added to the system, compared to the transfer approach described in the next section.

The transfer approach

The transfer approach is less ambitious than the interlingua approach, and consists of three stages. The analysis stage aims to convert a source-language text into an abstract source-language representation. Following this, the transfer of the source-language representation into its equivalent target-language representation takes place. The last stage is where a target-language text is generated. This approach is similar to the translation process described by Nida (1969; see also Chapter 2). Specific dictionaries are used at each stage: a source-language dictionary at the analysis stage, a bilingual dictionary at the transfer stage, and a target-language dictionary at the generation stage as illustrated in Figure 3.7.

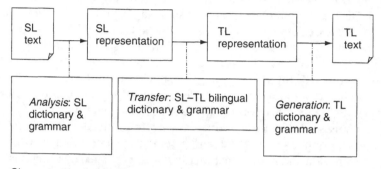

SL = source language; TL = target language

Figure 3.7   Transfer model

This approach uses contrastive knowledge of the two languages. As an example, Figure 3.8 shows the transfer stage where the source-language representation of the English phrase 'the beautiful little girl' undergoes a parsing process to restructure the English phrase into its Spanish translation, 'la pequeña muchacha hermosa'.

Like the other rule-based approach, the transfer approach is suitable for building a multilingual machine translation system. However, unlike the interlingua approach where only one interlingua is responsible for all the language pairs, the transfer approach uses different transfer models for each language pair. Figure 3.9 shows an example of a transfer-based multilingual machine translation system of three languages able to generate six language pairs (from Polish into Hungarian and Romanian; from Hungarian into Polish and Romanian; and from Romanian into Polish and Hungarian).

The transfer approach is not without problems. It relies on dictionaries, which may not necessarily contain sufficient knowledge to resolve ambiguities (Kit, Pan and Webster 2002: 57). Moreover, failure at the analysis stage may result in zero output because the transfer process cannot take place. Ariane by GETA and SUSY by the University of Saarbrücken exemplify the typical features of a second-generation transfer approach system. Other systems include METAL initially developed by

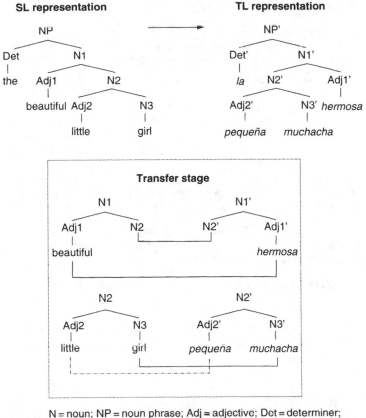

N = noun; NP = noun phrase; Adj = adjective; Det = determiner;
SL = source language; TL = target language
Note: ' = translation (e.g. NP' is the translation of NP).

Figure 3.8 Transfer using tree-to-tree parsing

the University of Texas in Austin, Atlas-I by Fujitsu and Duet by Sharp (Lewis 1992: 79).

It is important to remember that all interlingua machine translation systems to date are only of demonstration or prototype capabilities. The interlingua approach is still pursued by many researchers for machine translation systems and other natural-language processing applications, but in reality the transfer approach is often the choice of preference simply because it is the simpler approach (Bel *et al.* 2001). At the end of the 1980s, even though rule-based approaches had been overtaken by a number of successful experiments using other approaches, they had

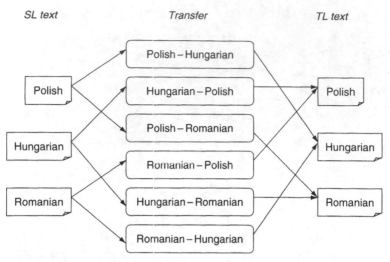

SL = source language; TL = target language

Figure 3.9   Transfer multilingual machine translation system model

gained some new uses for web-based information technology such as multilingual information retrieval and online translation (Streiter, Carl and Iomdin 2000).

Corpus-based approaches

The early 1990s saw corpus-based approaches gaining popularity in machine translation research. Statistical- and example-based approaches are two different methods that make use of linguistic information in a corpus to create new translations. All corpus-based machine translation systems use a set of so-called 'reference translations' containing source-language texts and their translations. Source and target-language texts are aligned and the equivalent translation is extracted using a specific statistical method or by matching a number of examples extracted from the corpus (Carl 2000: 997).

This approach is not new to machine translation researchers. In the early 1960s, experiments were carried out at IBM to investigate statistical methods, but on the whole these were not successful. Another attempt was made later with a newer stochastic technique called Bayes' theorem (Tomás and Casacuberta 2001) that, as a result, revived the use of statistical methods in machine translation research. The example-based approach was first proposed by Nagao in 1984, but it was not until the late 1980s that researchers began to employ this method (Trujillo 1999: 204). Corpus-based approaches provide an alternative to the intractable complexity of rule-based approaches at the analysis and generation stages (Hutchins 1994).

These two approaches (statistical-based and example-based) were explored by different groups of machine translation researchers on both sides of the Pacific. While the IBM group in the USA concentrated on experimenting with statistical methods with considerable success, at the same time researchers in Japan also experimented successfully using translation examples taken from corpora to generate new translations. Unlike rule-based approaches, the two approaches do not apply linguistic rules to the analysis of texts or to the selection of translation equivalents.

The statistical-based approach

Prior to the 1990s, attempts to use statistical methods in the development of machine translation systems were unsuccessful. As we have seen, working statistical-based machine translation came into being (see also Berger *et al.* 1994) when researchers at IBM introduced the use of Bayes' theorem in their Candide machine translation system. Candide was based on what was at the time a huge corpus, more than two million French and English sentences, of transcribed Canadian parliamentary debates known as 'Hansards'. The premise of this approach is that a translation can be modelled with a statistical process. Bayes' theorem deals with probability inference and defines how to combine knowledge of prior events, for example past translations with new data (new source-language texts) to predict future events (in this case, new translations). This method has, so far, been shown to work best in restricted subject fields.

In the statistical-based approach, a source-language text is first segmented into strings of words and phrases; the source-language segments are then compared to an existing large aligned bilingual corpus consisting of original texts and their translations, and a statistical method is then employed on the aligned bilingual corpus to obtain new target-language segments. From the new segments, using the theorem, a new target-language text is produced (Carl and Way 2003b: xix). This approach is clearly quite different from the rule-based approaches previously discussed that employ pre-determined linguistic rules to analyse source-language texts in order to generate translations (see Figure 3.10).

The principal hypothesis of this approach is that one source-language sentence (*S*) can have a large number of translations (*T*), and each of these

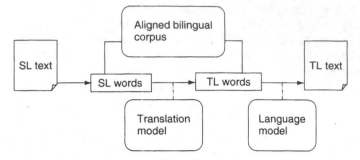

SL = source language; TL = target language

Figure 3.10   Statistical-based model

has a varying probability (*P*) of being correct. The probability is calculated using Bayes' rule, which states that:

$$P(T|S) = \frac{P(T) \times P(T|S)}{P(S)}$$

where *P*(*T*|*S*) is the probability of *T* given the translation *S*; *P*(*T*) is the probability of randomly selecting the text *T*, which is calculated from the frequency in the corpus; *P*(*S*|*T*) is the probability assumed by the translation model used by the algorithm assigned to *S* being translated into *T*; and *P*(*S*) is the frequency of observing the text *S* in the corpus.

Using this hypothesis, the highest probability of the target-language translation (*T*), for the source-language sentence (*S*), is calculated. In other words the algorithm selects the translation it regards as most likely by combining information from its translation model and information from its language model, both typical components of statistical systems. In the translation model (see Berger *et al*. 1994), a source-language segment (a word or a string of words) is matched with, or 'mapped' onto, its target-language segment. The model can be based on words, phrases or sentences, such as those in the IBM1 to IBM5 translation models (see also Brown *et al*. 1993). The translation model calculates the probabilities of every word that makes up, say, the target-language sentence in *T*, based on each of the source-language words in *S*. In most statistical machine translation systems, the lexicon of the translation model is single-word-based; that is, one source-language word corresponds to only one target-language word. Here the word-for-word translation approach seen in Chapter 2 is the basic method of selecting a pair of segments, often based on single words, which then get combined into sentences. However, most pairings between a source-language word and a target-language word are not one-to-one; the exceptions are certain technical terms, such as the German 'gefluder', the French 'flume', as the English 'flume' (Newmark 1996: 56). Other forms of pairing commonly occur, such as: one-to-zero equivalent, for example the Malay word 'songket' is a hand-woven fabric with gold and silver threads often worn during official functions or ceremonies in the Malay community and does not have an equivalent in English; one-to-many equivalents, for example 'love' has several equivalents in Malay – 'cinta', 'sayang' and 'kasih'; and one-word-to-one-phrase equivalent, for example the one-phrase equivalent of 'absent' in Malay is 'tidak hadir' (not present).

The problem of pairing words in this approach is similar to a number of translation procedures described by Vinay and Darbelnet (1958/2000) discussed in Chapter 2. Consider, for example, that target-language words sometimes appear in a different order from the source-language words; in statistical-based machine translation this phenomenon is called 'distortion'. The probabilities for distortion are also included in the translation model; for example, $P(3 \mid 4)$ in which the probability that the source word in position 3 will produce a translation word in position 4, or $P(3 \mid 1, 3, 4)$ in which the probability that the source word in position 3 will produce a translation word in position 1 when there are three words in the source language and four words in the target language (Somers 2003g). In general, only linguistic and contextual information such as surrounding words, parts-of-speech and syntactic constituents are used in the model. Semantics, however, is rarely included as part of the model.

The second component typical of statistical-based systems, the language model itself (see Berger *et al.* 1994), is then used to compute the likelihood of the results being a valid target-language segment (written as $P(T \mid S)$ as shown in the Bayes' rules earlier), following the operation of the translation model. The computation is best achieved through employing an algorithm, which uses '*n*-gram' statistics; an *n*-gram is a string of '*n*' letters. In practice, *n* is taken as a small number, for example from one to five where *n* is the number of letters in each of the chosen strings. Therefore, if $n=2$ it is called a '*di*gram', and if $n=3$ it is a '*tri*gram'. For example, the text 'the blue car' can be generated using a '*di*gram' as 'th', 'he', 'eb', 'bl' and so on; or a '*tri*gram' as 'the', 'heb', 'blu', 'lue' and so on. Note that *n*-grams ignore any spaces between letters.

The process of calculating all these probabilities can be visualized in Figure 3.11. The translation model, as we have seen, is derived from an

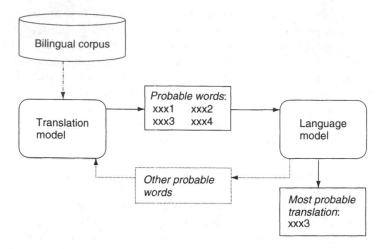

Figure 3.11   Probabilities workflow in the statistical-based approach

aligned bilingual or parallel corpus while the language model calculates the probabilities of word sequences from the target language. Only the most probable translation is usually suggested as the equivalent. Other probable words can also be tried repeatedly to seek better equivalents if necessary.

These *n*-gram-based models lack contextual information such as information on the words surrounding the target words, part-of-speech, syntactic constituents and semantics. A statistical-based approach also separates the monolingual and bilingual information. The monolingual information is located in the language model while the bilingual information comes from the translation model (Trujillo 1999: 210–11). The probability calculations used to evaluate a desired target-language text are vital to this type of approach. The goal is to harvest a list of possible translation equivalents for a new source segment. In other words, the task of a statistical machine translation system is to choose the source-language segment from the corpus that is the closest to the new source-language segment based on probabilities.

This approach is, however, not without problems. If the bilingual corpus is too small, the system may not be effective in generating good translations. The Candide machine translation system, for instance, has so far worked well in an experimental environment, but it is unsure if it will perform as well in a commercial environment. The move from an experimental to a commercial environment needs to be considered. Since 1994, attempts have also been made to include knowledge derived from linguistics in the Candide machine translation system. This has been shown to produce more successful results than the simple use of statistical methods (Bel *et al.* 2002).

The example-based approach

Example-based machine translation is also referred to as analogy-, memory-, pattern-, case- or similarity-based translation (Sumita and Imamura 2002). As noted earlier, Nagao proposed this approach in the mid-1980s, and it lies between rule based and statistical approaches (Carl and Way 2003b: xix). Matching rules that are used in rule-based machine translation systems are dispensed with. An example-based machine translation requires a bilingual corpus of translation pairs and employs an algorithm to match the closest example of a source-language segment to its target-language segment as the basis for translating the new source text. A matched pair of segments is called an 'example'. A segment can be of any length or operate at any linguistic level (see also Arnold *et al.* 1994), but according to one view, ideally, it should be at the sentence level (Carl and Way 2003b: xix).

Three main tasks are involved in the translation process of an example-based system (see Figure 3.12): matching segments from the new source text against existing pairs of examples extracted from an aligned bilingual corpus, then aligning corresponding translation segments and recombining them to generate a target text (Kit, Pan and Webster 2002: 60).

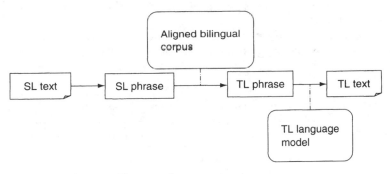

SL = source language; TL = target language

Figure 3.12   Example-based model

According to Sato and Nagao (1990), the basic idea of an example-based translation is to 'translate a source sentence by imitating the translation of a similar sentence already in the database'. However, in most cases, more than one 'imitation' may be needed to translate a completely new source-language sentence. Table 3.2 illustrates this.

Table 3.2   Imitation in the example-based approach

Sentence	English (source)	Malay (target)
Example	ES3.1: The lady *in the farmers' market* is my cousin.	MS3.1: Wanita *di pasar tani itu* ialah sepupu saya.
Example	ES3.2: *She sells flowers every day*.	MS3.2: *Dia menjual bunga setiap hari*.
New	ES3.3: *She sells flowers in the farmers' market every day*.	MS3.3: *Dia menjual bunga di pasar tani itu setiap hair*.

ES = English sentence; MS = Malay sentence

When an English sentence such as 'She sells flowers in the farmers' market every day' (ES3.3 in Table 3.2) needs to be translated into Malay, the database of examples is searched for similar but not necessarily identical source-language strings such as 'The lady in the farmers' market is my cousin' (ES3.1) and 'She sells flowers every day' (ES3.2). Along with source sentences such as these, their Malay translations are also extracted (see MS3.1 and MS3.2). By referring to these examples, the new source-language sentence may then be translated by 'imitating' the matching parts of the Malay examples and recombining them to turn them into new target-language sentence (see EM3.3; see also examples in Sato and Nagao 1990).

New source-language sentences can also be translated according to the 'semantic similarity' of examples in the database as shown in Table 3.3

Table 3.3   Semantic similarity in the example-based approach

Sentence	English (source)	Malay (target)
Example	ES3.4: Tigers born in the zoo for the past 10 years were all *males*.	MS3.4: Harimau yang lahir sejak 10 tahun yang lalu semuanya *jantan*.
Example	ES3.5: The villagers who attended the meeting were all *males*.	MS3.5: Orang kampung yang menghadiri mesyuarat itu semuanya *lelaki*.
New	ES3.6: Sarah's puppy is a *male*.	MS3.6: Anak anjing Sarah *jantan*.
New	ES3.7: The cooks are all *males*.	MS3.7 Tukang masak semuanya *lelaki*.

ES = English sentence; MS = Malay sentence

(see also examples in Turcato and Popowich 2003). This can be used to determine which target-language alternative is most suitable for the translation of a noun such as 'male', that is potentially polysemous when translated into a language such as Malay which distinguishes the words used to indicate gender for humans and for animals. Unlike in English, the specific terms to indicate a male animal ('jantan') and a male human ('lelaki') are not interchangeable in Malay. The term 'jantan' is only used to refer to humans in the metaphorical or derogatory sense, and the term 'lelaki' is never used to indicate a male animal. Therefore, based on semantic similarity with the word 'male', the Malay translation 'jantan' in 'Anak anjing Sarah jantan' (MS3.6) must share the same semantic feature of (+animal) as the 'male' in the English example sentence 'Tigers born in the zoo for the past 10 years were all males' (ES3.4). Similarly, 'lelaki' is the translation of 'male' that has the same semantic (+human) feature in sentences ES3.5-MS3.5 and ES3.7-MS3.7.

The example-based approach is very similar to that used in computer-aided translation tools like translation memory, which we will consider in the next chapter. However, while both allow translation examples to be extracted from the bilingual corpora stored in the system, only the example-based approach is capable of extracting more than one example to create a target-language sentence (Trujillo 1999: 203; Somers 2003f: 5). The other distinction between these two systems is that translation memory is an interactive tool used by professional translators while example-based machine translation is an automatic translation system (Sumita and Imamura 2002; see also Somers 2003c and 2003f).

The example-based approach is unlikely to succeed if no close matches can be found in the bilingual corpus or if the input sentences are metaphorical in nature. Adding new examples to an aligned bilingual corpus could either improve or degrade the performance of the system. Similarly, too many repetitions of the same or similar examples could either reinforce or jeopardize the performance of a system (see also Somers 2003f). Other areas of concern include how to estimate the size of the corpus, and whether the analysis of the corpus should be carried out before or during the translation process (Sumita and Imamura 2002). Lastly, the matching algorithm is based on the comparison of words through their proximity in meaning (see Tables 3.2 and 3.3), but problems may still occur; for example, the kind of numerous morphological variations found in languages such as Malay which make matching procedures more complex. A high degree of morphological variation is commonly found, for instance, in agglutinative languages such as Hungarian, Malay, Swahili and Turkish. Words in these languages are constructed by 'gluing' together several morphemes (the smallest units of grammar, such as a prefix) in a linear sequence. Each gluing process would generally alter the meaning as well as the part-of-speech of the word; for example, the Malay word 'berkeseorangan' (to be alone and feeling lonely) is made up of two prefixes ('ber-' and 'se-'), a root word ('orang', which means 'person') and a prefix and suffix pair ('ke-an'). The process of 'gluing' the affixes to the root word must also be done in the correct order. The first level of affixation begins with 'se-' and 'orang' to form 'seorang', which means 'a person'. This is followed by affixing 'ke-an' to turn 'seorang' into 'keseorangan', which means 'lonely', and the last stage is to add 'ber-' that once again changes its meaning – 'to be alone and feeling lonely' – to produce 'berkeseorangan'.

A number of example-based machine translation research projects have been described in the literature including, for example, the Chinese–English system for Hong Kong's legal code and various bilingual resources from the Linguistic Data Consortium (LDC) in Zhang, Brown and Frederking (2001); an example-based system for a German–Polish machine translation system in Gajer (2002); and an English–French example-based system in Gough, Way and Hearne (2002).

Corpus-based approaches also have problems with scalability, which means that a corpus can be either too small or too large for a particular task (Bel *et al.* 2001). Corpus-based machine translation systems, whether statistical- or example-based, should not, however, rely solely on the information found in the corpus. Words and structures from outside the corpus should also be included if it becomes apparent that they might occur in other texts in the same subject field (Lehrberger and Bourbeau 1988: 129).

Hybrid and interactive machine translation systems

A rule-based system is deductive in nature as it is based on a set of linguistic rules set up by its designers. Moreover, it does not in principle store any translation results or reuse previously translated segments. Such a system is difficult to adapt for new subject fields. A corpus-based system, on the other hand, is inductive in nature because the rules are derived from a given set of translation examples and modification is achieved through the addition of new translation examples. The rule-based approach is often expensive, and may produce inconsistent results when new linguistic rules are added. In contrast, the corpus-based approach is flexible enough to process sentences even if they are ill-formed. However, when long sentences are involved, the processing time tends to be lengthy (see also Carl *et al.* 2000).

Machine translation research is unlikely to progress significantly by the refinement of one approach in preference to another. Instead, 'hybrid' (Coloumbe 2001) and other innovative approaches may be the best way forward. Many of these hybridizations combining two different machine translation systems are still at an experimental stage; for example, hybrids such as a rule-based CAT2 machine translation system and an example-based Edgar machine translation system (Carl *et al.* 2000), or an example-based engine and an interlingua approach in one single system called Pangloss Mark II (Bel *et al.* 2001). Alternatively, different types of tools may be combined or integrated in a new system, such as Otelo, which is made up of two machine translation systems – IBM LMT and Logos – with a translation memory system called IBM Translation-Manager (Carl *et al.* 2000).

Another solution to compensate for the lack of understanding of natural languages on the part of computers is to involve humans in the process, that is to have interactive machine translation systems. The human input or intervention feature is similar to that of human-aided machine translation. However, there is one significant difference: interactive machine translation systems allow a translator to have control over the translation process and the output, while human-aided machine translation systems pause and ask the user (not necessarily a translator) to resolve the problem of lexical or syntactic ambiguity (see also Melby and Warner 1995; Macklovitch 2001). Examples of interactive machine translation systems include LING-STAT, TransType2 and WebDIPLOMAT (Web Distributed Intelligent Processing of Language for Operational Machine Aided Translation) from Carnegie Mellon University, and DBMT (Dialogue-based Machine Translation system) from the University of Grenoble (Melby and Warner 1995: 34–5).

Online machine translation systems

Machine translation was originally designed for formal written language, but the demand for the translation of e-mail messages that contain less formal syntactic structures has increased in recent years. Hence the developers of machine translation systems have created different systems to meet the needs of different end-users, for instance, client–server machine translation systems. In a client–server situation, an organization or a translation company hosts the machine translation system on a server. The 'client', either a company or an individual, can access the machine translation system using user identification and a password such as the client–server structure found in the European Commission Systran machine translation system which offers translation services to translators, administrators and the officials of European Union institutions and bodies. The system has 18 language pairs with English, French, German and Spanish acting as the main source languages (Petrits 2001).

Machine translation systems have also been made accessible to the general public who may need occasional translations through the Internet. Machine translation developers such as Systran, for example, offer a free online translation facility named Babelfish, which is located on the AltaVista search engine website (see http://www.altavista.com/). Babelfish is reported to have received over 500,000 visitors and handled more than four million web pages and a million translations of a wide range of web pages per day at the start of the millennium (McKinsey 2001). The growing number of online machine translation systems and improvements in their performance mean that millions of Internet users can now read pages originally posted in languages that they do not understand.

For end-users who occasionally require the translation of web pages, small chunks of text and e-mails, free online machine translation systems such as Babelfish, Promt-Online and WorldLingo are extremely helpful. Since most online machine translation systems are for general purposes, the translations generated may not be of the highest quality but there is enough information for the end-users to at least understand the overall content. As an example, a chunk of English text translated by two online machine translation systems, Promt-Online and World-Lingo Free Online Translator, into German is shown in Figure 3.13. The two German translations have a few differences: the spelling of specific words, such as 'dass' and 'daß'; the identification of parts of speech, such as '-unterstützungen' (plural noun) versus 'stützt' (third-person singular verb) for the English verb 'supports'; and the non-translation of words such as 'nicknamed' and 'Pigmy' in WorldLingo compared to 'Spitznamen' and 'Pygmäin' in Promt-Online. The German sentences translated by these two online systems are not grammatically correct and the terms used may not be accurate, but the overall message in the English text is more or less conveyed to a German-speaking end-user who does not read or understand English.

English text: The famous skeleton from Indonesia nicknamed the 'Hobbit' does not belong to a modern human pigmy with a brain disease. The study of the brain supports the idea that it might be a new kind of dwarf, which is one of the human species.

| *German translation by Promt-Online*: Das berühmte Skelett von Indonesien mit einem Spitznamen bezeichnet der 'Hobbit' gehört einer modernen menschlichen Pygmäin mit einer Gehirnkrankheit nicht. Die Studie von Gehirnunterstützungen die Idee, dass es eine neue Art des Zwergs sein könnte, der eine der menschlichen Arten ist. | *German translation by WorldLingo*: Das berühmte Skelett von Indonesien, das das 'Hobbit' nicknamed ist, gehört nicht einem modernen menschlichen Pigmy mit einer Gehirnkrankheit. Die Studie des Gehirns stützt die Idee, daß es eine neue Art Zwerg sein konnte, welches eins der menschlichen Sorte ist. |

Figure 3.13 Translations by online machine translation systems

Commercial machine translation systems

Much of the previous discussion has been about the development of machine translation systems from a research perspective. In this section, the focus is on commercial machine translation systems. Table 3.4 presents an indicative summary of the different types of commercial machine translation systems currently available (Hutchins, Hartmann and Ito 2004). The classification is based on the intended target market, for example home versus professional, and the number of languages involved.

The languages and direction of translation in machine translation systems are usually pre-determined. The direction of translation for the trilingual class varies from system to system and it is not possible to list each one. Similarly, the directions are not listed for the multilingual systems, which involve more than three languages. Almost all commercial systems are said to have rule-based rather than corpus-based architectures. Corpus-based systems are now being commercially developed and could make their appearance in the market in the future (Bennett and Gerber 2003: 176; Hutchins 2003: 163).

The type labelled as 'professional' in Table 3.4 caters for individual professional translators, while 'client–server' is primarily intended for external contractor companies or translation companies in order to support their teams of professional translators either in-house or working

Table 3.4   Classification of commercial machine translation systems

Language type	Bilingual (unidirectional)	Bilingual (bidirectional)	Trilingual	Multilingual	Total
General	18	31	7	12	68
Home	8	36	9	16	69
Professional		19	3	12	34
Internet (web, e-mail, chat-rooms)	12	25	6	45	88
Client-server	3	6	1	13	23
Portal, service		1		10	11
Mobile	2	3			5
Total	43	121	26	108	298

Source: Hutchins, Hartmann and Ito (2004).

as 'suppliers' of translation services on a freelance basis. The type labelled 'portal' refers to machine translation companies that supply machine translation systems to other companies or websites. The type labelled 'mobile' may refer to plug-in systems; for example, a palm pilot plugged into a networked computer using either a cable or wireless modem to remotely access a machine translation system.

In Hutchins, Hartmann and Ito's (2004) compendium, only two commercial integrated systems are listed. They are the ESTeam Translator© developed by a Swedish company called ESTeam AB, a machine translation system integrated with a translation memory system that supports European languages, and TransPen developed by a Taiwanese company called Otek International, Inc., a Chinese–English machine translation system integrated with an optical character recognition (OCR) tool. Most integrated systems mentioned in the previous discussion are still at the experimental or prototype stages. Some originally planned integrated systems did not even get past the experimental stage, such as the integration of Trados Translator's Workbench v1.07 for Windows with the Logos machine translation system (see also Puntikov 1999).

One of the main commercial functions of machine translation is to improve the productivity of human translators who are able to check and polish translations (Graddol 1998: 144–5). Although a machine translation system is unlikely to be as accurate as a professional translator, it is faster and cheaper. As we have seen, extensive research in machine translation, using a variety of techniques and types of technology, is now in progress at universities and large corporations in many countries. The successful use of any commercial machine translation system requires a large investment on the part of the end-user such as being committed to create, maintain and update terminology and translation databases in order to maximize the usability of a system. Training on how to use a machine translation system is essential, while regular after-sales service and technical support from the developers are equally important (Bennett and Gerber 2003: 189).

Reasons for using machine translation systems

In reacting to the possibility of machine translation, professional translators need to realize that today's translation demands include translation for many different purposes. For machine translation, in particular, at least four purposes have been identified: dissemination, assimilation, information exchange and access. With the exception of translation for information dissemination, where almost all information in the source texts is conveyed in the translation, translations for the remaining three purposes tend to be tailored to the need of an end-user, as we shall see below.

The type of text considered to be most cost-effective for machine translation is the informative text (see also Reiss 1977/1989), usually written in a 'restricted' form or variety of special language. As mentioned previously, this type of text includes instruction manuals, technical articles, abstracts, minutes of meetings and weather reports. In fact, the function of a text is crucial to generating a good output from a machine translation system. Informative texts have certain characteristics. They do not present any conflict of aims; they should be clearly written, objective, factual and neutral, and usually suffer minimal loss of meaning during translation (see also controlled language in Chapter 2).

Nearly all translations of this kind are meant to disseminate information. In order to successfully perform this task, translations into multiple target languages need to be accurate and well-written. When machine translation systems were first developed, the intention was to have the systems produce high-quality translation output for publication purposes. Unfortunately this did not materialize for reasons we have already discussed, and hence the outputs generated by machine translation today are often regarded as translation drafts that require humans to perform the task of post-editing.

However, careful translation is often not required for the assimilation of information, such as when, for example, the translation is required for the purpose of internal monitoring and information filtering inside an organization based on a variety of sources. Once all the gathered information has been machine translated, the output is manually sorted and the human translators only post-edit the portion of the output that contains valuable information identified from the raw machine translation output (see Chapter 6). Translation of the latter kind need not be of publishable quality; it is sufficient that the translation can be understood. In other words, basic comprehension is all that is required as long as the user understands the content or topic of the machine translation output. It is extremely effective for those who need to access foreign language documents, in particular information downloaded from the web. The goal of machine translation for assimilation purposes is to produce large, inexpensive volumes of rough translation automatically at a fast rate. Translation for assimilation purposes is cheaper and quicker by far than for dissemination purposes, most of it achieved by the cheaper PC-based machine translation systems. Keeping translation costs low is the main goal.

In recent years, the demand for the translation of web pages or of communications between two parties from different linguistic backgrounds carried out over the Internet has increased. Human translators are unable to meet this need since instantaneous 'real-time translation' is required to convey the basic contents of the message; the quality of translation is not an issue for this purpose. The exchange of information does not only involve the translation of electronically written texts online but also of bilingual phrases on handheld translation devices for tourists and to some degree, the interpretation of telephone conversations and business negotiations (see Chapter 6).

Speedy access to information, in whatever language, is important in the modern world, and in this context machine translation can facilitate information search and retrieval. Online multilingual machine translation systems retrieve and extract information from textual and non-textual databases, especially from the Internet, operating in conjunction with other tools to search and retrieve information from scientific and technical journals, to extract specific information from newspaper reports, to summarize reports and to listen to or view non-textual (audio-visual) material.

Conclusion

In the last five decades, the research and development of machine translation systems has undergone great changes in many respects: funding, evolution from mainframes to networks and the emergence of artificial intelligence, neural networks, corpus-based approaches and the application of linguistics (see also Bennett 2003). However, the results have been mixed. According to Tsujii (1991: 4), machine translation is believed to be one of the hardest dreams to realize in information science and is still likely to be difficult despite all the improvements made (see also Bennett and Gerber 2003). Nevertheless, despite the many drawbacks, machine translation is still important in the information world of today and will become increasingly important in the future (Haynes 1998; see Chapter 6).

In this chapter it has been shown that the development of machine translation systems has progressed steadily. We now see a variety of approaches used to generate if not the highest quality, then certainly the optimal quality of translation given the available knowledge and technology. For professional translators, the data-driven approaches of statistical-based and example-based approaches may be of more use than rule-based machine translation systems, because of the benefit of using previously translated material and other types of textual and non-textual data as corpora (see Chapter 6). We have also seen that online machine translation systems, mostly general-purpose ones, are more suitable for the general public who need to access information written in languages they do not understand or to obtain *ad hoc* translations.

Historically, the involvement of translators with mainframe or networked machine translation systems has largely been in the context of large organizations where the decision to use machine translation is made by the organization rather than the translators, who are then mainly engaged in editing roles. Since these systems are large and expensive, only organizations can afford them. Interestingly, when the more affordable smaller PC-based systems were introduced in the early 1990s, they were marketed aggressively to companies or small businesses. They were of little relevance to freelance professional translators as the quality of the output was poor. As a result, most professional translators did not consider PC-based machine translation systems as an option. The percentage of professional translators using any machine translation system may still be small even though in recent years their performance has been significantly improved. It was the appearance on the market of tools such as translation memory and the concept of the 'workbench' which finally grabbed the attention of translators, as well as companies. It is to such computer-aided tools that we turn our attention in the next chapter.

Suggested reading

Arnold, D., L. Balkan, R. Humphreys, S. Meijer and L. Sadler (1994) *Machine Translation: An Introductory Guide*. Manchester and Oxford: NCC Blackwell.

Hutchins, W.J. (ed.) (2000b) *Early Years in Machine Translation: Memoirs and Biographies of Pioneers*. Amsterdam: John Benjamins.

Nirenburg, S., H.L. Somers and Y. Wilks (eds) (2003) *Readings in Machine Translation*. Cambridge, Mass.: MIT Press.

Schwarzl, A. (2001) *The (Im)Possibility of Machine Translation*. European University Studies. Series XIV, Anglo-Saxon Language and Literature. Frankfurt am Main: Peter Lang.

Trujillo, A. (1999) *Translation Engines: Techniques for Machine Translation*. London: Springer-Verlag.

4
Computer-Aided Translation Tools and Resources

The approach taken in this chapter is different from that of the previous chapter. Instead of focusing systematically on a number of approaches, the emphasis here is on translation tools, resources and standards that may be useful to professional translators. Many professional translators of specialist texts can benefit from using computer-aided translation tools such as translation memory systems, terminology management systems and the standards for translation data interchange such as translation memory exchange (TMX). Certain tools, however, such as localization tools, are only of interest to professional translators who are involved in the localization industry. These tools are useful to know about but they may not be needed for all kinds of translation and would be of little use to professional translators working with creative texts. Some other resources and tools, such as parallel corpora and concordancers, are extremely helpful for professional translators in order to enhance their productivity and the quality of their translations. Another important topic that needs attention here is the standards that have been created to enable interoperability of lexical and terminology databases, translation memory databases and localization tools in the localization process. Since they are frequently upgraded, tools and resources discussed in this chapter are only described in general terms.

Workbenches

A 'workbench' or a 'workstation' is a single integrated system that is made up of a number of translation tools and resources such as a translation memory, an alignment tool, a tag filter, electronic dictionaries, terminology databases, a terminology management system and spell and grammar-checkers. Two major translation tools in a workbench, translation memory systems and terminology management systems, will be described here.

Translation memory systems

In the 1970s, one of the earliest computer-aided translation tools to emerge was translation memory, yet it was only commercially developed in the mid-1990s (Somers 2003c: 31). Translation memory has been defined as 'a multilingual text archive containing (segmented, aligned, parsed and classified) multilingual texts, allowing storage and retrieval of aligned multilingual text segments against various search conditions' (EAGLES 1996). Unlike machine translation systems, which generate translations automatically, translation memory systems allow professional translators to be in charge of the decision-making whether to accept or reject a term or an equivalent phrase or 'segment' suggested by the system during the translation process. Translators can also build their own 'memory'.

Virtually all translation memory systems are language-independent and support international character sets that represent many, if not all, alphabets and scripts digitally. For instance, the Arabic-based or Perso-Arabic languages such as Avestan, the oldest Iranian language used for writing the sacred texts of the Zoroastrian religion; the languages of Batak spoken in northern Sumatra, Indonesia; and Newari, a language spoken in central Nepal, have yet to be digitized for natural-language processing applications including computer-aided translation tools. Nevertheless, a tool like a translation memory system also has other limitations, in particular the fact that it functions optimally with texts written in some kind of 'special language' related to a particular subject field and with certain genres which require frequent updates and re-translation. Thus translation memory systems are extremely useful for translating texts that contain large numbers of repeated words or terms, extended phrases and even sentences. Legal documents, technical reports and manuals are good examples of texts that can benefit from the use of this type of translation tool.

Translation memory technology works by reusing previously translated texts and their originals in order to facilitate the production of new translations (Puntikov 1999: 64). It can also interface with databases of stored specialized terminologies that can be accessed and retrieved for reuse in new translations. Some terminology databases are empty to begin with and have to be filled or 'populated', while other databases may come with sets of terms from specific subject fields, to which new terms can be added. Clients are also known to supply their translators with terms often referred to as 'legacy data', although the data may be presented in different applications including word-processing software, spreadsheets or other databases and structured in different ways.

Generally, a database of terms is known as a 'termbase'; the tool which is used to build the termbase is a database management system which has been customized for storing and retrieving lexical data and is known as a 'terminology management system'. This tool will be described later in this chapter.

Characteristics

A translation memory system has no linguistic component, and two different approaches are employed to extract translation segments from the previously stored texts. These are known as perfect matching and fuzzy matching. Other characteristics such as filter, segmentation and alignment will also be discussed.

Perfect matching. A perfect or exact match occurs when a new source-language segment is completely identical including spelling, punctuation and inflections, to the old segment found in the database, that is in the translation 'memory' (Austermühl 2001: 136). Table 4.1 shows an example of a perfect match between a previously translated English source sentence stored in the database or memory, 'Close the filler cap' (ES4.1), and the new English sentence, 'Close the filler cap' (ES4.2). Therefore, the previously translated Spanish sentence, 'Cierre el tapón' (SS4.1), can be reused as the new translation without any changes (see SS4.2).

Table 4.1 Example of perfect matching

Sentence	English (source)	Spanish (target)
Old	ES4.1: Close the filler cap.	SS4.1: Cierre el tapón.
New	ES4.2: Close the filler cap.	SS4.2: Cierre el tapón.

ES = English sentence; SS = Spanish sentence

Fuzzy matching. Unlike a perfect match, a fuzzy match occurs when an old and a new source-language segment are similar but not exactly identical (Esselink 1998: 134). Even a very small difference such as punctuation leads to a fuzzy match.

Table 4.2 shows an example of fuzzy matching of two new source-language sentences: 'How to operate the appliance' (ES4.5) and 'There is water in the tank' (ES4.6) The tool searches in its memory for possible matches and finds 'How to assemble the appliance' (ES43) and 'There is no water in the tank' (ES4.4). The translator must now translate 'operate' into 'operar' to complete the translation (see SS4.5). In other words, the translator replaces 'ensemblar' (SS4.3) with 'operar' (SS4.5) to produce a new Spanish translation. In the case of the sentence 'There is water in the tank' (ES4.6), the Spanish word 'no' is dropped to produce the new translation (see SS4.6). If there is more than one pair of fuzzy matches, the translation with the closest similarity to the new source-language segment is usually suggested as the first choice (Austermühl 2001: 137; see also Somers 2003c).

Table 4.2   Examples of fuzzy matching

Sentence	English (source)	Spanish (target)
Old	ES4.3: How *to assemble* the appliance.	SS4.3: Como *ensemblar el* aparato.
Old	ES4.4: There is *no* water in the tank.	SS4.4: *No* hay agua en el depósito.
New	ES4.5: How *to operate* the appliance.	SS4.5: Como *operar* el aparato.
New	ES4.6: There is water in the tank.	SS4.6: *Hay agua en el depósito.*

ES = English sentence; SS = Spanish sentence

As the degree of similarity between old source segments in the database or memory and new source-text segments currently being translated may vary, an algorithm is used to calculate a percentage which expresses the degree of match. The higher the percentage of the fuzzy match, the closer the similarity between the two source-language segments. The threshold percentage can be set by the user at a high level, for instance at 90 per cent, to restrict the retrieval of old source-language segments to those containing only small differences from the new source-language segment. In contrast, the threshold can be set at a low level, for instance at 10 per cent, to allow the translation memory to retrieve segments only weakly related to the new segment. Examples in Table 4.3 show two thresholds for fuzzy matching.

For the higher percentage, only two English words 'pull' and 'out' (ES4.7) are different from the new sentence, 'push' and 'in' (ES4.8).

Table 4.3 Higher and lower threshold percentages for fuzzy matching

Percentage/sentence	English (source)	French (target)
High/old	ES4.7: *Pull* the control dial *out* to start.	FS4.7: *Tirer* le sélecteur pour mettre en marche.
High/new	ES4.8: *Push* the control dial *in* to start.	FS4.8: *Enfoncer* le sélecteur pour mettre en marche.
Low/old	ES4.9: If the *drum* does not stop moving, disconnect the electrical power.	FS4.9: Si *le tambour* est toujours en marche, couper le courant.
Low/new	ES4.10: If the *washer* does not stop moving *when the door is opened during the spin cycle*, disconnect the electrical power.	FS4.10: *Si pendant le cycle d'essorage la machine* est toujours en marche *lorsque le couvercle est ouvert*, couper le courant.

ES = English sentence; FS = French sentence

A lower threshold means that there is less similarity between the old and new source-language segments (see ES4.9 and ES4.10), with more work for the translator to do. In some cases, more time is needed to edit fuzzy matches than to translate them from scratch.

Segments that mean the same thing but differ in format such as dates (30 October 1961/October 30, 1961/1961, October 30), measurements (kg/kilogram), time (4.00pm/1600) and spellings (color/colour) all fall in the fuzzy-match category although they are differently categorized by Austermühl (2001) and Bowker (2002). Some systems also allow for the automatic processing of such changes. Examples of English–German fuzzy matches can be found in Esselink (2000) and Austermühl (2001), and English–French in Bowker (2002).

Polysemous and homonymous words, that is homographs, always need careful handling and present a challenge for all machine translation systems. However, in a computer-aided translation system, a translator can decide to accept or reject a match – either perfect or fuzzy – when it is suggested by the system (Bowker 2002: 97). Table 4.4 illustrates just such a case. Although three suggestions 'proa', 'arco' and 'laço' for 'bow' are given in the fuzzy matches, only 'laço', in 'They tie the rope around the tree in a *bow*' (ES4.14) would be selected.

Most translation memory systems have the perfect matching feature. However, a translation memory system that has the fuzzy matching feature will enable a translator to optimize the use of previously translated material by adjusting the threshold accordingly.

Table 4.4   Examples of matching suggestions for 'bow'

Sentence	English (source)	Portuguese (target)
Old	ES4.11: The big wave has damaged his _bow_ and stern.	PS4.11: A onda grande danificou a _proa_ e a popa.
Old	ES4.12: My music teacher told me not to hold the _bow_ too tightly.	PS4.12: O meu professor de música disse-me para não segurar o _arco_ com demasiada força.
Old	ES4.13: The hunter is using his _bow_ and arrows to kill the deer.	PS4.13: O caçador está a usar o _arco_ e as flechas para matar o veado.
Old	ES4.14: They tie the rope around the tree in a _bow_.	PS4.14: Eles atam a corda com um _laço_ à volta da árvore.
New	ES4.15: She made a _bow_ with the ribbon.	PS4.15: Ela fez um _laço_ com a fita.

ES = English sentence; PS = Portuguese sentence

Filter.   Some translation memory systems are equipped with filters for the more common formats. A filter is a feature that converts a source-language text from one format into another giving a translator the flexibility to work with texts of different formats (Esselink 2000: 362). A translation-friendly format contains only written text without any accompanying graphics. In order to obtain such a format, an import filter would separate a text from its formatting code. For example, a web document can be formatted with HTML code which is normally hidden from the end-user when browsing the web (to view the code, select the 'Source' option from the 'View' menu). The code marks the beginnings and ends of paragraphs, headings, text formats such as bold and italics, the position of graphs and links, so that the document assumes a certain appearance on screen. HTML is one of a number of so-called 'markup languages' to which we return later in this chapter. The HTML code for a web page is shown in Figure 4.1.

If the translator works on the document in the HTML format, there is a danger that the code might accidentally get removed or translated as part of the text, giving an incorrect translation. Furthermore, the translation might not then allow conversion back to a web page owing to the missing code. Therefore, when a web page requires translation, to make the translation task easier the page is usually stripped of the HTML code leaving only the text without any graphics or formatting information, as shown in Figure 4.2.

```
<!-- Side bar structure ends here --><!-- End of Math Side Bar --
><!-- Allow menubars in non-printable versions --><!--
Secondary Menubar handling--><!-- End of Secondary Menu
Bar Handling -->
<div id="CreatorContent"><!-- Content Section begins here --
><!-- Math Body Prefix file ends here -->
<h2> Teaching Assignment Winter 04<br>
</h2>
<b><a
href = "http://www.stats.uwaterloo.ca/%7Epmarriott/STAT231/">
STAT
231
Empirical Problem Solving</a> <br>
  <br>
Office Hours for STAT 231<br>
</b>
<ul>
<li>Tuesday 10-11</li>
<li>Thursday 10-11<br>
</li>
</ul>
<br>
```

Figure 4.1 Example of HTML code in a web page

Teaching Assignment Winter 04
STAT 231 Empirical Problem Solving
Office Hours for STAT 231
Tuesday 10–11
Thursday 10–11

Figure 4.2 Example of the web page without HTML code

When the translation is completed, the original formatting code can be reincorporated into the translation using the filter. The ability to preserve the format of a source-language text and apply it to the translation contributes to the robustness of a translation memory system (Puntikov 1999: 64). Robustness is the ability of the tool to function in specific conditions determined by a translator; for example, accessing a number of databases or applications simultaneously.

Segmentation.   Segmentation is the process of breaking a text up into units consisting of a word or a string of words that is linguistically acceptable. Segmentation is needed in order for a translation memory to perform the matching (perfect and fuzzy) process. A pair of old source and target-language texts is usually segmented into individual pairs of sentences. However, not all parts of texts, particularly specialist texts, are in a sentence format. Exceptions include headings, lists and bullet points. As a result, different units of segmentation are needed. A translator can decide the length of a segment but often punctuation is used as an indicator. A segment is then allocated a unique number or tag by the system as shown in Table 4.5 (see also Table 4.6).

Table 4.5   Example of segments

Segment	English
4.16	the translation of English affixes into Malay
4.17	in Malaysia
4.18	the terminology committee
4.19	the planning of the Malay language
4.20	scientific and technological terms
4.21	the translation of English affixes

It is important to note that while segmentation is quite natural for Latin-based alphabets, it is rather alien to languages such as Chinese, Thai and Vietnamese, which are written continuously without any spaces between characters. Thus, other methods of segmentation are required to determine the beginning and ending of a segment in such cases (see Gao *et al.* 2004).

New segments can be added to the translation memory while translating, an alternatively previously translated source-language texts and their translations can be entered into the memory through a process of text alignment.

Alignment.   Alignment is the process of binding a source-language segment to its corresponding target-language segment. The purpose of alignment is to create a new translation memory database or to add to an existing one. The corresponding pairs of source and target-language segments are called 'translation units' (see Table 4.6). Once the translator has loaded the parallel texts – an original and its translation – into the system, the tool makes a proposal for aligning the segments based on a number of algorithms such as punctuation, numbers, formatting, names and dates, for which the translator is offered various choices. The translator can then adjust the alignment proposed by the system before committing the aligned

Table 4.6 Example of translation units

Segment	English (source)	Segment	French (target)
4.16	the translation of English affixes into Malay	4.16a	la traduction d'affixes anglais en malais
4.17	in Malaysia	4.17a	en Malaisie
4.18	the terminology committee	4.18a	la commission de terminologie
4.19	the planning of the Malay language	4.19a	la planification de la langue malaise
4.20	scientific and technological terms	4.20a	termes scientifiques et technologiques
4.21	the translation of English affixes	4.21a	la traduction des affixes anglais

texts to the memory, either by creating a new one, for example for a new subject field or new client, or by adding to an existing one. Translation units are usually numbered or tagged as shown in Table 4.6 (see also Table 4.5). The collection of translation units is stored, in no particular order, in the database for future translations. Most commercial alignment tools allow alignment at the sentence level. However, in recent years the attention of researchers has also focused on alignment methods for translation memory systems below the sentence level (see Piperidis, Papageorgiou and Boutsis 2000).

Reviews of specific translation memory systems can be found in Esselink (1998), Benis (2003), Környei (2000), Austermühl (2001), Gerasimov (2002) and Wassmer (2004). Helpful sources for the latest information on translation tools and resources can be found on the web pages of the *Translation Journal* (see http://accurapid.com/journal/), and Multilingual Computing, Inc. (see http://www.multilingual.com/).

The translation workflow

A typical workflow of translation involving a translation memory system is described in Figure 4.3. Suppose that an English source text needs to be translated into French (see Figure 4.4). The English text is then compared to a database of previously translated English–French texts to find out if any of the segments in the new English source text matches the segments of old or stored English source texts in the database.

At this stage, identical or similar segments in English and French are identified and extracted by the translation memory system. The extracted translation units (a pair of source and target-language segments) may look like those in Table 4.7.

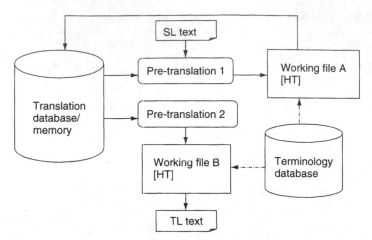

SL = source language; TL = target language; HT = human translator

Figure 4.3 Example of a translation workflow using a translation memory system

---

Translation in Malaysia has never been an important part of the planning of the modern Malay language. The Terminology Committee set up to deal with the borrowing of foreign words into the Malay language only focused on scientific and technological terms. However, one persistent problem since 1973 has been the translation of English affixes into Malay. Until today, Malaysian translators are facing problems translating English affixes.

Figure 4.4 Example of an English source text

Table 4.7 Example of English-French translation units from a database

Segment	English (source)	Segment	French (target)
4.22	in Malaysia	4.22a	en Malaisie
4.23	the planning of the modern Malay language	4.23a	la planification de la langue malaise
4.24	the Terminology Committee	4.24a	la commission de terminologie
4.25	scientific and technological terms	4.25a	termes scientifiques et technologiques
4.26	the translation of English affixes into Malay	4.26a	la traduction d'affixes anglais en malais

From these translation units, a pre-translation process takes place to produce pre-translation 1 as shown in Figure 4.5 (see also Figure 4.3).

La traduction en Malaisie *has never been* un rôle important de planification de la langue malaise. La commission de terminologie *set up to deal with the borrowing of foreign words into* la langue malaise only focused on termes scientifiques et technologiques. *However,* un des problèmes récurrents dopuis 1973 *has been* la traduction d'affixes anglais en malais. *Until today, Malaysian translators are facing problems translating* les affixes anglais.

Figure 4.5   Pre-translation 1

The remaining English segments which were not found in the database have to be translated manually by the translator. This is shown in Figure 4.3 as working file A. At this point if a search for terms is required, the terminology database can be accessed. The English–French translation units which have just been translated are then stored in the database to generate a second pre-translation (see Figure 4.3). This translation, the first draft of the target-language text in French, then requires revision by the translator. This is indicated in Figure 4.3 as working file B. At this point, the terminology database can be re-accessed if needed. After the completion of the translation task by the translator in working file B, a target-language text in French is produced, which may undergo further revision by the translator to produce a polished translation (see Puntikov 1999; Zerfass 2002).

The principal workflow seen in Figure 4.3 is reflected in almost all translation memory systems, but strategies can follow two models: database and reference (Zerfass 2002). The model shown in Figure 4.6 has a component that stores all previously translated material in one database. The segments are context-independent, which allows matching to occur in different translation contexts. Segments from a new source-language

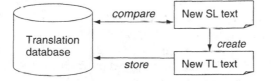

SL = source language; TL = target language

Figure 4.6   Database model in translation memory systems

text are compared to segments in the database, and translations are offered to the translator if identical and/or similar segments are found. Once the translation is completed, a new target-language text is produced and the new or revised segments are added to the database.

In the reference model, the translation database shown in Figure 4.7 is empty until relevant source and target-language texts are loaded into it in stage 1. For example, when translating an updated version of a source-language text such as a newer version of an instruction manual, the previous older versions can be aligned and segmented before being loaded into the translation database. Segments from the new source-language text are later compared to the old segments stored in the translation database. Once the translation is complete, a target-language text is created in stage 2.

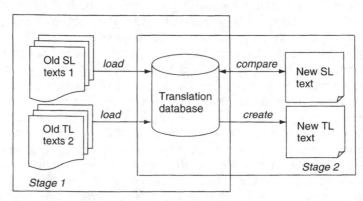

SL = source language; TL = target language

Figure 4.7   Reference model in translation memory systems

Terminology management systems

For professional translators who specialize in highly technical subject fields, terminology is a crucial component of their translation work. A terminology – that is a codified collection of terms – can be defined as 'a systematic arrangement of concepts within a special language. Concepts, not terms. Systematic, not alphabetic' (Bononno 2000: 651). In other words, terminology is arranged by concept. Each concept has a label – or set of labels if synonymous – called a 'term', which is a single word or a string of words used to represent it in the language of the specialized field. Concepts are arranged 'systematically' to reflect the organization of know-ledge in a particular subject field, for example to exhibit a hierarchical relationship of scientific classification or taxonomy. In biology, animals and plants, for example, are hierarchically classified. The most familiar one is the 'genus-species' hierarchy such as 'Zingiber officinale', the scientific name for ginger where the first word, 'Zingiber', refers to the genus (one hierarchical level above species, for which the first letter of the word is upper case) and 'officinale' refers to species (for which the word is usually written with initial lower case). In practice, however, most terminology collections do not exhibit a complex conceptual structure, hierarchical or otherwise. Instead, terms which label the same concept (for example synonyms, spelling variants, abbreviations) are grouped together in the same entry (or 'record' in the database), whereas polysemous terms (same form, different meanings – for example in different subject fields) are recorded in separate entries (or separate records in the database). This method of organization contrasts with that used in lexicography, in which the form of the word or term determines its position in the organization of the lexicon – usually alphabetical – regardless of meaning. So, in a terminology, for instance, the linguistic terms 'subordinate clause' and 'dependent clause' would be grouped together in the same entry/record as synonyms labelling the same (or very similar) concepts. The term 'clause', however, would have separate entries for the subject fields linguistics and law, as the concept and the system to which it belongs – and hence the definition – is different in each case. According to lexicographical practice, both senses would appear under an entry for 'clause'.

Terminology is an important field of study and most professional translators who are involved in technical translation know that terminology is crucial to their work. However, most professional translators prefer to use terminology without investing too much work in something that would take them away from their main priority, which is to translate. A tool like a terminology management system, therefore, helps professional translators to record and then integrate terminology into their translation work. A typical terminology management system consists of tools to structure the database according to need; a database, which once populated is known as a 'termbase', and a look-up feature (see Wright and Budin 1997 and 2001). The main functions of a terminology management system are to maintain a database, to manipulate terminology resources, to identify multiple equivalents, to establish terminological resources for dictionaries and glossaries, and to exchange terms efficiently (Galinski and Budin 1997: 397). If concepts are organized hierarchically, these functions cannot be performed by spreadsheet software such as Excel (Bononno 2000: 652).

A terminology database can be designed and populated from scratch during ongoing translation work. Additional information ('metadata') such as definitions, context, gender and synonyms can also be included. Most terminology management systems allow the user to define and structure the information categories needed for their work (see International Organization for Standardization (ISO) Technical Committee 37, which governs the standardized principles, methods and application relating to terminology and other language resources). A detailed description of how to build and manage a terminology database is found in Austermühl (2001) and Bowker (2002).

Alternatively, terms for specific subject fields and languages can be accessed by a translator via compact discs or online term banks. The European Commission Terminology Database (EURODICAUTUM), for example, currently provides terminology online for approximately 91 subject fields in 12 languages; it is now being relaunched as part of a new interagency online term bank called the Inter-Agency Terminology Exchange (IATE) which combines multilingual data from EURODICAUTUM with those of other European Union agencies (see http://www.unilat.org/dtil/etis/actasTDCnet/macphail.htm). Another well-known term bank is the Terminology of Telecommunications (ACRoTERMITE) containing data in six languages (Arabic, Chinese, English, French, Russian and Spanish) in the field of telecommunications. For a discussion of termbases and term banks in the context of translation, see Rogers (2005).

The database and look-up features are integrated in some terminology management systems while in others they are kept separate. Professional translators may prefer to use an integrated system that enables them to compile a terminology database while translating with a translation memory system. Systems that have separate facilities are more suitable for terminologists. Examples of commercial terminology management systems are Multiterm by Trados, and Termstar by Star, which can be used separately from their translation memory systems (Translator's Workbench and Transit respectively) while TranslationManager by IBM and SDLX by SDL International are integrated systems (Esselink 2000: 379).

Translation support tools and resources

The description by a professional translator of his working methods provided in Chapter 1 shows the importance of other tools to the translator such as spell, grammar and style-checkers, dictionaries, glossaries, concordancers and online search engines. In this section, we shall concentrate on parallel corpora and concordancers for professional translators while other resources such as dictionaries and glossaries will be mentioned more briefly.

Most of us are familiar with spell, grammar and style-checkers as well as dictionaries, and understand how they differ from each other. In the case of dictionaries, it is coverage, not size that is important to professional translators (Bennett and Gerber 2003: 187). The popular and high-demand languages of Western Europe such as English, French and Spanish and of Eastern Asia such as Chinese and Japanese have dictionaries with wider coverage than low-demand languages such as Singhalese of Sri Lanka and Warrungu, an Aboriginal language of Australia. As for the spell-checker, its main function is to compare a text against a large dictionary, or sometimes a number of different dictionaries, for misspellings. A grammar checker looks for grammatical errors occurring in a text such as repeated words or ungrammatical phrases that do not conform to the pre-determined set of grammatical rules stored for that particular language. A style-checker looks at irregular sentence aspects such as length of sentence, punctuation and other stylistic features, although 'styles' are generally not well-differentiated. The glossary, on the other hand, is a little different from the rest of the tools. In many cases, glossaries are custom-built either by a translator or a client. A glossary is a list of terms belonging to a specific subject field with or without definitions. It comes not only in text format but also in graphical format.

Parallel corpora

A corpus in the present context is a collection of written texts in a machine-readable format. In Translation Studies and linguistics, two terms are used to refer to corpora which consist of original texts and their translations: 'parallel corpus' and 'translation corpus'. In the field of computational linguistics the term used is 'parallel texts' (see Véronis 2000). Other design possibilities include corpora which consist of texts in two or more languages and are selected according to similar pre-determined design criteria, for example size, domain, genre and topic. This type of corpus has been called a 'multilingual corpus' or a 'comparable corpus' in Translation Studies. Multilingual corpora cannot, however, be aligned as there is no source text–target text relationship. However, this type of corpus is rich in useful information for translators (Bowker 2002: 46). The final type is the 'comparable corpus', which consists of texts in one language, but offering a comparison between original texts and translations into that language. Comparable corpora are useful for researching possible differences between original texts and translated texts with respect to the distribution of words and syntactic structures, for example. For a summary of the use of corpora in Translation Studies, see Kenny (1998).

Belonging to the broad field of language technology, parallel corpora are used as a linguistic resource for a wide range of applications including the compilation of termbases (see, for instance, Ahmad and Rogers 2001). Based on pre-determined criteria that reflect the design and purpose for which they are created, different corpora can be built for use in translation, as we have seen, for a range of purposes. For European languages there are many parallel corpora, for example INTERSECT (International Sample of English Contrastive Texts) French–English Corpus; English–Portuguese COMPARA; CRATER (Corpus Resources and Terminology Extraction) in English, French and Spanish; Linköping Parallel Corpora for English–Swedish; and the Scania Corpus for English, French, German, Spanish, Dutch, Italian and Finnish. Parallel corpora that involve at least one non-European language include TOLL (Thai On-Line Library) Parallel Text via the Internet for Thai and English; English–Turkish Aligned Parallel Corpora; Japanese–English Broadcast News Corpus; PESA (Portuguese–English Sentence Alignment) Parallel Corpora of Brazilian Portuguese and English; and the English-Inuktitut (a dialect of the Inuit of the Canadian Eastern Arctic) Parallel Corpus (see Godwin-Jones 2001).

Parallel corpora are beneficial to professional translators as resource material in addition to their own previously translated material, especially when there is a need to widen the search for the most suitable equivalent of a source-language term or segment. Some parallel corpora are available online, as indicated for example by the National Language Software Registry which collects and provides detailed information on a variety of natural-language processing software (see Godwin-Jones 2001). Another source of parallel corpora is the LDC (Linguistic Data Consortium) that collects and creates parallel texts such as United Nation proceedings, and the European Corpus Initiative Multilingual Corpus.

In order for parallel corpora to be of value to a translator, the corpora might have to be custom-designed. But it is important to bear in mind that constructing a parallel corpus from scratch currently involves a great deal of work, which most professional translators are not likely to undertake. Automated support for compiling corpora from the WWW is still at the research stage, and hence it is only natural that accessible online parallel corpora are preferred. However, translators who specialize in a narrow subject field or a less common language pair may not be able to enjoy the advantages of readily available parallel corpora and may be forced to build their own. A simple explanation of how to construct a parallel corpus is given in Figure 4.8.

At the corpus design stage, the desired characteristics of a corpus are determined. These include subject fields, language pairs, the size of the source and target-language texts, authors, genres, dates, the origin of texts (for example bilingual websites or printed bilingual materials) and copyright permission. Collecting texts such as web pages and previously translated materials, which are stored electronically, can save a lot of time and effort when compared to collecting printed material that has to be converted into electronic format using OCR.

When a printed document which is not available electronically needs a translation, the first thing a professional translator would do is to scan the document. An OCR tool is used to improve the scanning process in order to recognize all punctuation and other marks such as '~' (tilde), '\' (backslash) and mathematical symbols in the source-language text and transfer these correctly into the electronic version of the document. Non-Latin alphabets and scripts are also supported by some OCRs but

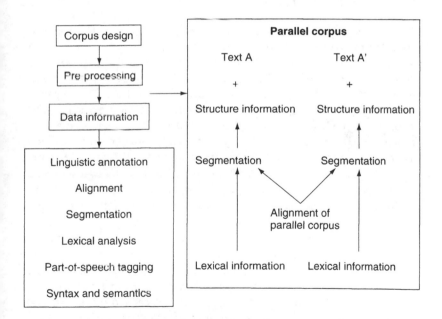

Text A = source-language text; Text A' = target-language text

Figure 4.8 Flowchart to illustrate how to build a parallel corpus
Source: Gamper and Dongilli (1999).

they are not necessarily as well-handled as the Latin alphabet. Therefore, after the scanning process a word-proofing tool like a spell-checker may be used for that language. OCR tools including Omnipage by ScanSoft and Finereader by Abbyy support Latin and some non-Latin alphabets and scripts (see Bowker 2002). At the pre-processing stage, the information recorded about each text may look like that in Figure 4.9.

```
<header type = "corpus" lang = "my"   id = "krm-e
   creator = "ck" status = "update" date.created = "2004
   date.updated = "2004 = -10-15"
   >
      <filedesc>
        <titlestmt>
          <title lang = "en"> Malay-English Corpus
          <title lang = "ms" >Korpus Melayu-Inggeris
```

Figure 4.9   Example of a text header in a corpus

The corpus may or may not need to be linguistically annotated, that is with a unique part-of-speech code provided for every word in the text (see Macklovitch 2001). Certain text-processing tools may operate without accompanying or hidden tags, but if annotation is required at the data information stage linguistic information for the language pair is selected for the purpose of linguistic annotation at the next stage. The part-of-speech code system is used to represent a grammatical category for each word. Examples of the Malay language part-of-speech codes such as NUM for numeral and NNN for common noun are illustrated in Figure 4.10. A tool such as a 'Treebank' that consists of 'a bank of linguistic trees' can be employed not only for morphosyntactic and syntactic annotations, but also semantic annotations based on a number of linguistic theories. Several Treebank projects are available in European and Asian languages such as the Penn Chinese Treebank, the Lancaster–Leeds Treebank for English, the Turin University Treebank for Italian, the Kyoto University Corpus for Japanese, the Prague Dependency Treebank for Czech and the METU-Sabanci (Middle East Technical University) Turkish Treebank.

The type of coding illustrated in Figure 4.10 is carried out for several reasons. For example, it allows the automatic extraction of an item matching the part-of-speech in the aligned translation and the alignment of bilingual sentences as a resource for professional translators (Gamper and Dongilli 1999). Once the linguistic information is ready, linguistic

---

Lima NUM *ekor* NUC *gajah* NNN *liar* ADJ *telah* AUX *memusnahkan* VVV *dua puluh*
NUM *ekar* NNN *ladang* NNN *getah* NNN *di* PRE *Johor* NPR. *Pengurus* NNN *ladang*
NNN *itu* DEM *menghubungi* VVV *Jabatan Haiwan dan Hidupan Liar* NPR *untuk*
PRE *menangkap* VVV *gajah* NNN *liar* NNN *ini* DET.

Translation: [Five wild elephants were found to have destroyed twenty acres of rubber
plantation in Johor. The manager called the Wildlife Department to trap these
elephants.]
NNN = common noun; NPR = proper noun; NUM = numeral; NUC = numeral
classifier; ADJ = adjective; AUX = auxiliary verb; VVV = verb; PRE = preposition;
DET = determiner

Figure 4.10 Example of part-of-speech tagging

annotation can be carried out at several levels. As an example, COMPARA
consists of bidirectional English and Portuguese texts (see Frankenberg-
Garcia and Santos 2003). In the case of the English–Portuguese corpus,
each English paragraph is aligned to its Portuguese counterpart. These
pairs of paragraphs are subsequently subjected to analysis using a corpus
tool called EasyAlign that aligns the corpus sentence by sentence. A unit
of alignment for COMPARA is an English sentence. The corresponding
units in the Portuguese translation, however, may contain more than one
sentence.

Concordancers

A concordancer is an electronic tool which has been used in language
learning, literary analysis, corpus linguistics, terminography and
lexicography. It allows the user to select a particular word or phrase
and displays the uses of that word or phrase in the selected corpus in
order to show where and how often it occurs, and in what linguistic
contexts it appears. The output is called a concordance. The concorded
word is shown in the centre of each line displayed in the concordance,
so that the user can quickly scan the results. The example in Figure 4.11
shows two words appearing on the left and right of the concorded
word 'round'. Other examples of concorded words can be obtained
from the Collins Worldbanks*Online* English website (see http://
www.collins.co.uk/Corpus/CorpusSearch.aspx) which has a corpus of
56 million words of contemporary written and spoken text in the
English language.

Concordancers usually allow the user to define the number of words
which they want to appear to the left and to the right of the concorded

A walk **round** its garden
I came **round**, I was
he hopped **round** the kitchen
other way **round**. The book
your friends **round** to witness
cloth wrapped **round** his head
the third **round** of the quiz
you this **round**-about route
needle spinning **round** and round
kids running **round** the back
she gets **round** to looking
twist Mary **round** with fingers
12-minute first-**round** win over
will buy a **round**, at a
to early-**round** matches, with
like going **round** the mansion
I'll turn **round** and run
the opening **round**, he was
people came **round** to the
been all **round** the country
one more – to **round** it off
very popular **round** here and
the year **round** with these
face too was **round**, her mouth
for another **round** of peace
I'll nip **round** and get a
other way **round** because I
the second **round** of discussion

Figure 4.11   Example of a concordance for the word 'round'

word or phrase and to sort the results in various ways, for example according to frequency or alphabetically according to the word immediately to the left or to the right of the concorded word. The tool has been applied to areas of study such as translation, language engineering and natural-language software development (see Wu *et al.* 2003). Concordances were originally done by hand to show the use of all the words in the Bible (see Tribble and Jones 1997).

While concordancers are strictly speaking used to produce concordances, such tools often have other functions, including typically the production of indexes (referenced lists of words from the selected corpus showing where they occur and their frequency distributions) and wordlists, which are like indexes without any indication of text location. A description of monolingual and bilingual concordancers and their key features and abilities is given in Bowker (2002).

In translation, a bilingual aligned corpus is a rich resource for professional translators. In order to mine this resource, two types of tool can be used: a translation memory system as discussed earlier, and a bilingual concordancer. Translation memory systems and bilingual concordancers are found to be more widely used in the academic setting where translators-to-be are taught translation-related tasks using both tools; in the professional setting, however, bilingual concordancers are less widely used than translation memory systems (Bowker and Barlow 2004). One reason for this is that many of the concordancers have been built specifically for particular research projects set up by universities and through individual initiatives. Examples include TotalRecall, an English–Chinese concordancer built by National Tsing Hua University and Van Nung Institute of Technology in Taiwan, and also Multiconcord, which was developed by David Wolls.

Commercialization of these research products is limited, with a few exceptions such as TransSearch, an English–French bilingual concordancer developed by the University of Montreal which is now offered as an online service by a company called Terminotix, Inc. specializing in computer tools for translation. There are, however, some concordancers which have been developed for general and educational uses, such as WordSmith and the Oxford Concordance Program (OCP) by the Oxford University Press. Nevertheless, unlike translation memory systems, which are marketed by commercial companies like Trados, the majority of concordancers are not widely advertised to professional translators. This is gradually changing, however, as bilingual concordancers are getting more exposure in particular with Translation Studies students training to become professional translators. The introduction of concordancers to students of translation started in the late 1990s in a number of universities and may eventually become a support tool a translator cannot do without (Bowker and Barlow 2004).

Localization tools

Localization tools have been developed in order to support the translation of software applications, product documentation and websites. Localization tools are used in conjunction with other computer-aided translation tools such as translation memory systems and terminology management systems.

Figure 4.12 shows an example of how different types of tool fit into the workflow of a localization process, divided here into two parts. The first part involves the planning and management aspects of the process while the second involves the translating aspects. The management and translation tools are displayed individually to show their use. In order to manage several languages at any one given time for the same source-language material, operational or management tools are used. Examples of such tools are LTC (Language Technology Centre) Organiser and LTRAC (Language Translation Resource Automation Console); these project management tools can be used with any translation project, not just localization. Translation memory, terminology management and localization tools are used in the translation of source-language material, while management tools are used to schedule and monitor the entire localization project based on a pre-determined deadline, and to test the product or check websites after the localization process has been completed.

A typical localization process involves three stages, namely project preparation, the translation proper and quality assurance. In the project preparation stage, the hardware and software may need to be reconfigured depending on the format of the source-language material, and references

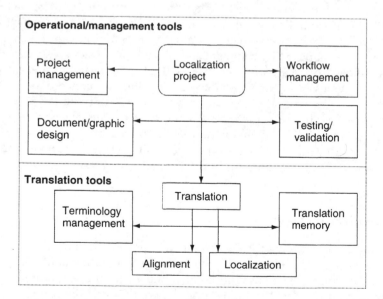

Figure 4.12   Types of tool used in a localization project

related to the subject field of the material may also need to be collected; translators may be required to get training if they are unfamiliar with the subject or with hardware or software applications. In order to prepare the source-language material of the translation proper, it undergoes a process called 'localization-enablement' or 'internationalization'. This process entails, for instance, stripping all graphics from the text which is to be translated. The purpose is to make it easier to localize and translate a document into a specific language (Esselink 1998: 2).

At the stage of the translation proper, a translation memory system needs to be prepared by either creating a new database (that is, memory) or using an existing database from another project. A similar step is taken for the terminology database. In the first case, if no existing translation or terminology database is available, the translator can store translations and enter terms into a newly created database during the translation process. In the second case, the translator may find that the source-language material can be pre-translated by a machine translation system or compared to an existing translation database. If this is the case, the translation draft may contain some segments that have been translated into the target language while the remaining segments are still in the source language (see Figure 4.5). Once the source-language material has been completely translated into the target language, quality assurance is performed either internally by professional translators and engineers or externally by vendors and clients. At this stage, the translation is reviewed and checked for content accuracy, grammar and spelling. If, for instance, the translation is of an operating manual, the operating procedures of the product are also performed and checked.

Some writers on translation issues consider localization to involve no more than is required for all translations if a functional view is adopted (see Chapter 2) with the emphasis on fitness for purpose. However, some translation jobs do require special attention in at least three respects, and may therefore be considered as localization. The first issue is language. Consider the case of Chinese, which has two different scripts – Traditional and Simplified – used by different countries. Singapore and the People's Republic of China use Simplified Chinese, while Taiwan uses Traditional Chinese. Therefore, the correct script for a translation is determined by the country in which the product will be marketed. As an example, Microsoft Xbox, a video game console, requires specific descriptions, information and configurations of the product to be translated into many different languages for its consumers around the world. The Xbox console sold in Singapore includes Chinese interfaces, and all games (for example, Halo, Blix and MechAssault) have been fully localized with speech dubbed into Chinese. The Xbox documentation for the Singapore market has been translated into the Simplified Chinese script, while the Traditional Chinese script has been used for the Taiwan market.

The second issue is cultural. Icons, product names, colours, speech and possibly sound effects have to be adapted to suit local users. At times product names have to be changed for cultural reasons. For example, the 2003 Subaru car model called 'Subaru Baja' (pronounced as /baha/) when launched in the USA would be likely to have its model name changed if marketed in Malaysia but may be able to retain its name for the Indonesian market. In Malaysian Malay, the term 'baja' (pronounced as /baja/, /j/ as in 'jump') means 'fertilizer'. In Indonesian Malay, however, this term could work quite well. There the term 'baja' (with the same /j/ pronunciation as the Malaysian Malay) means 'armour', which conveys the idea of strength and protection.

The third issue is technical. In order to support local languages (especially non-Latin scripts), online or print documentation may still require redesigning. In Thai, additional typographical symbols, some of which are ancient symbols, are needed to mark the beginning of a sentence, stanza or paragraph when writing with a computer keyboard. Thai letters displayed on a computer screen are of different sizes and written on four levels (top, above, base line and below). This creates a number of problems such as the position of the cursor when typing a character. A wrongly positioned cursor could result in spelling errors (Kosavisutte 1996/2001). Adaptations are also needed for language scripts that are written from right to left, with the exception of numbers which are written from left to right, for example in Arabic, Hebrew, Persian and Urdu.

Some translation memory systems are integrated with other tools for localization purposes. An integrated tool allows translation memory to be utilized during the localization process, as already indicated in Figure 4.12. Professional translators who are involved in the localization industry prefer this type of integrated application or workbench. Some of the products falling into this category include GlobalSight System by GlobalSight, SDLX from SDL International and Alchemy Catalyst by Alchemy Software Development. Reviews of specific localization tools can be found in Wassmer (2000) and Austermühl (2001), while the uses of localization tools are described in Esselink (1998 and 2000).

It is also common to find localization companies using both translation memory systems and machine translation systems; for example, workbenches that are integrated with several machine translation components or machine translation systems that are integrated with translation memory systems. In some cases, integration with other tools such as

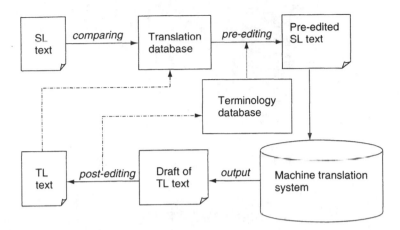

SL = source language; TL = target language

Figure 4.13 Example of the translation process using a machine translation system, a translation database and a terminology database

terminology management systems can also be found. Figure 4.13 is an example of a translation process accessing previously translated material stored in a translation database to pre-edit a source-language text before it is automatically translated by a machine translation system. The terminology database can still be accessed at the post-editing stage if the use of specific terms needed to be reconfirmed. The post-edited target-language text is also stored in the translation database as resource material for future translations.

Commercial computer-aided translation tools

The increased demand for technical translation has been the catalyst for the widespread use of translation tools. Unlike machine translation systems, computer-aided translation tools are language-independent, allowing professional translators to use them regardless of the languages they work with. Table 4.8 is a classification of tools currently available on the market.

The usefulness of these tools varies greatly in accordance with the translator's needs. For example, if localization is only a small part of a translator's work, a translation memory system may be sufficient. On the other hand, if localization is the only translation work a translator does, a specialized localization tool would be needed in addition to

Table 4.8 Classification of commercial computer-aided translation tools

Language tool	Bilingual (unidirectional)	Bilingual (bidirectional)	Trilingual	Multilingual	Language-independent	Total
Electronic dictionary	1	15	5	36		57
Translation memory					39	39
Alignment				1		1
Localization					39	39
Terminology management system					22	22
Total	1	16	5	37	100	159

Source: Hutchins, Hartmann and Ito (2004).

a translation memory system. If the bulk of the translation work comes from a particular client, the tool preference of that client will have to be taken into account by the translator. Other considerations such as cost may also determine which tool a particular translator chooses to use. In order to provide a range of choices, many translation and localization tools come in different versions from basic to full systems. It is often the case that a basic version is the cheapest solution as it contains only a limited number of features. The higher the number of features a version has, the higher the cost. Most tools can also be upgraded when an improved feature or a new feature is introduced.

Standards for data interchange

In this chapter we have seen that translation and terminology data can be stored using a large number of tools in a variety of formats using different operating systems. A similar situation is also found in the localization industry where numerous types of tools are used. In order for the translator to have access to translation and terminological resources that are stored in different translation, terminology and localization tools, several attempts have been made to support the transfer of data between these tools – in other words, to introduce interoperability. These attempts have led to the creation of a number of standards. A standard is a universal format that has been agreed and approved by either an international standards organization such as ISO or the relevant industry such as the localization industry. In the case of data exchange, the aim of a standard is to facilitate exchange using a common markup language to structure the data in each document using a set of agreed tags as annotations (see, for instance, the HTML code in Figure 4.1 above). XML (eXtensible or eXtensive Markup Language) is one such standard – developed by the WWW Consortium (W3C) – which describes the structure of different types of electronic documents and hence facilitates the sharing of data between different software applications in a consistent way. It does not contain a fixed set of elements like HTML. Essentially, XML defines 'what the information is', while HTML defines 'what the information looks like'. XML is an abbreviated version of SGML (Standard Generalized Markup Language), an international standard for describing the structure of electronic documents.

While XML is one standard in widespread use, there are different standards or sets of standards for data interchange which are of particular interest to any professional translator: the standard for the interchange of translation memory data, the standards for the interchange of lexical and terminological data, and the standard for the interchange of localization information. These are, in turn, Translation Memory eXchange (TMX), TermBase eXchange (TBX), and XML Localisation Interchange File Format (XLIFF), and are all described below.

Translation memory exchange

Until recently, most computer-aided translation tools were not compatible with each other, and as a result the import and export of files into and from different software applications presented great problems. In 1998 this prompted OSCAR (Open Standards for Container/Content Allowing Reuse) to create the translation memory exchange (TMX), an intermediate format to facilitate the sharing of translation memory data. Having TMX in a translation memory system increases its flexibility to combine with other computer-aided translation and localization tools. One goal of TMX is to maximize the reusability of previously translated material, which may have been stored in different formats.

Figure 4.14 illustrates how TMX facilitates the sharing of data between different formats. A text in Word format stored in Database 1 is exported to the TMX format and then imported into an HTML format. The HTML text is stored in Database 2. It is important for the import and export processes to apply the same TMX specification to prevent the loss of information during the importation and exportation processes.

In 2004, the latest specification of TMX version 1.4b was published, describing the features of TMX in two parts (see also the 2005 OSCAR Recommendation at http://www.lisa.org/standards/tmx/tmx.html). The first is a specification of the format of the 'container', the higher-level elements where information about the file is stored. The second is a specification of the low-level meta-markup format for the content of a

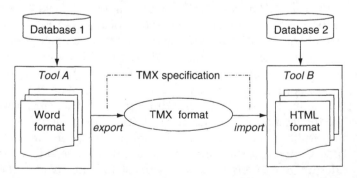

Figure 4.14   Example of TMX data-sharing

segment of a translation-memory text. These are known respectively as the header and the body. A header contains information about the entire document, and several required attributes must be included in a TMX specification. In Figure 4.15, the segments in bold are the obligatory attributes in a header. The attributes contain information such as the date of creation of the text, the identity of the creator, and so on.

```
<tmx version – "1.4">
<header
creationtool = "ToolA"
creationtoolversion = "123"
datatype = "PlainText"
segtype = "sentence"
adminlang = "en-BR"
srclang = "en"
o-tmf = "XYZ"
creationdate = "01-01-2005"
creationid = "PKM"
changedate = "21-03-2005"
changeid = "DD"
>
</header>
</body>
</body>
</tmx>
```

Figure 4.15   Example of a header in TMX

The body contains a collection of 'translation units' or <tu> elements. This collection can come in any order. Each <tu> has at least one 'translation unit variant', a <tuv> element that contains the segment and the information pertaining to the segment. One required attribute in a TMX body is the language element: 'xml:lang' specifies the language of the text using two-letter codes, such as MS for the Malay language. The language code is adopted from the Internet Society's RFC 3066 (Request for Comments: 3066) – Tags for the identification of languages, which is based on ISO 639 (Language Codes). The actual text of a given segment is stored in a segment element, <seg>. Figure 4.16 is an example of a body in TMX.

The display of a TMX logo in association with a tool indicates that it has undergone TMX certification testing. Computer-aided translation tools that have TMX certifications include Déjà Vu by Atril, MultiTrans

```
<body>
<tu
tuid = "0001">
<tuv
xml:lang = "en-BR">
<seg>The <bpt i = "1" x = "1">{\b </bpt>fat<ept
i = "1">}</ept>
<bpt i = "2" x = "2">{\i </bpt>boy<ept i = "2">}</ept>
sleeps.</seg>
</tuv>
<tuv>
xml:lang = "MS"
<seg>Itu <bpt i = "1" x = "2">{\i </bpt>budak<ept
i = "1">}</ept>
<bpt i = "2" x = "1">{\b </bpt>gemuk<ept i = "2">}</ept>
tidur.</seg>
</tuv>
</tu>
</body>
```

Figure 4.16   Example of a body in TMX

by MultiCorpora, Prolyphic by Prolyphic, SDLX by SDL International, WordFast by Champollion and Partners, and Wordfisher by Környei. A detailed description of TMX can be found on the LISA website (see http://www.lisa.org/tmx/).

Termbase exchange

Each day new terms are created around the world in various languages to provide inventions, discoveries and new conceptualizations with linguistic labels. For many years the terminology community has been developing term banks or termbases to store and manage these terms. However, termbases are created in different formats, that is using different subsets of possible information categories such as linguistic data, examples, definitions, sources, administrative data, and so on, and using different data structures, that is the information is differently organized or distributed between the different fields in the database. Nevertheless, they may contain similar although not necessarily identical information. When users access these different termbases, a problem of incompatibility may arise. Thus, a standard is needed to provide a format that can facilitate access to all termbases regardless of how they are stored.

Between professional translators, sharing terminology is important, and it is also beneficial to anyone wishing to upgrade his or her own terminology databases. This sharing of terminology is called 'terminology interchange'. Since terminology management systems vary, standards for terminology interchange have been created based on ISO 12620 (Data Categories). Such standards include:

- MARTIF (Machine-Readable Terminology Interchange Format) – (also known as ISO 12200 – Computer Applications in Terminology), a format for platform-independent and publicly available terminological data interchange. It functions as a channel for transferring data from one terminology management system to another.
- GENETER (Generic model for Terminology) – a tool to represent terminological data which serves as an intermediate format between different applications and platforms.
- OLIF (Open Lexicon Interchange Format) – a tool that exchanges lexical and terminological data. It addresses data management needs for basic terminological exchange and lexicons for machine translation.
- XLT (XML representation of Lexicons and Terminologies) – a standards-based family of formats that represents, manipulates and shares terminological data. It is able to merge and extract OLIF, GENETER and MARTIF, and provides the basis for the TermBase eXchange (TBX; see below).
- Termado – a tool that manages and publishes term catalogues, lexicons and dictionaries. It also imports and exports terms to and from external applications such as other terminological standards (MARTIF and OLIF).

Given the variety of existing standards, TBX (TermBase eXchange) is an XML-based standard format created to provide a common or standard format to share terminological and lexical data among users of different tools. TBX is a joint-effort between OSCAR and the SALT Group (Standards-based Access service to Lexicons and Terminologies), a consortium of academic, government, associations, and commercial groups in the USA and Europe.

The terminological framework for TBX (LISA 2002: 6) was provided by two international standards, ISO 12620 (Data Categories) and ISO 12200 (Computer Applications in Terminology). A forthcoming standard known as the Terminological Markup Framework (TMF), which is being developed by the ISO Technical Committee 37 (Terminology – Principles and Coordination), will be added soon. ISO 12620 is used to describe a system of concepts, which is hierarchical such as genus-species. The TMF specifies the structures and mechanisms that allow terminological data to be represented in a computer. The main task of TBX is to analyse, represent, manipulate and share terminological data. There are plans that it should eventually support the extraction and merging of other files such as OLIF files and TMX files (LISA 2002: 6).

Similar to TMX, the interchange standard for translation memory data, a TBX document also has a header and a body. The header usually contains global information about the terminology such as the origin of the data, the client, the language(s) involved, and so on. Figure 4.17 illustrates a typical TBX document header (LISA 2002: 9). The first line indicates that the type attribute is a TBX document and that the 'xml:lang' attribute indicated is 'en' for English as the default language based on ISO 639 (Language Codes). It can also have an attached second language code taken from ISO 3166 (Country Codes), for example 'fr-CA' for Canadian French. The second line provides the information about the specific file and its source, for example the company name and the file number.

```
<martif type = 'TBX' xml:lang = 'en' >
<martifHeader>
  <fileDesc>
    <sourceDesc>
      <p>Black Walnut Homes termbase</p>
    </sourceDesc>
  </fileDesc>
</martifHeader>
```

Figure 4.17   Example of a header in TBX

The second part, or body of a TBX document, is shown in Figure 4.18 it contains specific information about the data in an entry in a concept-oriented termbase, based on the data model in ISO 16642 (Representing Data Categories).

The 'id' feature contains a unique value identifying the document (in this case an entry for a particular concept in civil engineering in English and Swedish). The document is divided up according to various information categories in ISO 16642 which are labelled by description type elements such as 'subjectField', which contains the description of the subject field 'civil engineering', and 'definition' where the meaning of the

```
<body>
<termEntry id='BWH1'>
<descrip type='subjectField'>civil engineering</descrip>
<descrip type='definition'>A wide layer of load-bearing material laid at the
bottom of a wall or column so as to distribute its pressure more widely over the
foundation </descrip>
<langSet xml:lang='en'>
<tig> <term>footing</term> </tig>
</langSet>
<langSet xml:lang='sv'>
<tig> <term>fundament</term> </tig>
</langSet>
</termEntry>
</body>
```

Figure 4.18   Example of a body in TBX

concept is given. The term information group or the <tig> element
contains information such as the term 'footing' in English shown as <tig>
<term>footing</term> </tig> (LISA 2002: 9–10). The language section
element 'langSet xml:lang' begins with the English language code 'en'. The
translation of 'footing' in Swedish – 'fundament' – is given in the line <tig>
<term>fundament</term> </tig>. Detailed information about TBX specifi-
cations can be found on the LISA website (see http://www.lisa.org/tbx/).

Localization exchange

Not infrequently, many technical and logistic challenges arise during
localization, and one such challenge relates to the problems of transferring
texts between different translation and localization tools. Texts are often
stored in different file formats, some of which are proprietary, for
example reports belonging to a company, while others are commonly
shared such as HTML files. These files are not necessarily easily transferable
from one tool to another. In order to eliminate such challenges, a
standard called XLIFF (XML Localisation Interchange File Format) has been
developed by OASIS (Organization for the Advancement of Structured
Information Standards). OASIS is the largest independent, not-for-profit
consortium in the world that is dedicated to overseeing the standardization of XML applications and web services. It has about 150 companies
and individuals in the localization industry as members including
Alchemy Software, Hewlett-Packard, IBM, Oracle, Microsoft, Novell, Sun
Microsystems and Tektonik.

XLIFF is another XML-based format that allows the interchange of localization information and is tool-neutral, enabling what is claimed to be a seamless transfer of information between tools (OASIS 2003: 14). One of its uses is to store texts that have been extracted from their original formats and to move these texts from one stage to another in a localization process without losing any information, as shown in Figure 4.19 (for more information on XLIFF, see http://www.oasis-open.org/committees/ xliff). The extracted data can be in the form of text or graphics. The advantage of using XLIFF is that it separates a text from its formatting for translation purposes, enables the use of multiple tools and stores information during a localization process.

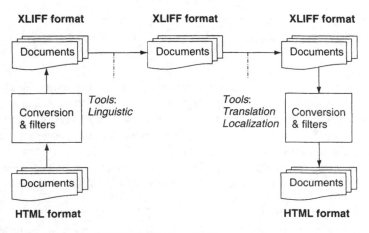

Figure 4.19   Example of XLIFF in the localization process
Source: Jewtushenko and Reynolds (2002).

Using filters, the text and layout in documents in HTML format are separated. The section with translatable text is converted into an XLIFF format while the non-translatable data (the layout) is kept in a separate file. An XLIFF file consists of one or more file elements and each of these has a head and a body section similar to TMX and TBX standards. A head section contains information about the text such as project number, contact information and so on, as shown in Figure 4.20.

A body section contains the main elements where localizable or translatable texts are kept. It is called the 'translation unit' or <trans-unit> element in the XLIFF format file. It contains an identity, 'id' attribute, to map where a segment is located in the source language text. Figure 4.21 illustrates this. The trans-unit element has a source element, which is the segment that is to be translated, and a target element, which is the accepted translated segment.

```
<head>
 <project-title>
  <project-name = "Living healthy">
 </project-title>
</head>
```

Figure 4.20 Example of a header in XLIFF

```
<body>
  <trans-unit id = "n3">
    <source>This is a good exercise.</source>
    <target xml:lang = "ms">Translation of "Ini satu latihan jasmani yang
bagus."</target>
   </trans-unit>
```

Figure 4.21 Example of a body in XLIFF

Sometimes, a second translation element, 'alt-trans', is given as an alternative translation for the source segment, as shown in Figure 4.22. An alt-trans element also contains a source and a target segment. This element can be matched from a translation memory, machine translation system or be suggested by a translator.

In Figure 4.22, the alt-trans element is matched from a translation database of a translation memory system. Using specific matching algorithms, an alternative translation is found but the matching, which is not perfect, only measures at about 60 per cent (match-quality). This indicates that the alt-trans element is a fuzzy match at best. Alt-trans is also a way of keeping track of the changes made during the stages of the localization process, a useful mechanism for keeping a record of what

```
<alt-trans match-quality = "60%" tool = "TM_System">
 <source>This is an exercise.</source>
 <target xml:lang = "ms">Fuzzy TM match for "Ini satu latihan."</target>
</alt-trans>
```

Figure 4.22 Example of an alternate translation element in XLIFF

the changes were, who did them, which tools were used to make them, and so on (OASIS 2003: 13). Once the translation work has been completed, the XLIFF format file is reconverted into the original file format (HTML) and the non-translatable portion (layout) of the source-language text is reincorporated. An XLIFF format contains only one source language and one target language. It is different from the TMX format that is able to support many languages in the same document.

Conclusion

This chapter has shown that there is a range of computer-aided translation tools and resources for the translator to consider. With such a wide range available, it is important that professional translators carry out careful research to discover which tool would suit them and their work best and what type of resources would enable them to translate faster and produce higher quality work. While most translators realize the usefulness of common linguistic tools such as spell- or style-checkers and electronic dictionaries, as well as the value of online searches to solve translation problems, awareness of other tools and resources such as bilingual concordancers and parallel corpora is often still low. On a more technical level, the usefulness of understanding the standards discussed here cannot be underestimated as they are crucial for the management of translation memory data and terms. If the translator is involved in translating technical texts and/or localizing texts in the translation industry – even if they do not specialize in the translation of technical texts – tools such as translation memory and terminology management systems may still prove to be useful, especially since companies that outsource translation jobs are increasingly incorporating such tools into their workflow patterns.

Suggested reading

Austermühl, F. (2001) *Electronic Tools for Translators*. Manchester: St Jerome Publishing.

Bowker, L. (2002) *Computer-aided Translation Technology: A Practical Introduction*. Ottawa: University of Ottawa Press.

Wright, S.E. and G. Budin (eds) (1997) *Handbook of Terminology Management. Vol. 1: Basic Aspects of Terminology Management*. Amsterdam: John Benjamins.

——(2001) *Handbook of Terminology Management. Vol. 2: Application-oriented Terminology Management*. Amsterdam: John Benjamins.

Esselink, B. (2000) *A Practical Guide to Localization*. Amsterdam/Philadelphia: John Benjamins.

Véronis, J. (ed.) (2000) *Parallel Text Processing: Alignment and Use of Translation Corpora*. Dordrecht: Kluwer Academic.

5
Evaluating Translation Tools

In the previous chapter, we looked at some of the technical and operational aspects of various translation tools. This chapter is devoted to the evaluation of both machine translation systems and computer-aided translation tools. In other words, how well do they work? Attention will be given to the different groups of stakeholders involved in the development of machine translation systems from researchers to end-users, as well as to different translation evaluation methods. Finally, sets of general guidelines or procedures designed by research groups and government agencies as the basis for planning more detailed, customized evaluations are considered. These are known as 'evaluation frameworks'.

For anyone interested in evaluation, it is important to bear in mind that there is still no standard method of evaluation that is reliable and acceptable, as will be shown in this chapter. Nevertheless, it is generally agreed that evaluation is important for translation tools. One reason for the lack of any standard method is the existence of a wide variety of tools; another is the range of groups with an interest in testing. So, for example, 'evaluation' is the term used by machine translation researchers and developers, while it is more common to find professional translators using 'review' when computer-aided translation tools are tested.

Machine translation systems

The evaluation of machine translation has a long research history. Early evaluations were found to be difficult and at times misleading (White 2003: 211). The harshest evaluation of machine translation came in the infamous ALPAC report mentioned in Chapter 3, which highlighted the misconceptions about language, usage and the system requirements of fully automatic high-quality machine translation systems. However, the report did illustrate the importance of evaluation.

For a number of groups, including researchers, developers and end-users, evaluation is of crucial importance. For researchers, evaluation can reveal if the theories applied yield the desired results; for developers, evaluation is a means of showing how good the system is for potential buyers; and for end-users, evaluation can provide useful information as to which system best suits their needs (Hovy, King, Popescu-Belis 2002a: 1). Since the ALPAC report, many large-scale evaluations of machine translation systems have been carried out, some of which are briefly described below:

- Van Slype (1979) established the methodology of evaluation which was state-of-the-art at the time and made a number of recommendations concerning the methodology to be used to evaluate machine translation systems and what research was required to improve the efficiency of the evaluations. The study, conducted by a committee headed by Van Slype, had three aims: to present an outline of methods of evaluation, to provide a critical appraisal of the evaluation methods and to make a recommendation to the European Commission as to which evaluation method to adopt. To fulfil these aims, the study was divided into three phases: the collection of relevant literature, critical analysis of the literature and recommendations for an evaluation methodology (Van Slype 1979: 20–1). The evaluation report included a survey of the definitions of evaluation and a survey of the measurement scales of 'intelligibility' (comprehension) and 'fidelity' (message) conveyed in the target-language texts generated by machine translation systems.

- Lehrberger and Bourbeau (1988) developed three forms of evaluation methodology: evaluation by the designer of the system, linguistic evaluation by the end-user, and cost–benefit evaluation of the system.

- JEIDA (Japan Electronic Industry Development Association) or JEITA (Japanese Electronics and Information Technology Association) as it has been known since 2000, developed comprehensive questionnaires to evaluate machine translation systems in 1992. A total of 14 categories of questionnaires on economic and technical factors were given to end-users, and questionnaires on technical factors were given to developers. Evaluation of the economic factors is concerned with the economic benefits of introducing a machine translation system, while the evaluation of technical factors sets out to investigate which system best fits the needs of a group of end-users once the decision has been taken to introduce machine translation. Evaluation of the technical factors by developers measured the performance of a system that fulfils internal development objectives (Hovy, King and Popescu-Belis 2002b: 45; see also Hovy, King and Popescu-Belis 2002c; White 2003).

- DARPA (Defense Advanced Research Projects Agency) compared the performance of three machine translation prototype systems from French, Spanish and Japanese into English. An evaluation exercise was undertaken to measure intelligibility and fidelity. Intelligibility measured how well the target language had been translated linguistically using a scale of one to five. Two other evaluation exercises measured fidelity involving 'adequacy' and 'informativeness'. Adequacy measured the faithfulness of a source-language text to the target-language text using a scale of one to five, while informativeness measured how much of the information contained in the source-language text was found in the target-language text. The DARPA evaluation of machine translation conducted between 1992 and 1994 was said to be the largest and most expensive project in the area of evaluation of translation tools ever carried out (White 2003: 236).

In the past, there has been a tendency to concentrate on only two aspects of evaluation for machine translation: intelligibility – the quality of the translation generated by a system, and fidelity – the closeness of the translation to its original text. For researchers, if a system is proven to produce syntactically and lexically well-formed sentences, then such an evaluation may be considered sufficient. For end-users, on the other hand, this type of evaluation is often insufficient as other measurements such as coverage (specialization of subject field) and extensibility (the ability to add new words and grammar rules) are equally important (Hovy, King and Popescu-Belis 2002a: 1).

Computer-aided translation tools

The results of evaluations of computer-aided translation tools are not as easy to obtain as those for machine translation systems, as the commercial companies that develop these tools do not make their findings public. These types of tools are aggressively marketed to professional translators and the unique features of a tool are usually highlighted. Reviews are normally undertaken by the translators themselves and can generally be found in translation journals, consumer and professional magazines, in newsletters and on the web. To add to the complexity of evaluation, computer-aided tools are available on the market in different versions, as indicated in the previous chapter. For example, SDLX Translation Memory is available in three versions: elite, profession and standard, catering for different types of end-users. Also, each version is frequently updated, making reviews of previous versions less useful.

Evaluations by researchers, developers and research sponsors often serve the purpose of improving the systems being developed. For computer-aided translation tools most such evaluation reports are available only to researchers and developers. Since competing companies develop their own tools, evaluation reports on the performance of the tools they have designed are considered highly confidential. Thus publicly available reports only appear once the tools are ready to be released or are already in the market as product reviews for end-users. Normally, these reviews of computer-aided tools are based on specific types of texts, language pairs and tool versions. The benefit of such reviews is, therefore, restricted to professional translators who share the same needs and criteria. Other evaluations of computer-aided translation tools are available but scarce, and are limited to reports such as the evaluation of translation memory and translator's workbenches by EAGLES (Expert Advisory Group on Language Engineering Standards, 1996) and Rinsche (1997), and the evaluation of an integrated machine translation and translation memory in the software localization industry by Bruckner and Plitt (2001). Another review by Whyman and Somers (1999) uses Trados Translator's Work-bench as a case study, demonstrating how to measure functionality and usability, and reviewing the performance of the tool by executing fuzzy matches. Schmitz (2001), on the other hand, focuses on assessing the criteria for evaluating terminology database management programs, that is terminology management systems. The criteria include:

- terminological aspects – the suitability of the software to perform a terminological task;
- technical aspects – the hardware and software environment required when using a certain tool;
- user interface aspects – documentation on how to operate a particular tool;
- organizational aspects – compatibility with existing hardware and software; and
- economic aspects – purchasing and operating costs.

There are other ways in which a translator can find out about evaluations of translation memory tools. One is by joining professional translator's mailing lists and another is by testing a demonstration version of a tool (Zerfass 2002; see Somers 2003c).

Stakeholders

In the evaluation of machine translation systems, there are at least four groups with an interest in the matter, each with their own set of criteria and goals which may or may not overlap. The groups described below are largely based on those suggested by Trujillo (1999) and White (2003).

Researchers

There has always been a close relationship between researchers and system developers; the former build prototype systems based on certain approaches or models (see Chapter 3). A prototype is an experimental design of a partial or a whole system that is used for testing purposes before a complete system is built. Experiments based on a variety of criteria are used to investigate the performance of prototypes at various stages of development. Usually evaluations performed by researchers are reported in the form of papers written in academic or research journals, in books and/or presentations at conferences and workshops. Amongst researchers, evaluations of this kind serve as a platform for testing, benchmarking and discussion.

Developers

A developer (an individual or organization) normally decides on which prototype is to be turned into a complete system. The quality of the system built must comply with the relevant ISO (International Organization for Standardization) software standards, which are described later in this chapter. When a prototype is selected, a detailed study of economic viability is carried out on the capabilities and limitations of the system. Based on a series of different methods of evaluation, the performance of the prototype as compared with systems built by competitors is also obtained.

Research sponsors

The funds to build prototypes and complete systems are provided by research sponsors. Usually research organizations, government agencies and large corporations are the main sponsors. One issue that concerns a research sponsor is deciding which research project to fund or which prototype machine translation systems to fund. Ongoing progress reports play an important role in helping to show that the hypotheses and methods employed have produced the expected results. The research sponsors also need to know if the system is able to meet projected translation demands. Other information of importance to a sponsor includes the organization and management of a research project at different stages of the development process, and the relevance of the project to other areas of natural-language processing research.

End-users

End-users are made up of several groups, the major ones consisting of translators and translation managers. The evaluation criteria that interest these groups include the 'hows' and the 'whats' (Trujillo 1999: 254). The 'how' questions include:

- how easy is it to operate a tool;
- how user-friendly is a tool;
- how long does it take to learn;
- how compatible is it with other hardware and software applications;
- how good is the design of the working environment (the layout of the interfaces and display of windows);
- how good is the support for Latin and non-Latin based languages; and
- how easily can a tool be extended or upgraded.

The 'what' questions include:

- what is the processing speed;
- what are the linguistic capabilities;
- what is the required operating system;
- what is the performance reliability; and
- what are the costs and benefits.

The suitability of a certain tool is not universal to all types of text; it is important to investigate if tool customization is possible in order to meet the required needs of a particular translator. Translation managers also need to discover if the tool they intend to purchase is compatible with the equipment already installed in the company and if their translators will be comfortable using it. Evaluation of system performance and the overall performance of the translation team are equally important to translation managers.

Evaluation methods

There is no doubt that evaluation is the driving force behind the development of natural-language processing technology (see Hovy, King and Popescu-Belis 2002b). Previous work shows that evaluations have been carried out for a variety of reasons by different groups of people and organizations, for example governmental campaigns (ALPAC and DARPA), industrial forums (LISA) and joint research institutes (EAGLES). A survey of the literature on the evaluation of machine translation systems by Church and Hovy (1993) suggests that the success of evaluating a system often depends on the selection of the most appropriate approach. Another aspect is the scope of the evaluation. This includes cases of humans evaluating machines, that is translations generated by machine translation systems; machines evaluating humans, in which tools like spell or grammar-checkers 'evaluate' the performance of translators; or machines evaluating machines, in which fully automated approaches are applied to assess the performance of machine translation systems. Comprehensive human evaluations can be extremely time-consuming and costly, such as those by ALPAC and DARPA. In recent years, researchers such as Elliott, Hartley and Atwell (2003) have investigated the use of partial or fully automatic methods to conduct evaluations. Below some of these methods involving humans and machines are described.

Human versus machine

In the early days, human evaluators were used to evaluate translations generated by machine translation systems. As I have mentioned previously, intelligibility and fidelity are the two main criteria used in evaluation. One example of human evaluators judging the intelligibility and fidelity of machine translation output relates to a number of early Russian–English machine translation systems evaluated in the ALPAC report. To measure intelligibility, 18 English monolinguals were selected to judge six translated texts (three by machine translation systems and three by human translators) using a scale from one, 'Hopelessly unintelligible...', to nine, 'Perfectly clear and intelligible...' (ALPAC 1966: 68–9; see also White 2003). The higher the score, the more intelligible the translation.

In order to assess fidelity, two groups of English native speakers were used. Members of the first group, who were bilingual (English and Russian), were asked to extract information from the English translations and compare this with the information in the Russian originals. The second group, English monolingual evaluators, were asked to assess the informativeness of the two sets of English translations (one set translated by machines and the other by humans) using a scale from zero, 'The original contains ... less information than the translation ...', to nine, 'Extremely informative ...' (ALPAC 1966: 68–9; see also White 2003). The higher the score, the more informative the translation.

Although helpful in some respects, the ALPAC report showed that human evaluation could be very subjective. This subjectivity stems from the fact that the method relies on evaluators who have variable levels of language proficiency, resulting in different evaluation scores. Furthermore, different scales, such as those reported in Van Slype (1979: 57–9), have been used to measure intelligibility, for example three-, four-, five, seven-, eight- and nine-point scales, while fidelity is measured on five-, nine-, 25- and 100-point scales. Sometimes non-scale methods can also be used to measure intelligibility, for example the Cloze test (in which blank spaces at regular intervals must be filled in by the evaluator), multiple-choice questionnaires and knowledge tests. For fidelity, the methods include the correctness of the information transferred, retranslation and direct questioning. A quantitative evaluation performed by machines is often seen as preferable and is considered to be more stable, reliable and cost-effective. Developers especially are interested in inexpensive automated evaluation methods that are fast, language-independent and comparable to evaluations performed by human evaluators.

One of the automated evaluation methods that has been designed is BLEU (Bilingual Evaluation Understudy), the thinking behind which was that 'the closer a machine translation is to a professional human translation, the better it is' (Papineni *et al.* 2002). In order to show that BLEU is a reliable and objective evaluation method, two criteria were used: an evaluation of the 'closeness' between a translation produced by a machine translation system and a translation translated by a translator, and an evaluation of a translation produced by a machine translation system using bilingual and monolingual human evaluators. Here, 'closeness' was measured using the *n*-gram algorithm (see Chapter 3). The human evaluators, on the other hand, evaluated the translation using a five-point scale of measurement. The automatic evaluation performed by BLEU was shown to be quite close to the evaluation performed by the monolingual human evaluators (Papineni *et al.* 2002).

Test suite versus test corpus

A test suite consists of a carefully constructed set of examples that represent some pre-determined 'linguistic phenomena', meaning lexical and structural components such as nouns and clauses further classified as, for instance, types of nouns (proper noun, pronoun or common noun), types of utterances (interrogative, imperative and declarative), word order, and so on. A set of examples is usually annotated according to their specific linguistic categories. Normally, an evaluation is carried out on selected linguistic phenomena, which can be tested one at a time, or alternatively in combination with another phenomenon, giving the evaluator full control at every test point (Elliott, Hartley and Atwell 2003). A test suite is the most suitable evaluation tool for researchers and developers because it enables them to see how a system performs using a range of controlled examples to discover where errors occur. They can also test the system's performance after changes have been introduced to rectify any errors. A test suite can be used on a single linguistic phenomenon such as pronouns in an exhaustive and systematic way.

Syntactic and morphological phenomena are structurally easier to characterize than semantic and pragmatic phenomena as they can be divided more easily into classes and levels. The fact that segments may be broken down morphologically and syntactically makes them ideal candidates for testing using the test-suite approach. The same cannot be said about semantic and pragmatic phenomena, as they tend to be context-dependent and ambiguous. A test suite, therefore, is more useful for the evaluation of systems that have large syntactic and morphological analysis components (Balkan, Arnold and Meijer 1994). As a result, it is not always easy to construct an appropriate test suite that can test precisely what needs to be evaluated in a translation, where message and meaning are important. According to Prasad and Sarkar (2000), a test suite also has some weaknesses. While it has to be constructed manually to achieve systematic variation within a particular range of grammatical phenomena, there is no standard method for constructing such a system. And since the same lexical items can be used repeatedly, findings can be misleading, resulting in an inaccurate evaluation (Arnold *et al.* 1994).

In contrast to a test suite, a test corpus is essentially a collection of texts which attempts to represent naturally occurring linguistic data. The test corpus methodology is based on the assumption that if a corpus is large enough, it is possible for any linguistic phenomenon of interest to occur at least once. Moreover, a test corpus can be used numerous times to test a variety of linguistic phenomena, and is usually also cheaper to construct than a test suite. Furthermore, a corpus can be compiled to reflect a user's needs (Elliott, Hartley and Atwell 2003). Note that both these evaluation methods are complementary rather than competitive in nature as exemplified in the work of Prasad and Sarkar (2000).

Glass-box versus black-box

The evaluation of natural-language processing tools can also be carried out using either a 'glass-box' or 'black-box' approach (see Arnold *et al.* 1994). A glass-box is sometimes referred to as a 'white-box', 'structural-box' or 'clear-box'. Its purpose is to test the structural components of a system by looking inside the box. To illustrate this, let us imagine that a system is a rectangle, made up of smaller rectangles, as shown in Figure 5.1. These smaller rectangles are called components or modules. A glass-box evaluation is performed in order to test specific components of a system (rectangles highlighted in solid lines).

The glass-box approach to testing requires intimate knowledge of the programming code and algorithms in the selected component in order to examine its performance. The approach is very useful to researchers and developers because they can identify the components that are experiencing problems. It also allows researchers to access each component and to evaluate its performance, while providing an understanding of how to tune, extend and maintain the tool (Trujillo 1999: 256; White 2003: 225). An example of a glass-box evaluation would be the testing of one or more components such as the parser, lexical look-up or semantic interpretation in a system (Palmer and Finin 1990: 177).

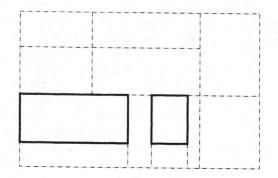

Figure 5.1   Example of a glass-box evaluation

Black-box evaluation, on the other hand, is more suitable for end-users. It is also known as functional or behavioural testing. The evaluation focuses mainly on the overall performance of a system by looking at only the input (the source-language text) and output (the target-language text), according to White (2003: 225). Imagine again that a system is a rectangle made up of smaller rectangles as shown in Figure 5.2.

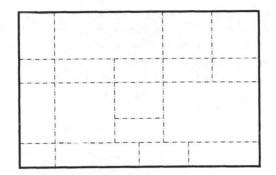

Figure 5.2   Example of a black-box evaluation

A black-box evaluation is carried out in order to test the performance of the system as a whole (rectangle highlighted in solid lines).

Often a system that is about to be released or has already been released onto the market is tested in this way to discover any incorrectly generated output or the reasons why the system does not work. Other characteristics of a system such as portability, maintainability and usability are also evaluated in this way (Palmer and Finin 1990: 176). One example of assessing the performance of machine translation systems in this way is the evaluation of the quality of target texts from three different machine translation systems in the European Commission. The aim was to compare the translation quality using certain linguistic criteria and then decide if the systems satisfied the needs of translators and administrators of the European Commission (Yuste-Rodrigo and Braun-Chen 2001). The linguistic criteria used were defined on two levels, sentence and text. At the sentence level, accuracy was rated taking into account factors such as punctuation, morphology and syntax. At the text level, the accuracy of elements such as coherence, intelligibility, fidelity, readability, style, terminology and usability was rated. Rather unsurprisingly, the evaluation experiment showed clearly – using a scale of one to five on both levels – that if a machine translation system is tailored to the needs of a specific group of users, the quality of the translations is usually better than a system that has been built to meet the requirements of 'all' users (Yuste-Rodrigo and Braun-Chen 2001).

General frameworks for evaluating translation tools

The idea of creating a general 'framework' for evaluating translation tools came into being as the result of evaluators having to design their own evaluations from scratch. Over the years, a great deal of literature has focused on the purposes, criteria and measurements in machine translation evaluation. Each time an evaluation was required, the evaluation literature had to be extensively searched to find suitable evaluation criteria, measurement and methods. Hence the non-existence of a standard evaluation method available for use and/or adaptation to all evaluators has been viewed as a serious problem (Hovy, King and Popescu-Belis 2002b: 44). As a result, a number of projects have been initiated to establish some form of general framework, method or set of guidelines to evaluate natural-language processing tools.

Most of the frameworks described here incorporate software standards from ISO as the foundation for a general evaluation framework. ISO is the world's largest developer of standards with the aim of ensuring that the development, manufacture and supply of products and services are efficient, safe and environment-friendly. In ISO, the quality and evaluation of natural-language processing tools is regulated by two series of standards, ISO 9126 (Software Product Quality) and ISO 14598 (Software Product Evaluation). Machine translation and computer-aided translation tools fall under the large umbrella of natural-language processing tools and, therefore, are required to achieve the standards set by these series. In order to fulfil the standard requirement of software quality, most evaluation frameworks existing today are based on these standards. Each series is briefly described below.

The ISO 9126 series (Software Product Quality) provides definitions of six key characteristics used in evaluating the quality of software products (see Trujillo 1999; Hovy, King and Popescu-Belis 2002a and 2002b):

- *Functionality*: meeting stated or implied needs of an end-user when functions of the system operate under specific conditions.
- *Reliability*: maintaining the level of performance by the system when operating under specific conditions.
- *Usability*: the ease of operating, understanding and learning each task of the system as a whole.
- *Efficiency*: the performance of the system in relation to the amount of resources available.
- *Maintainability*: the capability of the system to undergo modifications such as corrections, improvement and adaptations for different requirements and working environments.
- *Portability*: the ability to transfer the system from one environment to another such as to different operating systems.

The ISO 14598 series (Software Product Evaluation) provides guidance on the practical implementation of software evaluation that takes into consideration different points of view. It can also be used in conjunction with the six key characteristics described in ISO 9126. The evaluation process may include the evaluation of specific components within a system or of the entire system, a process broken up into five stages as shown in Figure 5.3 (see also Hovy, King and Popescu-Belis 2002b: 50).

The evaluation requirement stage of the process shown in Figure 5.3 is where criteria are identified for evaluation purposes. The criteria are for measuring the capability of a specific machine translation system in which its strengths and weaknesses are discovered. It means that an evaluation is performed either on selected components of a system or an entire system. A list of criteria includes adequacy to evaluate user-friendliness, efficiency to evaluate the consumption of resources, and linguistic quality to evaluate the coverage of the lexicon, syntax and semantics of the source and target languages of the system (Vertan and Hahn 2003). Since it is not easy to measure quality, the characteristics suggested in the ISO 9126 series are used as a quality measurement.

In the specifications stage of the evaluation, the type of measurement used is often dictated by pre-determined criteria and quality characteristics

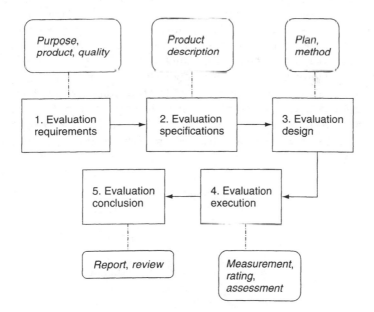

Figure 5.3 Example of an evaluation process

such as scale-based scores, to measure items that include word or sentence errors in the target-language text (Tomás, Àngel Mas and Casacuberta 2003). Based on the description of the components undergoing evaluation, plans are scheduled and methods are selected in the evaluation design stage that include the length of time to complete an evaluation, the order of components being evaluated and appropriate methods such as test suite or black-box. All these will be determined by whether the evaluation is for end-users or researchers. Once the evaluation design is agreed upon, the actual task of evaluating can take place. Measurement refers to the scores that are obtained from the metrics defined in the second stage. Rating concerns the interpretation of the scores, and assessment is the written summary of the ratings (see Tomás, Àngel Mas and Casacuberta 2003). Upon completion of the evaluation, the reports of the findings are written up. In addition, a detailed description of the problems occurring in the system during the evaluation is also given. In some cases, the whole evaluation process is reviewed to ensure that the initial objectives of the evaluation are met and the problems encountered are confirmed (see Vertan and Hahn 2003).

As I have mentioned previously, ISO evaluation standards were used as the basis for producing this kind of standard for machine translation evaluation. A number of related projects were involved in this process over time; these are all described below. The sequence of development started with EAGLES, in which ISO standards were adapted to the translation environment; the resulting new standards were later carried forward by the International Standards for Language Engineering (ISLE) and the Test-bed Study of Evaluation Methodologies: Authoring Aids (TEMAA). Another initiative was the Framework for the Evaluation of Machine Translation (FEMTI), an extension of ISLE. The way in which these project extensions relate to each other is shown in Figure 5.4. Most of these projects were collaborations between European research organizations and US government agencies.

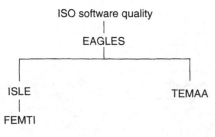

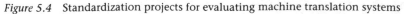

Figure 5.4   Standardization projects for evaluating machine translation systems

Let us now consider each of these projects in turn. As we have seen, one of the earliest efforts to provide evaluation standards for machine translation was through the EAGLES project (1993–96) funded by the European Commission in response to the lack of standards in language-technology evaluation. Since no general framework or set of systematic procedures suits all evaluations, it was felt that creating an evaluation framework that can be flexible and modifiable might be the answer. One of the initiatives taken by EAGLES was to define the means of evaluating resources, tools and products. A general quality model for natural-language processing systems was created which contained a hierarchical classification of features and attributes. From the model, specific features and attributes can be extracted for evaluation purposes to match the needs of any specific end-user (Hovy, King and Popescu-Belis 2002b: 47). In other words, EAGLES aimed at producing an evaluation package in which different features and attributes could be combined to reflect the needs of an end-user.

As a user-oriented evaluation system, the general framework proposed by EAGLES has three main components. The first is a set of attributes that fulfils specific conditions in order to evaluate a translation tool. There must, for example, be sufficient attributes to express all requirements that have been listed by an end-user. The attributes must also be general enough to enable repetition of similar evaluations by different groups of end-users. Attributes identified will determine the second component, that is the requirements. These are concerned with the needs that the system is designed for. The requirements can be divided into two categories, functional and non-functional. Functional requirements are about specific tasks that the system needs to support (see functionality under ISO 9126), while non-functional requirements are about constraints the system encounters when performing certain given tasks (see efficiency under ISO 9126).

Once the requirements have been listed, the third component, which is the method of evaluation, can be selected. The methods have three sub-components: test types, instruments and test materials. The test types are usually determined by the motivation behind the evaluation, for example, whether to assess the usability of the system in daily work, to examine the behaviour of the system under strict working conditions or to check the functionality of the system in general. In response to these motivations, three types of testing can be carried out, scenario testing, systematic testing and feature inspection.

Scenario-testing involves using the environment of the end-user as the basis for carrying out the evaluation. This can be conducted in the field or in a laboratory. A field test uses the actual working environment of the end-user and it is only applicable for a system that is already fully operational. A laboratory test uses the task-based environment where each task is tested in isolation and this type of test is only appropriate for a system that is only partially operational. Systematic testing involves testing under very specific conditions and the results are usually as expected. There are three ways to achieve this: task-oriented, menu-oriented and benchmarking testing. In task-oriented systematic testing, a pre-defined task in an actual working environment is given to a system to perform. The system is expected to produce the expected results. This type of test can also be used to evaluate components of a system during the developmental stage. Menu-oriented systematic testing involves testing each function of the system in a pre-determined sequence. It can be performed regardless of whether the system is still at the developmental stage or already fully operational. In benchmarking testing, the performance of individual functions, system modules or the entire system can be evaluated. In contrast, the last type of testing, feature inspection, is about describing the technical features of a system in detail. The purpose is to allow an end-user to compare the system with other systems of a similar kind. For the comparison of systems, a feature checklist is provided.

Evaluation data can be collected manually or automatically. Manual collection of data involves the use of questionnaires, checklists, interviews and observations, while automatic collection of data consists of recording the interactions between the end-user and the system that can be printed or replayed at a later date. The type of test material is usually made up of a collection of naturally occurring texts in electronic form. However, the type of evaluation carried out is still influenced by factors such as the reason for the evaluation. The description of the general framework by EAGLES can be summarized as shown in Figure 5.5.

ISLE was a transatlantic project (2000–3) between the European Commission and the US National Science Foundation. One of the main aims of ISLE was to propose standards, guidelines, recommendations for evaluating resources, tools and products, building on the results obtained from EAGLES and ISO standards. Under ISLE, a working group called the Evaluation Working Group (EWG) was set up to concentrate on formulating such standards (Calzolari *et al.* 2003: 6–8). The EWG worked in a sequence of phases beginning with a state-of-the-art investigation. In this phase, relevant technical, scientific and engineering literature was studied, also including reports on systems and their requirements in past evaluation exercises as well as the problems encountered

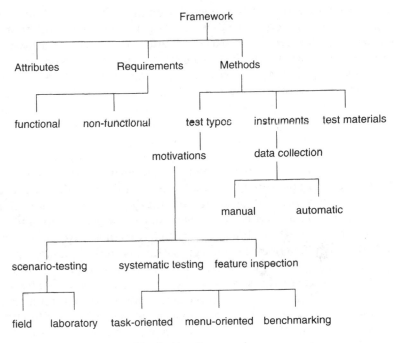

Figure 5.5 EAGLES general evaluation framework

during the evaluation and their solutions. At the stage where the proposal for a standard evaluation methodology and framework was being elaborated, the end-users in the working environment were invited to become involved by providing feedback on the proposal. The EWG worked on the principle that when end-users feel that they are part of the making of a standard, it is much easier for them to accept it. For the validation phase, the proposal was subjected to testing in a controlled actual working environment. The results, in turn, were used to improve the proposal for the benefit of both end-users and developers. In the maintenance phase, the refinement of the proposal was carried out by the EWG with input from end-users and developers. Although not 'final', the resulting proposal is at least a 'consolidated' one among all parties involved and will be valid for a period of time until further modifications or additions are needed. The proposal will continue to be maintained even after it has been turned into a fully-fledged standard. The activities of the EWG were published in what is known as the dissemination phase. Collaborations with related projects with other bodies were also encouraged (Calzolari *et al.* 2003: 10–1).

While EAGLES focused on the evaluation of several application areas such as translators' aids and writers' aids, the EWG of ISLE concentrated on methods and metrics for machine translation evaluation. Instead of using a committee of experts to suggest a general framework, the EWG runs workshops as the main means of refining the evaluation methodology and framework. The purpose is to provide a training platform for practitioners and to test the evaluation methodology and framework on actual evaluation tasks. The feedback from the workshops, in turn, enables EWG to improve on the evaluation methodology and framework.

Like EAGLES, the EWG realizes that the framework they have worked on remains very general, so much so that an evaluator would still have to customize the framework to suit the purpose of the specific evaluation to be undertaken. The reason for this is that machine translation evaluation 'is characterised by a severe degree of complexity and by many local contextual difficulties, which together have until now caused many different evaluation approaches and techniques to appear' (Calzolari *et al*. 2003: 15). As the ISLE project shows, further work is needed to discover the strengths and the weaknesses of evaluation systems as well as to establish correlations between evaluation metrics such as rating scales, or between evaluation attributes such as intelligibility. In addition, it remains necessary to choose relevant metrics and to understand the amount of work and costs involved in applying each metric. And finally, as pointed out by Calzolari *et al*. (2003: 5–16, 21), there is a need to understand whether the rating scales used would be appropriate and acceptable to those who requested the evaluation.

Within the duration of their projects neither EAGLES nor ISLE produced a complete evaluation framework. As a result, FEMTI was set up to continue the research – as an extension of the EWG and the ISLE projects – funded by the Danish and Swiss governments and the US National Science Foundation. FEMTI was established to organize all methods of evaluating machine translation systematically. It aims at assisting end-users in choosing the machine translation system that suits them best, assisting end-users in comparing several machine translation systems and assisting developers in upgrading an old machine translation system or designing a new one. It also has a structured collection of methods and serves as a platform for discussion among evaluators (Hovy, King and Popescu-Belis 2002b: 44).

In FEMTI two important questions have been asked: why is an evaluation needed and what is being evaluated? The answer to the first question ranges from a researcher wanting to assess what a particular set of procedures or algorithms is supposed to do, to an end-user wanting information on which system to buy. The answer to the second question may be for a researcher to evaluate a component in a system or for an end-user to evaluate the performance of a system (Hovy, King and Popescu-Belis 2002b). FEMTI is made up of two sets of criteria, evaluation requirements and system characteristics, which are related to these two questions. The first set defines the intended context of use (types of task, user and input) for the machine translation system that is under evaluation (see King, Popescu-Belis and Hovy 2003). The second set is related to the first and is concerned with internal and external characteristics and with the corresponding metrics associated with quality. Box 5.1 is a concise description of the framework and the groups of stakeholders who will benefit from each requirement and characteristics. A detailed description of FEMTI can be found at http://www.issco.unige.ch/projects/isle/femti/, although it is still an on-going project at the time of writing.

Box 5.1   FEMTI evaluation framework

1   Evaluation requirements

(a)   Evaluation purpose: to enable decisions to be made

- *Feasibility evaluation*: to discover if the approach used can be successful after further research and development. The stakeholders are mainly researchers and research sponsors.
- *Requirements elicitation*: to obtain reactions from potential stakeholders via the prototype system. The stakeholders are mainly developers and end-users.
- *Internal evaluation*: to perform periodic or continual evaluation at the research and development stage. The stakeholders are mainly developers and research sponsors.
- *Diagnostic evaluation*: to discover the causes of a system not producing the results as expected. The stakeholders are mainly developers.
- *Declarative evaluation*: to measure the ability of a system to handle a sample of real text especially the linguistic capability. The stakeholders are mainly researchers, developers and research sponsors.
- *Operational evaluation*: to discover if a system serves its intended purpose. The stakeholders are mainly researchers, developers and research sponsors.

Box 5.1   (Continued)

- *Usability evaluation*: to measure the ability of a system to be useful to the intended end-user. The stakeholders are mainly developers and end-users.

(b) Evaluation objects: to identify the context of use, for example, a system that translates weather bulletins.

(c) Translation task characteristics: to discover from the end-users' point of view the purpose of the translation output. The stakeholders are mainly developers, research sponsors and end-users.

- *Assimilation*: to supervise the large volume of texts produced in more than one language. The stakeholders are mainly end-users.
- *Dissemination*: to deliver translations to others. The stakeholders are mainly end-users.
- *Communication*: to support speakers of different languages. The stakeholders are mainly end-users.

(d) User characteristics: to identify different groups of end-users.

- *Machine translation users*: interactions between end-users and the system. The stakeholders are mainly translators and post-editors.
- *Translation consumers*: end-users who use the translations.
- *Organizational user*: organizations who provide translations such as translation agencies.

(e) Input characteristics: to identify the format of the source-language texts and information about the authors.

- *Text types*: genres, subject fields.
- *Authors*: level of proficiency in the source language and level of knowledge in the subject field.
- *Sources of errors*: linguistic errors and typographical errors.

2   System characteristics

(a) Machine translation system-specific characteristics: components in the system and process flow of the system.

Box 5.1 (Continued)

- *Translation process*: the underlying methodology (see rule-based and corpus-based approaches in Chapter 3) behind the development of the system. In other words, how the knowledge of the translation process is represented and acquired in the system and when a particular type of knowledge is applied during the translation process. This also includes the language coverage such as dictionaries, glossaries, terminology databases and grammar.
- *Translation process flow*: the processes, such as pre-translation preparation, post-translation output and dictionary updating, that enable a system to operate successfully.

(b) External characteristics: the six qualities of translation based on ISO 9126 mentioned earlier in this chapter (functionality, reliability, usability, efficiency, maintainability and portability). In addition, cost is another characteristic that plays a major role in deciding whether a system can undergo a detailed evaluation.

Another extended project developed from EAGLES is TEMAA, co-funded by the European Commission and the Federal Office for Education and Science of Switzerland. The aim of TEMAA is to develop a general evaluation procedure and to test methodologies for evaluating natural-language processing tools. Like EAGLES, ISLE and FEMTI described earlier, TEMAA also uses the ISO 9126 series as the basis for evaluation design. Case studies have, for instance, been conducted on spell-checkers for Danish and Italian and two other natural-language processing products. In order to evaluate spell-checkers, a set of programs called Automatic Spelling Checker Checker (ASCC) is employed to convert a list of valid words into invalid words automatically. The invalid words are used as input to the spell-checker in order to test its error-detection feature. The detailed results of the evaluation of a spell-checker can be found at http://cst.dk/temaa/D16/d16exp.htm.

In the past few years, two other major evaluation standards have been introduced, the National Institute of Standards and Technology (NIST) in the USA, to which we return below, and an evaluation project called the 'Campagne d'Evaluation de Systèmes de Traduction Automatique' (CESTA) in Europe. CESTA is one of eight campaigns to evaluate human-language technologies within the EVALDA (Infrastructure d'EVALuation à ELDA) project, which is one of the numerous projects undertaken by ELDA (Evaluations and Language resources Distribution Agency). One of the core businesses of ELDA is carrying out the missions and tasks of ELRA (European Language Resources Association), which is evaluating human-language technologies. Its objectives are to assemble reusable evaluation components such as methodologies, protocols and metrics, and to promote collaborative research by improving and setting up new evaluation campaigns (Dabbadie, Mustafa El Hadi and Timimi 2004).

CESTA is financed by the French Ministry of Research and Education to carry out evaluations of six machine translation systems (five commercial and one experimental). It aims at providing an evaluation for commercial machine translation systems and to set up reusable machine translation evaluation protocols. The campaign is divided into two stages; the first was the evaluation of the system's default dictionary in 2004 while the second was planned for 2005, following terminological adaptation. The evaluation corpus consists of 50 texts, each is approximately 400 words, involving a 'major' or primary language pair, that is French as the source language and English as the target language, and what is called a 'minor' or secondary language pair with English as the pivotal or relay language for the translation of Arabic into French (Arabic–English–French). The major language pair evaluation is being used to test the six machine trans-lation systems, while the minor language pair is being used to measure the robustness of the chosen metrics. The CESTA project began in 2003 and is scheduled for completion at the end of 2005. Its details and work-in-progress reports can be found in Mustafa El Hadi *et al.* (2004).

As an agency of the US Commerce Department, NIST offers a training course on how to evaluate machine translation systems. Interested indi-viduals and organizations are required to attend in order to learn how to plan and perform an evaluation. Most of the evaluation exercise itself is conducted through e-mails between the participants and NIST. After enrolling, the participants receive the source-language texts from NIST. Using machine translation systems of the participants' choice, the source-language texts are translated into target-language texts. Usually the language pair for the evaluation exercise is determined by NIST. Upon completion, the translations are sent back to NIST for eval-uation. Human evaluators and automatic *n*-gram statistics (see Chapter 3) are used in the evaluation. The evaluation results produced by the automatic methods are available within minutes of submission by the participants while the human evaluation results are presented at a workshop at the end of the course. All participants are required to attend the workshop to review and discuss the evaluation results.

Conclusion

For some time efforts have been made to create a framework for the evaluation of natural-language processing tools like machine translation systems and computer-aided translation tools. The main difficulty is that evaluation can be performed for a wide range of reasons by different groups of individuals. No evaluation is suitable on all occasions for all interested parties and for all purposes. The evaluation methods described in this chapter have indicated that there are many aspects of a system that can be evaluated, from a single component to an entire system. In fact, evaluation is a complex issue with more than just a single solution. Therefore, no research project can claim to have created a complete framework. Still, each effort must be applauded and encouraged. Building a standard framework is no easy undertaking since 'setting up a global methodology for evaluating all types of computerised translation systems for all end-users is a task that [*sic*] may not be possible to carry out completely' (Lehrberger and Bourbeau 1988: 192). Nothing has changed much since then.

Suggested reading

EAGLES (Expert Advisory Group on Language Engineering Standards) (1996) *Evaluation of National Language Processing Systems: Final Report.* At http://issco-www.unige.ch/projects/ewg96/index.html.

Lehrberger, J. and L. Bourbeau (1988) *Machine Translation: Linguistic Characteristics of MT Systems and General Methodology of Evaluation.* Amsterdam/Philadelphia: John Benjamins.

Sparck Jones, K. and J.R. Galliers (1996) *Evaluating Natural Language Processing: An Analysis and Review.* Berlin: Springer-Verlag.

Van Slype, G. (1979) *Critical Study of Methods for Evaluating the Quality of Machine Translation: Final Report.* At http://www.issco.unige.ch/projects/isle/van-slype.pdf.

6
Recent Developments and Future Directions

In this chapter we explore some future directions in a number of major areas of translation technology, building on recent developments. We start with developments in two translation 'types' that are by now very familiar, namely machine translation systems and computer-aided translation tools, before moving on to systems that incorporate speech technology. Translation tools for minority languages are an increasingly important topic as the demand for translation grows worldwide. This therefore also deserves attention in a chapter focusing on future trends. The increasing multilingualism of the Internet has direct implications for the volume of translation demand as the 'content' of web pages needs to be made available to speakers of other languages. The use of web content as a resource for online machine translation systems is also discussed, before the chapter concludes with one of the fastest growing areas of translation today, the localization industry.

Machine translation systems

If the prejudices and misgivings that still linger among professional translators concerning machine translation are to be countered, a new image of machine translation systems including a realistic view of their capabilities is needed. The different purposes for which machine translation is used – as discussed in Chapter 3 – are particularly relevant here, as this diversity will ensure the continuation of machine translation research. Furthermore, universities such as Carnegie Mellon University, the University of Maryland, Kyoto University, the University of Essex, the University of Montreal and Korea Advanced Institute of Science and Technology, as well as private sector companies such as AT&T, IBM, Microsoft, NTT, Rank Xerox, Systran Software and Sony are all still actively involved in machine translation research. However, as we have seen, many projects are still at the prototype or experimental stage and are therefore of little interest to anyone not immediately involved in the early stage of development. Since the systems are prototypes, their architectures and output performances are still a subject for discussion among the researchers involved, and are not yet available to the general public. For this reason, it is difficult to predict how this research will develop.

Currently, operational machine translation systems are found on mainframe computers, workstation and/or client–server systems on the intranets of large organizations. Machine translation systems are available for professional translators as well as occasional users, alongside online machine translation services. However, in the future, integrated multitasking commercial and online machine translation systems that will fulfil the range of translation purposes discussed in Chapter 3 are likely to become more common. Developed from current experimental interactive machine translation systems, commercially available systems will evolve which will allow a translator full control over the translation process. These systems are likely to have some forms of control more advantageous to translators than those currently provided by machine translation systems which require translations to be post-edited extensively for publishing purposes (Macklovitch and Valderrábanos 2001). Since interactions between the system and the human translator would allow the translator to make changes during the translation process, interactive machine translation systems are likely to reduce the amount of post-editing required. It has also been suggested that a primary factor behind the renewed interest in machine translation is the failure of translators to meet the high demand for translation, which opens up a tremendous opportunity in the market for language technology businesses to ease 'the translation bottleneck' (Macklovitch 2001).

The emergence of data-driven methods has motivated more research in the area of natural-language processing. Retrieving information from the WWW is currently achieved through the use of search engines such as Google (Macklovitch 2001). However, the availability of extensive information has shown that there is a need for more robust information retrieval methods across different languages. One method for achieving this is called multilingual information retrieval (MLIR). MLIR refers to the ability to retrieve relevant multilingual textual and non-textual (for example, sound and images) material on the Web or stored in a database by processing a query written in just one language. For an end-user to read the multilingual material collected, the material has then to be translated into the language of the end-user, and machine translation system is one of several methods used to achieve this. However, there are limitations in translating all languages. A machine translation system is language-dependent, since it is built for a specific number of language pairs and translation directions. Even online machine translation systems, despite the large number of languages they can translate, are still mostly restricted to popular languages. Therefore, not all materials can be translated into the end-user's language. Also, machine translation systems are especially liable to errors when processing languages that use a variety of diacritical or accent and tonal marks written above, below, before and after letters or words in order to distinguish, for example, between similar words. As a result, the translation may turn out to be less than useful to the end-user who initiated the query in the first place. In recent years, research and experiments have been carried out on MLIR and the use of machine translation systems as the device to translate the collected material. At this time, the results are promising but more work is still needed to discover how to optimize the collection of material, especially from the Web, and how to produce adequate translations using on- or offline systems that an end-user can understand (see Lin 1999; Nie 2003; Zhou *et al.* 2005).

The question we now ask is, what does the future hold for machine translation research? One suggestion, from Schäler, Way and Carl (2003: 104), is illustrated in Figure 6.1. The model presented in the figure divides translation quality into three levels: high, medium and low, corresponding to three different types of text. At the top level, a

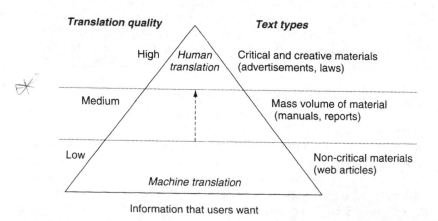

Figure 6.1   Future-use model of translation technology
Source: Schäler, Way and Carl (2003): 104.

human translator is chosen over a machine to translate texts that are of a creative nature where, for example, the use of metaphors is abundant. Examples of such texts include advertisements and plays. At the middle level, a combination of human translator and machine is used to translate large amounts of subject-specific texts for which accuracy and presentation, especially graphics, are important. Examples of such texts include laboratory reports and manuals. At the bottom level, a machine is chosen over a human translator to produce rough translations at very little or no cost, such as those offered by online machine translation systems. Examples of non-critical texts are, according to Schäler, Way and Carl (2003), web pages for products, services and general information. As translation technology research and development progresses and produces more reliable systems, it is to be expected that the use of machine translation will increase as indicated by the upward arrow.

This view of the future of machine translation is optimistic and is based not only on a change in the public understanding of the difficulties of translation and of the limits of automation, but also on an awareness of different types of translation needs (Macklovitch 2001). Moreover, most machine translation systems contain a large vocabulary, and provide broad coverage, and are capable of generating low or moderate-quality translations. In order to achieve high-quality translation, a machine translation system must be designed for a very narrow subject field where vocabulary and grammar is based on a controlled language (Sumita and Imamura 2002). Accordingly, many commercial systems have been designed for certain subject fields or for users with specific needs (Hutchins 1994). Over a decade ago, the problems of complex sentence analysis, optimum target-language equivalents and generating idiomatic output had yet to be resolved, as pointed out by Hutchins (1994); this is still the case today (Somers 2003g; see also the forthcoming proceedings of the 2005 International Workshop on Intelligent Linguistic Technologies). As a part of this process of problem-solving, researchers have realized that automating translation is not an easy task. Despite all the knowledge, expertise and technology, there are still many problems to overcome, working with languages that often do not express the same thing in the same way consistently. Computers are essentially devices that follow rules that have been programmed by humans, as we shall see in the last section of this chapter, and have difficulties with such 'inconsistency'. Furthermore, problems of language analysis, transfer and synthesis, learning and common-sense reasoning, especially for machine translation systems, are yet to be fully resolved. These are described in Arnold (2003).

We can recall that attempts have been made with a new generation of corpus-based machine translation systems to replace the older rule-based systems but that this has met with limited success. It is important here to be aware that corpus-based approaches should not be viewed as an alternative but as a complement to rule-based approaches (see Chapter 4). Although the advantage of corpus-based approaches is that they are able to create new translations from previously translated materials, linguistic knowledge is still needed to make corpus-based machine translation systems more robust. Thus current research in machine translation has tended to move in the direction of integrating corpus-based and rule-based approaches, that is 'hybrids'. As a result, over time many machine translation systems have changed their architectures, some turning into hybrids, while others have continued to retain their individual approaches.

Technological changes have given rise to changes in opinion even among machine translation sceptics with respect to the economic feasibility and the advantages of using machine translation systems in particular ways. In fact, according to some experts, machine translation is a central tool of the emerging world of multifunctional natural-language processing applications in a multilingual world (Bel *et al.* 2001).

Computer-aided translation tools

To enhance their performance and increase translation productivity, translators are usually in favour of using effective tools, although reservations are sometimes expressed about the personal investment needed in equipment, training and set-up time. In the foreseeable future, workbenches (incorporating many computer-aided translation tools) will continue to be the main translation support for professional translators. Apart from workbenches, however, the development of speech technology to analyse and synthesize human speech will also be of help to professional translators in their work. In the past, some professional translators orally recorded the first draft of a translation using what was called a 'dictaphone' machine (originally a trademark of the Dictaphone Corporation but now used eponymously). From the dictaphone, the recorded translation draft was then typed up – usually by a secretarial assistant – to produce the written version of the translation. In contrast, the current technology of 'dictation equipment', that is voice-dictation software, serves as an alternative to typing, having the ability to convert recorded speech into text automatically ('text' in this context always referring to written text). It can also be used to create, edit, revise and save translation documents based on the voice commands of the translator. Such a facility can reduce the time taken listening to the recording and in typing up, but only once the system has been trained to recognize the accent, pitch and tone of voice of the speaker/end-user (see Chapter 4).

The success of a tool such as voice-dictation software is due to advancements in speech recognition, a process by which a computer recognizes an acoustic speech signal (human utterances of a pre-determined language) into text. The reverse situation is also possible so that text is converted to speech: a text-to-speech system, based on speech synthesis. Furthermore, integrating computer-aided translation tools, such as translation memory systems, with voice-dictation software could be extremely useful to professional translators especially if the translator wants or needs to multitask, for example by translating the first draft of a text with the help of the dictation software, while the translation memory system is performing a matching operation for a specific word or phrase.

At present, speech-to-text and text-to-speech technology mostly caters for Western European languages, although a limited number of products with Asian languages such as Hindi and Thai can be found. Voice-dictation software is highly language-specific (Somers 2003c: 17). Also, it is voice- and accent-specific necessitating, as indicated, training of the system by the individual translator. It is difficult to predict when voice-dictation software will become available for more languages outside Western Europe, although in recent years researchers in China, Hong Kong, Japan, Taiwan and the USA have begun working on Chinese and Japanese with this objective. Reviews of early generations of dictation software can be found in Benis (1999) for British English, French, German, Italian and Spanish. Examples of commercial voice dictation software for these languages include Express Dictate by NCH Swift Sound and FreeSpeech by Philips.

In the next section, we look at developments in speech technology and its growing role in translation technology in more detail.

Translation systems with speech technology

In the past few years, speech technology has attracted the attention of natural-language processing researchers especially in Canada, Europe, Japan and the USA. Their general aim is to provide a technology that is not only able to convert speech into text, and text into speech, but also speech into speech within the same language or between different languages. Traditionally, translation is understood to be text-based while interpretation is speech-based. However, this dividing line has been blurred by speech technology, as well as by developments in screen translation (for a recent account, see Gambier 2003).

In the previous section we saw how the integration of current mono-lingual (at any one time) dictation software with existing computer-aided translation systems could support the translator in certain tasks. In this section we are concerned with speech technology which operates between languages. Figure 6.2 shows the connection of speech technology to computer-aided translation and machine translation systems.

In the speech-technology literature, terms like 'speech-to-text trans-lation', 'text-to-speech translation' and 'speech-to-speech translation' refer to systems that involve the conversion of text and speech where each input and each output is in a different language. Speech-to-text translation refers to the translation of speech in one language (the source input) into text in another language (the target output) where spoken words are converted into text for individuals with hearing or motor-skill disabilities. Examples of speech-to-text translation systems are IBM ViaVoice and Dragon NaturallySpeaking that both translate between seven languages.

A recent application of speech-to-text technology is in the conversion of spoken language on television into 'closed captions' for the deaf and

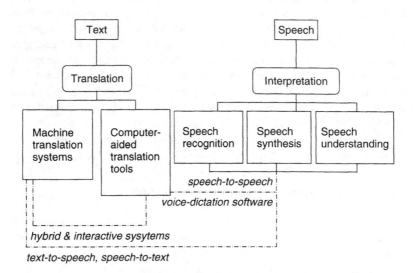

Figure 6.2   Speech technology in translation

hard-of-hearing community, not strictly-speaking a translation application but one which has clear links to the human activity of interpreting. The system currently relies on a kind of intralingual interpreting (see Chapter 2), in which a trained intermediary rephrases and simplifies the speech of live broadcasts, for example news programmes, as the input to the speech technology software which then converts the simplified and deliberately more monotonous speech into text for the captions (although still with a number of errors). Closed captions are the written version not only of what is being said on television but also of relevant sounds such as 'PHONE RINGING' and 'FOOTSTEPS' for the benefits of people with a hearing disability. These captions can be activated by the viewer, sometimes with a special decoder. The technology may soon be able to cope with live, real-time television and cable/satellite transmissions. Products of this capability could be appearing on the market very soon as they have already been advertised on the web, such as the SoftNI Live Subtitling Suite™ by SoftNI Corporation.

Text-to-speech translation refers to the translation of a text (the source input) into speech (the target output) where a text is converted into a voice message, primarily for those with visual disabilities. Examples of text-to-speech translation systems include Talking Translator Pro by AbhiSoft Technologies that translates between eight languages, and AT&T Labs' Natural Voices™ that translates between five languages.

Speech-to-speech translation refers to the translation of speech (the source input) into speech (the target output) for bi- and multilingual speakers of different languages. Examples of speech-to-speech translation systems include MASTOR (Multilingual Automatic Speech-to-Speech Translator) by IBM that is used to facilitate speech between individuals who share no common language, and HealthComm Healthcare Patient Communication Platform by Spoken Translation, Inc., which provides communication between Spanish-speaking patients and English-speaking healthcare workers. The function of a bi- and multilingual speech-to-speech system is similar to that of an interpreter, for example in business negotiations between individuals who do not understand each other. A text-to-text translation system is, of course, a conventional machine translation system, as discussed in Chapter 3.

In its early stages, the focus of speech-recognition research was on single-language systems that provided 'hands-free' control of computers and other electronic devices for end-users with physical disabilities. The possibilities were explored concerning computers receiving and interpreting spoken commands to perform certain tasks such as deleting a word or saving a document when word-processing. Research activities later moved on to multilingual speech recognition such as the Global-Phone system developed at Carnegie Mellon University and the University of Karlsruhe in Germany, which handles at least 15 languages. Global-Phone contains a database of 'speech transcriptions' of political and economic newspaper articles recorded by native speakers. The purpose of the database is to train and test speech recognition systems based on large vocabularies and to aim for speaker-independence. More databases of transcribed speech in the form of spoken corpora are available from ELRA and LDC. These corpora consist of transcribed speech data and pronunciation dictionaries for at least ten languages, and of text corpora for at least 20 languages (Somers 2003b: 7).

There are numerous research projects in speech recognition, many of which are still at the developmental stage, while the uses of some are limited to particular environments. The following projects can be noted:

- A Japanese–English and Japanese–Chinese multilingual speech translation system developed at Matsushita Electric Industrial Co., Ltd. and Osaka City University. This experimental system was tested on 1,000 expressions covering the domains of transportation, hotels, restaurants and other areas of interest to tourists.

- Speechlator, a hand-held two-way Arabic and English speech-to-speech personal digital assistant (PDA) device incorporating a translation system under the Babylon project developed at Carnegie Mellon University. The Speechlator is currently designed for medical interviews between English-speaking doctors and Arabic-speaking patients.

- LingWear by Carnegie Mellon University, a language support system that includes translation, navigation assistance and information access for military personnel and/or humanitarian aid workers in foreign environments. Access is possible via voice or written commands.

- A speech-to-speech system called TONGUES (Act II Audio Voice Translation Guide Systems), which contains a speech recognizer that converts Serbo-Croatian words into text, translates this text into English and broadcasts it via a speech synthesizer. This system was first developed at Carnegie Mellon University under the DIPLOMAT (Distributed Intelligent Processing of Language for Operational Machine Aided Translation) project, now located at Lockheed Martin Systems Integration-Owego for the second phase. It is designed for US Army Chaplains to provide religious support and humanitarian aid. This system now has other languages such as Arabic, Dari, Farsi, Kurdish and Pashto to be used in countries where US military bases are located.

- Mandolin, a prototype automated text and speech translation system that can be integrated with telephony systems, the Internet, broadcasting and video-conferencing in both written and speech formats developed by AT&T Government Solutions.

As a result of the 11 September 2001 attack on the USA, the amount of research on automated speech transcription has increased. The Babylon project at Carnegie Mellon University is developing a portable speech-to-speech translation device and the EARS (Effective, Affordable Reusable Speech-to-Text) project aims to turn speech recordings into digital texts which can then be searched for information, particularly in Arabic.

Translation technology has also been designed where the source input is a sign language and the target output is speech or text. In the USA, a system called 'Paula', developed by DePaul University, is a computer-generated synthetic interpreter of translated spoken English into American Sign Language for use at airport security checkpoints. Other examples are the 18-year old Ryan Patterson's 2002 prize-winning design in the Siemens Westinghouse Science and Technology Competition of a sign-language translator glove that works through sensing the hand movements of the sign language alphabet. Similarly, AcceleGlove is a sensor-studded glove for American Sign Language developed by Jose Hernandez-Rebollar in 2003 as a doctoral student at George Washington University. The glove transfers or 'translates' information using a computer into spoken and written English. Similar tools can be found for other languages, for example, there is a device developed by the Silesian University of Technology called THETOS (Text into Sign Language Automatic Translator), formerly known as TGT-1 (Text-into-Gesture Translator), which translates written Polish into Polish Sign Language, and an experimental automatic sign recognition and translation device for Chinese Sign Translation developed by Carnegie Mellon University.

Using speech technology, some commercial companies have produced products for more general use. Such portable translation systems have gained popularity among tourists, for example the Ectaco Partner® Voice Translator for Pocket Personal Computer, and among foreign language learners, for example the Lingo 16-Language Pocket Translator. Early in 2003, the NEC Corporation developed a two way Japanese and English automatic speech-translation application that can be incorporated into mobile phones, PDAs and Internet terminals for travellers.

As has been shown, speech technology has been influential in the development of new types of tools for translation. The above examples are testament to the future direction of some machine translation archi-tectures. At this moment, most speech technology has been incorporated into machine translation systems only for specific uses, but it is only a matter of time before online machine translation systems such as Babelfish, WorldLingo and Promt-Online will also offer speech translation services. The benefits of this type of integration will not be reserved for special groups of individuals such as professional translators, but will extend to the general public.

Translation systems for minority languages

To date, natural-language processing and machine translation research and development have focused on major or popular languages, as dictated by socioeconomic factors (Somers 2003b: 8). For various economic, cultural and political reasons, many other languages are still not covered, especially those from Central, South and Southeast Asia, and Africa.

Let us look at the Southeast Asian region. In Laos, for example, machine translation research activity is non-existent. While Lao–French translation research has been conducted in the Papillon project by GETA at Grenoble University, the particular form of Lao for which the system has been developed is spoken in northern Thailand and is written with the Thai alphabet (Berment 2002). Other countries in Southeast Asia such as Vietnam have only limited natural-language processing research. Research in natural-language processing related to the English–Vietnamese machine translation system developed in 1972 in the USA (see Chapter 3) during the Vietnam War or the French–Vietnamese and English–Vietnamese machine translation system developed by the University of Geneva (see Doan-Nguyen 2001) was conducted outside Vietnam. Some research has recently started in Indonesia, while Thailand is the only Southeast Asian country that has successfully developed several machine translation systems. For example, there is an online English–Thai system called Parsit and a Thai/English/German system called AbcThai.

One country that has shown a decline in machine translation research is Malaysia (Sornlertlamvanich 2002). The English–Malay machine translation system called Jemah, the English–Malay and French–Malay workbench called Siskep, the Jemah/Siskep hybrid jointly developed by *Universiti Sains Malaysia* (Science University of Malaysia) and GETA did not survive beyond the prototype stage owing to a lack of funding. Another casualty was the experimental Japanese–Malay machine trans-lation system called ALT-J/M (Automatic Language Translator Japanese to Malay) by NTT of Japan and NTT MSC (Multimedia Super Corridor) of Malaysia. Owing to the lack of commercial viability, this project was stopped in 2002. There are many factors that contributed to its demise, including the fact that the building of a Japanese–Malay bilingual corpus proved to be costly. Buying existing corpora was equally expensive and there was a lack of experts proficient in both the Japanese and Malay languages. Furthermore, NTT MSC is a profit-making company that needs to see returns on its investments; a system that has limited use and a small number of users is not a profitable endeavour. However, there are still some research activities in other areas of natural-language processing in Malaysia such as information retrieval.

In the South Asian region, one country that is active in machine translation research is India, where a number of research projects involving major Indian languages and English can be found. Anusaaraka, developed at the International Institute of Information Technology in Hyderabad, has two different machine translation systems, one that involves translation between major languages spoken in India (Bengali, Hindi, Kannada, Marathi, Punjabi and Telegu) and another which translates from English into Hindi. Other systems include MANTRA (Machine Assisted Translation) developed at the Centre for Development of Advanced Computing in Pune that translates government appointment letters and the daily proceedings of *Rajyasabha* (the Upper House of the Indian Parliament) from English into Hindi, and MaTra developed at the National Centre for Software Technology in Mumbai, which is a human-aided machine translation system that translates news from English into Hindi. All the systems mentioned above contain dictionaries and employ grammar rules. This is not the case with Anglabharti, developed at the Indian Institute of Technology in Kanpur, a machine translation system from English into major Indian languages that applies a modified interlingua approach (see Chapter3) where the English language is analysed only once to create an intermediate structure. This intermediate structure is then converted into each Indian language through a process called text-generation. In addition, there is Anglahindi, the English into Hindi version of Anglabharti. The other non-rule-based machine translation system is the example-based system for translating news from Bengali into Assamese called Vaasaanubaada, developed at the Assam University in Silchar.

In recent years, several less well-known or 'low-density' languages have also caught the attention of researchers working in the area of natural-language processing. In this field, low-density languages are those that have very few or no resources containing linguistic information, such as dictionaries and texts in an electronic format (McEnery, Baker and Burnard 2000). It means that any texts in print of a low-density language would have to be converted into an electronic format and be tagged before they can be of any use to the researchers in the area of machine translation development. Such an exercise is time-consuming and costly. Moreover, according to Jones and Rusk (2000), commercial market forces are unlikely to provide much incentive to work with low-density languages. Nevertheless, certain low-density languages have been selected for machine translation, corpus-building and dictionary research. These include Haitian Creole (see Mason and Allen 2000), Uighur (see Mahsut *et al.* 2001), Galician (see Diz Gamallo 2001), Amharic (see Alemu, Asker and Getachew 2003) and several South American languages such as Aymara spoken in Bolivia, Mapudungun in Chile, Huao (one of several alternative names for Waorani) and Quichua in Ecuador, and Quechua in Peru in the Avenue project at Carnegie Mellon University. This issue has been discussed at length in the works of Somers (1998c and 2003d), Berment (2002) and Streiter and De Luca (2003).

Translation on the web

The translation industry, like any other, is not spared the effect of global changes. The world is increasingly technologically driven, opening up new possibilities, opportunities, needs and demands. Information is becoming more flexible and fluid via the electronic medium. On the web, a multilingual global community has access to information which in turn requires translation. A multilingual environment on the web promotes many things, from products and services to understanding of and communication between different ethnic communities. As the speed of telecommunication increases, fast translation is a service offered by many translation companies and professional translators over the web. Hence, the electronic nature of much translation work and of communication between translators and their clients has also resulted in information which was at one time preserved only on paper now being stored digitally.

A multilingual marketplace such as the web caters for the language needs of different groups of end-users. Demand for information access and retrieval has made online machine translation systems almost indispensable, allowing many end-users to obtain almost instantaneous translations, although they are often of poor quality. For individual users, free online machine translation services are the window on another cultural and linguistic world. For corporate end-users, gathering information and communicating is of great importance. In order to be competitive, they rely heavily on having access to the latest information and services available on the web. Thus machine translation is an essential tool, as the Internet is becoming the main medium of communication and the information hub for various groups of users around the world.

One type of product that provides an instantaneous summarized translation is known as automated real-time translation. This system is especially useful to organizations where global communication is critical and time is of the essence in their daily business operations. Hence, instantaneous translations of web pages, documents, e-mails and other types of information are crucial. The system has several advantages, such as obtaining a translation of formal, as well as colloquial texts within seconds, rapid translation of foreign-language articles and real-time online communication (e-mails and chat-room messages) in multiple languages.

For the development of machine translation, the Internet is a major driver; machine translation is fast becoming a communication-enabling technology. In addition, since the early 1980s renewed interest in machine translation has been triggered by improvements in computational hardware and software, developments in computational linguistics and corpus linguistics, as well as changes in translation needs and demands. So, like a domino effect, more products lead to more documentation, more sophisticated products lead to more comprehensive documentation, increased globalization leads to the translation of documentation into more languages, and the shortage of human translators leads to the development of a variety of multifunctional translation tools. This has enabled new markets involving machine translation and integrated translation tools to flourish.

A question of concern to many countries is the monopoly of English on the Internet since its inception, although this dominance has been partly due to accidental factors such as the Internet originating from the USA (Nunberg 1996). Moreover, English is the accepted 'international lingua franca' in the fields of science, communication, aviation and medicine. The type of English language often used on the web has been described as a 'free-floating lingua franca' or 'International English', a language that has lost a large number of cultural and grammatical elements that tie it to its native speakers (Snell-Hornby 2000: 109). However, according to the Internet Society's preliminary findings on the language of home pages on the web, languages other than English are now becoming more widely used and this trend will grow in importance.

In recent years, non-English speakers are beginning to account for ever-higher proportions of Internet users; the amount of information available in languages other than English, such as Japanese and Spanish, has increased.

The 2004 global Internet population shows that Asia is leading with 31.7 per cent followed by Europe with 28.4 per cent and North America with 27.3 per cent. In Asia, three countries, China, Japan and the Republic of Korea, make up close to three quarters of the total Asian Internet population (Internet World Stats 2004). Based on the survey by Global Reach (see http://global-reach.biz/globstats/index.php3) of the popularity of languages on the Internet as of September 2004, Chinese is already rated as the second most popular after English. Indeed, according to some predictions, Chinese might even overtake English to become the primary language of the web by 2007 (Eisele and Ziegler-Eisele 2002). Estimating the number of pages on the web is, of course, notoriously difficult.

Machine translation systems and the semantic web

Without a doubt, the Internet is the current medium of global communication, and natural-language processing applications such as machine translation systems are one of the key technologies that has benefited from this. In early 2004, a survey in the magazine *Technology Review* showed that machine translation is one of the leading top-ten emerging technologies. As the number of languages on the Internet and the number of non-English Internet users and resources on the WWW grows, it is likely to increase in importance.

Two important points concerning developments in machine translation were noted earlier in this book: that most machine translation systems are currently restricted in terms of subject fields and language pairs, and that the trend of future machine translation research seems to be moving towards hybridization between rule-based and corpus-based approaches. Online machine translation systems, however, may be following a slightly different path. Current online machine translation systems generally produce poor-quality translations that do not reflect the real capabilities of the majority of machine translation systems. The reason is that almost all online machine translation systems rely on limited sets of linguistic rules of dictionary look-up and simple syntactic transfers following the rule-based approach. Corpus-based approaches are now seen as a serious challenge to the present rule-based online systems as a result of new technology. This new technology not only benefits current online machine translation systems but also current corpus-based and knowledge-based systems (Vertan 2004; see also Chapter 4).

As early as 1989, Tim Berners-Lee of the W3C, the creator of the WWW, HTML and other important web ideas, had already introduced the idea of what is now known as the 'Semantic Web'. In 2001, after formalizing this idea, Berners-Lee together with his co-authors James Hendler and Ora Lassila defined the Semantic Web in *Scientific American* as 'an extension of the current Web in which information is given well-defined meaning, enabling computers and people to work in better cooperation' (see also Berners-Lee and Miller 2002). With the Semantic Web – a universal medium for information exchange, providing meaning to the content of documents on the web that can be 'understood' by machines – scientific communities, in particular the natural-language processing community, realized it had the potential to improve natural-language processing applications, especially machine translation systems.

Currently, information is stored on the web in only a limited way, hidden within HTML (see Chapter 4) the markup language used to describe the layout of a document such as text interspersed with visual images and interactive links. Information on the web is written in this way in order that a computer can 'read' or process it. However, at present the computer is not yet capable of 'understanding' the information or content stored on the web (Vertan 2004), that is it cannot make links between items based on meaning. One way of making web content 'machine-understandable' is by using emerging Semantic Web technology.

One potential beneficiary of the Semantic Web is example-based machine translation systems. Current example-based systems rely on generating new translations automatically via examples extracted from aligned parallel corpora. This approach is limited by the availability of such corpora, which are found only in certain subject fields and languages (see Chapter 4). According to Vertan (2004), the Semantic Web promises improved opportunities to use any document on the web as additional corpus material, by, for example, improving the automatic identification of the translations of source documents. She also suggests that improvements in translation accuracy in relation to word meanings will also become more viable, so that, for instance, words like the German adjective 'groß' can be semantically disambiguated in phrases such as 'große Schlösser' as 'important castles' or 'large castles'. But how is all this to be achieved? The basic idea is to add semantic coding to documents and data in other applications such as databases, and then

to exploit this in various ways to allow more relationships to be established within and between these documents etc. which begins to relate
their content through meaning links rather than just structural links.

The technical means for achieving this are complex and cannot be
explained in any meaningful detail here. A good introduction is provided
in Berners-Lee, Hendler and Lassila (2001). Briefly, the architecture
consists of several components of different technologies, including:

- XML (see Chapter 4), a customizable general-purpose markup language
  that is used to enhance the meaning of the content of a document.
  For example, without such enhancement, the computer does not
  know who 'I' is or what 'cats' mean in the sentence: 'I have two cats'.
  But this sentence can be enhanced with meaning using an XML-based
  markup language as follows:

  ```
  <sentence>
  <person  href = "http://quah.com/">I</person>have  two<animal>
  cats</animal>.
  </sentence>
  ```

  The computer now knows that 'I' refers to a 'person' and 'cats' refers
  to a type of 'animal'. XML enables information in RDF (see below) to
  be exchanged, for instance, between computers that use different
  operating systems.
- Resource Description Framework, a framework for describing and
  representing information on the web so that a computer can read
  and understand it (Vertan 2004). It is used to describe features on a
  web page, for example properties such as price and other information
  such as its author. Information on the web written in RDF, which is
  also known as an 'RDF statement', is annotated in 'triples', in the
  structure of subject–predicate–object. The subject is the resource that
  is being described, the predicate is the property of the thing that is
  being described, and the object is the value of that property. This can be
  written, for example, as: 'The author of http://www.pkmstats.com/ is
  Paul Marriott' where the subject is 'http://www.pkmstats.com/', the
  predicate is 'the author' and the object is 'Paul Marriott'.
- Web Ontology Language (OWL), an extension of RDF, has a larger
  vocabulary and stronger syntax than RDF. Since early 2004, OWL
  has been a web standard as recommended by W3C (see http://
  www.w3schools.com/rdf/rdf_owl.asp). According to Vertan (2004)
  this annotation in the Semantic Web helps example-based machine
  translation systems in three ways: creating additional sources of

aligned parallel corpora from documents on the web, generating rough translations from example-based systems by using the documents on the web as corpora, and disambiguating words or phrases in translation.

- Ontologies (of which many are available), as domain or subject field structures that map out how terms relate to each other in particular subject fields, typically but not exclusively in hierarchies which allow the computer to work out through the use of inference rules that two terms are related, even if this is not explicitly stated; for instance, if a 'sandal' is mentioned in a text as a kind of 'shoe', and elsewhere 'shoes' are mentioned as a kind of 'footwear', then the rules would link 'sandal' with 'footwear'. In other words, ontologies concern the description of things and their relationships (see Gómez-Pérez, Fernández-López and Corcho 2002). Terms or codes occurring in documents can be linked to a relevant ontology – in this sense, a file or document containing the subject field structure – through a 'pointer' mechanism, enabling them to acquire some kind of meaning from the ontological structure. The terms to which various documents are linked in this way may still not link up, however, if each ontology uses a different term for the same concept, that is synonyms, or if the ontology is differently structured. The example of synonymy given by Berners-Lee and his colleagues is 'zip code' and 'postal code', if the system is trying to work out particular locations. Consistency is therefore a problem, even within one language. As any translator knows, establishing equivalents across languages is often difficult, as concepts (and hence terms) do not necessarily map directly. The problem is no less serious for machines, as Vertan (2004) points out: 'The main challenge in the design of ontologies with multilingual instances is that...there is no one-to-one mapping to the meaning in the other language'. Nevertheless, projects are underway – such as the one at the University of Hamburg described by Vertan – to build demonstrator systems to, for instance, automatically extract translation examples from texts annotated in RDF in order to 'improve the quality of online systems' by extending the example base.

In a similar way to example-based machine translation systems, knowledge-based systems can also benefit from the ontologies of the Semantic Web, since the current ontologies for these systems are extremely language- and subject-field-dependent. The Semantic Web is therefore a technology that has the potential to advance the development of machine translation onto another level: if this technology were successfully applied to machine translation and other natural-language processing applications, the benefits could be enormous (see Dori 2003).

The localization industry

Ever since products began to penetrate markets in different countries, the notion of translation and the nature of the translation industry have become increasingly complex. The role of the computer cannot be ignored here. Products – including related documentation – that are to be sold in a specific market have to undergo certain changes as required by the trade regulations of that country. The changes involved concern not only the translation, for example of user manuals accompanying certain products, but also packaging; the changes must be carried out in a manner appropriate to the target market, a process known as 'localization', as we have seen earlier in Chapters 1 and 4. The need for localization has been growing at such a rapid rate that in recent years we have begun to talk about a 'localization industry'.

Since the early 1990s, the localization industry has undergone, and is still undergoing, far-reaching changes. The future of this industry is not easy to predict since it is a very dynamic. Even assessing the current localization industry market can be difficult. What is certain, however, is that progress in the localization industry depends on several factors, including language-technology tools, the standardization of tools, training and the web. Tools like translation memory systems and terminology management systems are important to the localization industry, but they need to be improved either through upgrading or integration with other relevant tools. With the hybridization of translation tools as discussed earlier, we know that this is already happening. In other words, the future development of translation tools will dictate the form that the localization process will take. With better technology, new and more sophisticated tools are being developed. Data interchange standards such as XLIFF and TMX (see Chapter 4) that are designed to facilitate the use of different tools during the localization process may not be adequate in the future. In addition, as new tools emerge in the market, well-trained people to handle such tools are needed. This means that training must be provided, taking into account time and cost, to ensure that only qualified individuals are involved in the localization process in order to increase productivity and quality. For this to happen, there must be enough incentive to attract talent to be trained in this field. Recognition of such professional training would be one way of making sure that the individual doing the localization work is skilled and trained.

The world we live in today is increasingly dependent on the web, in particular through the ways in which people communicate, information is stored and business is conducted. The high demand for rapid translation and the localization of services and products constitute a challenge for the localization industry. Whatever happens to the web in the future cannot fail to affect this growing industry (LISA 2003).

Conclusion

The development of translation technology is advancing and will continue to grow. Numerous projects presented in this book are still in progress with the aim of discovering the extent of its capabilities and evaluating its benefits. The idea is to design better and more robust systems for a multitude of human users, ranging from the simple translation of words to covert activities of intelligence-gathering, and from text to speech to sign language. It is important to remind ourselves that no technology can entirely replace human translators, for the simple reason that humans are still needed to produce high-quality translations. Human languages are multilayered in usage and meanings, and current technology remains unable to decipher the finer nuances of human languages in the same way as humans can. Technology is restricted to its specific uses and, as a result, is destined to remain as a tool.

Suggested reading

Branchadell, A. and L.M. West (2004) *Less Translated Languages*. Amsterdam: John Benjamins.

Carl, M. and A. Way (eds) (2003a) *Recent Advances in Example-based Machine Translation: Text, Speech and Language Technology*. Vol. 21. Dordrecht: Kluwer Academic.

Cronin, M. (2003) *Translation and Globalization*. London: Routledge.

O'Hagan, M. and D. Ashworth (2002) *Translation-Mediated Communication in a digital World*. Clevedon: Multilingual Matters.

Schäffner. C. (ed.) (2000) *Translation in the Global Village*. Clevedon: Multilingual Matters.

7
Translation Types Revisited

In Chapter 1, the classification of translation into different types on a linear continuum reflecting degrees of human and machine interaction was shown to present certain difficulties once current translation tools were incorporated. It was agreed that an alternative way of presenting the four basic translation types – machine translation, human-aided machine translation, computer-aided translation and human translation – was needed. One of the main weaknesses underlying the linear continuum model is that current translation tools are more sophisticated than those of the early 1990s. In this chapter, a revised, multidimensional perspective of translation types will be presented, reviewing the many topics discussed in previous chapters in relation to the four main translation types and their sub-types, where relevant. The depiction of translation types differs from the linear model in Hutchins and Somers (1992) in at least one further respect: a new medium for translation, the Internet, has now emerged, radically changing the way translation operates, as seen in earlier chapters. It is also likely to change the architectures and functions of specific translation tools, particularly online machine translation systems.

The purpose of this chapter is to show the characteristics of each translation type, taking into account developments since Hutchins and Somers first proposed their typology by relating these types to the topics discussed in previous chapters. We will see that the boundaries between the original types are breaking down and that different groupings emerge when they are viewed from different perspectives in relation to particular topics, reflecting the complexity of translation activities today. In order to best capture these relationships, a series of tables will be presented in which a common 'strand' or set of related topics is considered systematically in the context of each of the four translation types. The topics include automation, theory, texts, the role of particular languages, standards for data interchange and evaluation methods. This analysis is followed by a different set of tables setting out the relationships specifically between what Hutchins and Somers defined as one translation type, namely machine translation – this time according to its sub-types – and a further set of topics, also discussed in previous chapters, including selected features of such systems from algorithms to modules, and language coverage. We shall see that the distinction between machine translation and human-aided machine translation is hard to sustain with some sub-types. We then turn to computer-aided translation tools, which are presented in the same way, that is according to sub-types, covering the texts translated, the degree of language dependency and language-pair coverage. The chapter ends with a brief conclusion taking stock of the current situation.

Relationships between topics and translation types

We will start by briefly reviewing the principal characteristics of the four translation types, as discussed in Chapter 1, before going on to reconsider these established types in the light of current developments. In Chapter 1, we discovered that many different terms are used to refer to any one type of semi-automated or fully automated system, leading to considerable confusion. It was therefore decided to follow the suggestion by Schadek and Moses (2001) to identify machine-aided human translation (MAHT) as computer-aided translation (CAT), and to distinguish this from human-aided machine translation (HAMT), which has more in common with machine translation. To recap the original linear model:

- Machine translation (MT) systems are purely automatic with no human intervention during the actual translation process. They are conventionally divided into specific-purpose systems for highly specialized technical and subject-field-specific texts on the one hand, and general-purpose systems for general-purpose texts on the other hand. The general-purpose systems now also include online machine translation systems found on the Internet.
- Human-aided machine translation systems (HAMT) are essentially a form of machine translation with an interactive mode; the principal contribution to the translation is made by the machine but a human can intervene during the translation process.

- Computer-aided translation (CAT) includes translation tools, linguistic tools and localization tools such as translation memory systems, electronic dictionaries and concordancers; the translator makes a much greater contribution here than in HAMT.
- Human translation (HT) refers specifically to translations performed by translators.

In the following section, the 'strand' which is under consideration at any particular time is viewed from various perspectives, each broken down into a number of topics, listed in the first column of each table. While these share a common theme, the translation types across the top of each table have specific characteristics. It is not difficult to indicate whether a translation type fulfils certain criteria, as indicated in the topics listed in each table, but it is important to realize that not all factors can be included at any one time as each table is designed to highlight one perspective only. Furthermore, it is easier to comprehend one perspective at a time.

Automation

Automation can be defined as the activities of machines that are self-acting or without human supervision. The different perspectives which we will be considering under this heading – each in turn – are the degree of automation, the level of human intervention and possible system combinations. We start in Table 7.1 by looking at how the different types of translation are related to the degree of automation, ranging from fully automated to non-automated. According to our definition, only machine translation is fully automated, while human-aided machine translation and computer-aided translation are partially automated to different degrees, depending on the level of human involvement. As for human translation, translators may or may not be using tools to assist their translation work, again blurring the

Table 7.1   Degree of automation

	MT		HAMT	CAT	HT
	Specific	**General**			
Fully automated	Y	Y	N	N	N
Partially automated	N	N	Y	Y	Y
Non-automated	N	N	N	N	Y

Y = yes; N = no

computer-aided translation/human translation distinction. Thus both 'partially automated' and 'non-automated' features apply here.

When a system has only partial automation, the element that completes it will be the human element. Hence, human intervention (see Table 7.2) is required in human-aided machine translation and computer-aided translation, although to different degrees. Clearly, 'intervention' is not applicable to human translation.

Table 7.2 Human intervention

	MT		HAMT	CAT	HT
	Specific	**General**			
Human intervention	N	N	Y	Y	n/a

Y = yes; N = no; n/a = not applicable

From previous discussions in Chapters 3, 4 and 6, we know that some translation tools may be combined to create new tools. To recap, these new tools are known as 'hybrids' when two machine translation systems of different architectures are combined, or as 'integrated' tools when a machine translation system is combined with a computer-aided translation tool, or a computer-aided translation tool is combined with another computer-aided translation tool. Table 7.3 shows which tools and technologies can be integrated with other tools/systems. Linguistic tools and translation tools are both common parts of computer-aided translation, but translators choose to use them in various combinations. Hence, the relevant cells are marked as Y for integration. Some translators, for example, use Translation Memory but without the Terminology Management

Table 7.3 Integrated tools

	MT		HAMT	CAT	HT
	Specific	**General**			
Machine translation	n/a	n/a	Y	Y	n/a
Translation tools	Y	Y	Y	Y	n/a
Linguistic tools	Y	Y	Y	Y	n/a
Localization tools	P	P	P	Y	n/a
Speech technology	Y	Y	Y	Y	n/a

Y = yes; P = possible; n/a = not applicable

System, and not all commercial systems include the same combination of tools.

At present, most localization tools have yet to be integrated with machine translation and human-aided machine translation systems. In some localization processes, machine translation systems have been used as separate tools to produce the first drafts of target-language texts. Therefore, there is a possibility (marked with 'P') that in the future these tools could be integrated.

In the previous chapter, it was shown that the integration of speech technology with translation tools, in particular machine translation systems, has produced a number of useful tools that can be used to translate textual and non-textual material. One example is TranSphere™ by AppTek (Application Technology, Inc.), which integrates machine translation with speech recognition and text-to-speech technologies. A versatile aspect of speech technology is that it can be integrated with the three translation types ranging from fully automated machine translation systems to partially automated computer-aided translation systems (see also Chapter 6).

Theory

In earlier chapters, the application of theory – both translation and linguistic – to the development of machine translation and other systems was discussed in some detail. This section looks at theory from two perspectives, firstly in relation to all four basic translation types (Table 7.4), and secondly specifically in relation to machine translation and its various sub-types (Table 7.5).

Based on the literature consulted for this book, there was no evidence of translation theory being used in the development of machine translation, human-aided machine translation or computer-aided translation. The relevance of translation theory to professional translators in their daily work is a controversy of long-standing (see Chesterman and

Table 7.4   Application of theory

	MT		HAMT	CAT	HT
	Specific	**General**			
Translation theory	N	N	N	N	P
Linguistic theory	Y	Y	Y	Y	P

Y = yes; N = no; P = possible

Wagner 2002). However, it can probably be assumed that most translators have some familiarity with translation theory through their training; whether they consider it useful is a separate matter. Moving on to linguistic theory, certain machine translation and human-aided machine translation systems have linguistic components that analyse the source language and synthesize the target language to generate translations. Computer-aided translation tools also contain linguistic components, in particular linguistic tools such as grammar-checkers. It is unlikely that formal linguistic theory will have any relevance for human translators. However, linguistics understood more broadly to include sociolinguistics (for example regional and social varieties), socio-pragmatics (for example politeness conventions), sense relations (for example polysemy, synonymy), text linguistics (for example genre conventions, cohesion) and contrastive linguistics (for example regular linguistic correspondences) provide a useful framework for decision-making in many aspects and types of human translation.

Another way of considering the contribution of theory to translation technology is to focus on the particular type 'machine translation' in the form of its various sub-types (Table 7.5), as it is in machine translation that formal linguistic theory features most strongly.

We know that the direct translation approach uses a very minimal application of linguistic theory, as it is largely based on word-for-word translation. Maximum use of linguistic theory is found in the rule-based approaches via a number of formal grammars, as described in Chapter 2. With regards to the corpus-based approaches, only the example-based approach uses linguistic analysis while the statistical-based approach relies on algorithms. The description in Table 7.5 applies only to traditional machine translation and not to hybrid and integrated systems.

Table 7.5 Application of theory in machine translation systems

	Direct translation	Rule-based		Corpus-based	
		Interlingua	Transfer	Statistical	Example
Translation theory	N	N	N	N	N
Formal linguistic theory	M	Y	Y	N	Y

Y = yes; N = no; M = minimal

Texts

In this section we look at the four types of translation from the point of view of the texts involved in the translation process, that is the source texts and their translations. We first consider the relevance of various types of editing to source and target texts (Tables 7.6 and 7.7), before moving on to editing in relation to the different stages of translation (Table 7.8) and then reviewing the degree of technicality or creativity of the source-language texts (Table 7.9). All these various perspectives are considered in relation to the four translation types.

Table 7.6 shows different possibilities for source-language texts with respect to the degree of editing which is needed for optimal performance in each of the four translation types. We recall from Chapter 2 that some source-language texts undergo a pre-editing process to reduce potential translation problems, especially when a translation tool such as machine translation is used. In other cases, a source-language text does not need to undergo any editing, although this may still facilitate the translation process.

A controlled language text may be the result either of editing a text using the restricted vocabulary and rules of a particular controlled language, or of authoring a text using a particular controlled language from scratch. Either way, the result is a controlled language text. A pre-edited text is understood here as having been subject to some simplifications, and/or the elimination of obvious grammatical and typographical errors (as we saw in Chapter 2), but not according to the rules of a particular controlled language.

If a machine translation system has been developed specifically for the same subject matter as the source-language text, a good output can be produced with a source text which has been edited into or written in

Table 7.6   Source-language texts

	MT		HAMT	CAT	HT
	Specific	**General**			
Controlled language texts:					
edited	O	LO	O	O	LO
authored	O	LO	O	O	LO
Pre-edited texts	O	LO	LO	O	O
Unedited texts	NO	LO	LO	O	O

O = optimal; LO = less than optimal; NO = not optimal

a controlled language. Controlled language source texts, if available, can also produce good results with human-aided machine translation and computer-aided translation. Pre-editing of texts would not normally be carried out for human-aided machine translation and computer-aided translation, as human intervention during the translation process is possible. A general-purpose machine translation system is likely to perform less well than a specific-purpose system even with a controlled language source text, simply because a general-purpose system is not designed to translate texts from narrow subject fields. General-purpose systems can cope with a broader range of input texts but with expectations of lower quality. With respect to human translation, it is possible for translators to work with a source-language text that has been produced in a controlled language format but they may find that working with such texts can be monotonous owing to a rigid style and limited vocabulary. Pre-edited source-language texts are likely to facilitate the translation process for most translation types. However, fully automatic machine translation systems may still face residual ambiguities or other problems which, in human-aided machine translation can be solved during the actual translation process.

Unedited source-language texts are not suitable as input to specific-purpose machine translation systems since the output is likely to be very poor. As for general-purpose machine translation, the output from an unedited source-language text can also be poor. We see this often in the quality of translations produced by online machine translation systems, although, as already noted, the quality of the translation is not critical here since the translation is usually for information purposes only. An unedited source-language text would not cause the same problems for a human-aided machine translation system as it would for specific-purpose machine translation because of the possibility of human intervention during the translation process. There is no doubt that human translators are able to deal with unedited source-language texts. Similarly, since in computer-aided translation a human is the principal translator, an unedited source-language text would not pose significant difficulties.

Let us now turn to target-language texts and the degree of editing, in this case after the actual translation process has been completed (see Table 7.8). The quality of a target-language text produced especially by semi- or automated systems mostly hinges on a number of factors such as the coverage provided by the dictionary or dictionaries in a system, the coverage of terms in a terminology database, the capabilities of the analysis and synthesis modules in a system, and the quality of the source-language text, as well as its type. The relationship between the source and target texts is complex and it is not realistic here to map all the possible interactions.

For target-language texts we are, of course, concerned with post-editing, which has been described in Chapter 2. To recap, the post-editing task is divided into 'rapid', referring to a minimum amount of editing to correct obvious grammatical errors, and 'polished', entailing sufficient editing of the target-language text to turn it into a high-quality translation. For human translation and computer-aided translation, making changes after the translation has been produced is usually called 'revision' if those changes are carried out with reference to the source text (see also Chapter 2). Somewhat confusingly, 'post-editing' is therefore much closer to 'revision' than 'editing' in the human context, which does not need to be done with reference to the source text.

Table 7.7 shows for which translation type the target-language text may need to undergo post-editing to produce the required quality of translation. Rapid post-editing can be performed on target-language texts generated by both specific- and general-purpose machine translation systems, and also human-aided machine translation systems where the text is needed for information only according to a specific purpose, for a specific group or for a specific period of time. Polished post-editing, on the other hand, is almost always required for the translations generated by specific-purpose machine translation systems: where the subject matter is highly technical, such as in operational manuals, accuracy and clarity are crucial.

Target-language texts generated by general-purpose machine translation may undergo polished post-editing but they are more likely to receive only rapid post-editing for information purposes. However, if the content of the target-language text is already broadly comprehensible and matches the user's needs, neither rapid nor polished post-editing is

Table 7.7   Target-language texts

	MT		HAMT	CAT	HT
	Specific	**General**			
Post-editing:					
Rapid	R	R	R	n/a	n/a
Polished	R	MR	R	n/a	n/a
Revision	n/a	n/a	n/a	R	R

R = required; MR = may be required; n/a = not applicable

required, as in the case, for example, of the output generated by online machine translation systems, for which post-editing is in any case not normally available. The same, however, cannot be said about human-aided machine translation. Target-language texts produced as a result of human-aided machine translation tend to be post-edited for publication purposes, that is for clients who commission the translation in the first place, such as those by the US Patent and Trademark Office mentioned in Chapter 1. In the case of computer-aided translation and human translation, revision is usually performed by a second translator to produce the required high-quality translation.

When the various stages of the translation process were discussed in Chapter 2, it was shown that certain tasks performed before, during and after the actual translation can influence the quality of the target text generated by a translation tool. In Table 7.8 we show which task, performed at a certain stage of the translation process, is important to which translation type. We extend the meaning of 'interactive' here beyond the conventional understanding of human–machine interaction in human-assisted machine translation to the use of any tool involving both human and machine.

Pre-editing, discussed in Chapter 2, is exceptionally important for specific-purpose machine translation and human-aided machine translation. Machine translation systems are 'sensitive' to any lexical ambiguities and typographical errors in the source-language text. If a source-language text contains too many errors and is not pre-edited, human involvement in human-aided machine translation can get tedious. For this reason, source-language texts are often extensively pre-edited based on the grammar and vocabulary of a controlled language in preparation for machine translation or human-aided machine translation.

In contrast, it is less important to edit the source-language text prior to translation for general-purpose machine translation and computer-aided

Table 7.8   Stages of the translation process

	MT		HAMT	CAT	HT
	Specific	**General**			
Pre-editing	I	LI	I	LI	LI
Interactive	n/a	n/a	I	I	I
Post-editing	I	LI	I	n/a	n/a

I = important; LI = less important; n/a = not applicable

translation. For general-purpose machine translation, accuracy and clarity may not be as crucial as long as the output can be understood, unlike specific-purpose machine translation. Pre-editing of source-language texts is also less crucial to computer-aided translation since the human translator expects to make a considerable contribution during the translation process. In fact, editing the source-language text in such circumstances could even be counterproductive, as the system would be less likely to match units from the original source text with units in the new source text, meaning that fewer translations would be proposed by the system. While human translators do not tend to pre-edit texts they are about to translate, they would normally check the accuracy of the information with the client and correct obvious factual errors when dealing with grammatical and/or typographical errors. For general-purpose machine translation systems, post-editing is shown as 'less important' in Table 7.8. The point is that post-editing is not as crucial for general-purpose machine translation as for specific-purpose machine translation as the purpose of the translation usually requires a lower quality.

Most translation tools are effective and efficient when used to translate or to support the translation of certain types of texts and, in some cases, certain subject fields. In Table 7.9, some different types are examined, whereby 'type' is described on a scale from highly creative to highly technical.

As mentioned in previous chapters, highly creative persuasive texts such as advertisements or expressive texts such as poems are not suitable for either specific- or general-purpose machine translation systems for a number of reasons, including novel or unconventional uses of language such as non-standard syntax patterns or neologisms, for which there is no equivalent word or phrase in the other language. Machine

Table 7.9   Types of text

	MT		HAMT	CAT	HT
	Specific	General			
Highly creative	NS	NS	NS	NS	S
Semi-creative	NS	NS	NS	NS	S
General-purpose	NS	S	P	S	S
Semi-technical	S	P	S	S	S
Highly technical	S	NS	S	S	S

S = suitable; NS = not suitable; P = possible

translations systems, in particular, have not yet achieved the ability to decipher ambiguities in which a word or a sentence can have more than one interpretation; for example, lexical ambiguity (more specifically, homographs) as in 'Beth goes to the bank everyday' where the word 'bank' could mean 'the edge of a river' or 'a financial institution', or syntactic ambiguity as in 'He knows more beautiful women than Samantha' where the sentence could mean 'he knows women more beautiful than Samantha' or 'he knows more beautiful women than Samantha does'. Homographs can sometimes be resolved by the user directing the system to one of its specialist dictionaries according to the topic of the text (for example economics for 'bank' as financial institution), but syntactic ambiguity is less easily resolved.

In contrast, semi-technical and highly technical texts are the most suitable types of text for specific-purpose machine translation systems. These texts are mainly scientific and technical, for instance articles on 'myrmecology' or 'the scientific study of ants' (a branch of entomology – the study of insects) for myrmecologists or manuals for engineers operating water desalination plants.

Most specific-purpose systems are built with pre-determined subject fields in mind (see also Chapter 3). Therefore, they cater for texts that contain a high number of specific terms and repeated or formulaic phrases. As for general-purpose machine translation systems, it is possible for them to handle semi-technical texts, such as articles in *Scientific American* that contain some common words that have acquired one or more new meanings within a subject field, but with the limitation that the systems may or may not have the right terminology coverage. Highly technical texts are not suitable for general-purpose machine translation systems because their dictionaries are mainly general and they are unlikely to contain specialized dictionaries in the appropriate subject field. For example, in a Portuguese medical journal the specialist medical term that refers to 'a pathologic condition resulting from an accumulation of acid or a depletion of the alkaline reserve (bicarbonate content) in the blood and body tissues, and characterized by an increase in hydrogen ion concentration' is 'acidoce' ('acidosis' in English). If the same concept were to be referred to in a general-purpose text such as a newspaper article about health in Portuguese, a synonym would be used: 'alteração do equilíbrio ácido básico do sangue e líquidos teciduais' (see http://allserv.rug.ac.be/~rvdstich/eugloss/multi002.html).

As in the case of machine translation systems, most human-aided machine translation systems are not suitable for translating semi-creative and highly creative texts. Extensive human intervention would be necessary owing to the higher number of creative metaphors or the higher degree of lexical and syntactic ambiguities in such texts, with which a human translator is clearly better able to deal than a machine (see also Chapter 6). On the other hand, it is possible for general-purpose texts to be translated by translation systems but with human intervention in order to deal with some degree of lexical ambiguity.

Translation tools like translation memory systems have not been developed for the purpose of translating semi- and highly creative texts. On the other hand, tools such as concordancers, electronic dictionaries and glossaries – which we have included here in the concept of computer-aided translation – can be extremely helpful in exploring the uses of words and phrases in the translation of such texts. General-purpose texts such as press releases, and semi- and highly technical texts such as popular scientific articles and scientific articles for other experts are also, of course, suitable for human translation.

Language dependency

Some tools are designed for specific languages. Spell-checkers are an obvious example, as are also electronic dictionaries and glossaries. Others, such as translation memory systems and concordancers, can be used with any language, assuming that the relevant character sets are digitally available. Such tools do not have any content except the input provided by the user. Any 'knowledge' that a translation memory system, for example, contains, such as 'this unit in language X is the equivalent of that unit in language Y', is based on the translator's own input, either through the alignment of previously translated texts and their sources using an alignment tool, or through the new units added to the translation memory database as the translator is working. So the translation memory system itself has no knowledge of any particular language. For example, a translation memory system such as the Heartsome Translation Suite developed by Heartsome Holdings Pte. is capable of handling an unlimited number of languages.

Table 7.10 reviews each translation type with respect to their degree of independence from particular languages.

Machine translation systems, human-aided machine translation systems and human translation are clearly highly language-dependent. The systems are usually developed for the translation of specific language pairs. The fact that some machine translation and human-aided machine translation systems offer translation between many language pairs does not alter the fact that they are still language-dependent. TranSphere™, for example, is a multilingual machine translation

Table 7.10   Language dependency

	MT		HAMT	CAT	HT
	Specific	General			
Language-dependency	H	H	H	H/L	H

H = high; L = low

system covering 18 languages including popular Western European and East Asian languages, as well as Arabic, Dari, Hebrew, Pashto, Persian, Turkish and Ukrainian, but it can't deal with any other language pairs. It is also not uncommon to find human translators working with more than one language pair, but usually with only one language as the target language. In the case of computer-aided translation, this is marked with 'H' for 'high' or 'L' for 'low' since some linguistic tools such as electronic dictionaries, and spell and grammar-checkers are language-dependent, while translation memory systems and concordancers are not.

A further aspect of language dependency concerns the development rather than the use of certain tools. We can, for example, recall the development of rule-based machine translation systems following the first generation direct machine translation systems. While direct systems had to be built from scratch for each language pair and direction, we recall that the idea behind the design of interlingua systems was to build a single module to analyse texts in each source language, and another module for the synthesis of texts in each target language, mediated by a universal interlingua module. The interlingua was supposed to allow the analysis of any source text for which an analysis module was available to be related to the chosen target language and synthesized into a target text, meaning that any language pair could be automatically translated, given an analysis module and a synthesis module (we return to modularity later in this chapter). As is now clear, this ambitious scheme did not lead to any full working systems (see Chapter 3), but the idea had been appealing: to create a large number of translation pairs from a minimal number of analysis and synthesis modules. Hence, there was still a degree of language-dependency in the form of the source-language and target-language modules, but their permutability made the potential coverage of such systems much less dependent on specific language pairs. In the end, the compromise was the less ambitious transfer system.

When discussing computer-aided tools such as translation memory, it was pointed out that the accompanying tool used to automatically align parallel texts (usually with a bit of help from the user), is independent of any particular language. Corpus-based and statistically-based machine translation systems are also language-independent in so far as they use algorithms as a method of extracting translation equivalents, as we have seen in Chapter 3 (we return to algorithms later in this chapter).

Our last perspective on language-dependency – see Table 7.11 – concerns controlled language, for example for highly specific purposes such as ASD Simplified English, compared with 'natural' language, as in standard British English for example.

Table 7.11 Types of source language

	MT		HAMT	CAT	HT
	Specific	**General**			
Controlled language	Y	P	Y	Y	P
Natural language	N	Y	P	Y	Y

Y = yes; N = no; P = possible

For specific-purpose machine translation systems, controlled language is more suitable for source-language texts than is natural language. On the other hand, natural language is best suited for general-purpose machine translation systems. Controlled language can facilitate both human-aided machine translation and computer-aided translation. The same, however, cannot be said about natural language, which is more suitable for computer-aided translation than for human-aided machine translation. Both varieties of language are acceptable to human translators. As mentioned above, for stylistic and other reasons, a natural-language text presents more of a challenge than a restricted controlled language text and human translators may therefore prefer it.

Standards for data interchange

The growing importance of language industry standards for reusing – or 'leveraging' – data previously processed by other tools cannot be underestimated in the modern world of the translation industry. These standards function as a bridge, connecting tools that are built using different programming codes and operating across a variety of platforms or systems, such as Microsoft Windows or Unix. The existence of numerous tools has made it necessary for specific standards to be created to help the operational flow when several tools are used concurrently in a translation process. Tables 7.12 and 7.13 focus on this aspect but from different perspectives.

Table 7.12 shows how important standards are for each translation type, referring to three different types of standard: TMX, TBX and XLIFF, as described in Chapter 4. Within machine translation, the need for particular standards may vary according to the sub-type. So, whereas direct translation and rule-based machine translation systems do not use previously translated material or corpora to generate new translations, corpus based machine translation systems do have a use for data interchange standards, as do also computer-aided translation systems, including some linguistic tools such as electronic dictionaries and termbases. At present, however, the TMX standard for the interchange of translation data is applicable mostly to translation memory systems as they store previously translated material in a database of translation examples, rather than to full machine translation systems.

Table 7.12 Data interchange standards in translation

	MT		HAMT	CAT	HT
	Specific	General			
Translation standard (TMX)	P	P	I	VI	VI
Terminological standard (TBX)	VI	VI	VI	VI	VI
Localization standard (XLIFF)	P	P	I	I	I

VI = very important; I = important; P = possible

We can recall that machine translation systems are increasingly being used to generate the first drafts of translations in the localization process. In such cases, the output data from the machine translation system – the raw translation – needs to be imported into the localization tool for further processing. For this to happen, the XLIFF standard is needed. The terminological data interchange standard TBX, on the other hand, is extremely important to all translation types, especially for the translation of technical texts. For computer-aided translation and human translation, both translation and terminological data interchange are very important, especially when linguistic tools or resources such as electronic dictionaries, glossaries and thesauri are used to assist the translator during the translation process, since most are compiled and structured in different ways. Furthermore, they may be accessed via different operating systems. The localization standard XLIFF is important for computer-aided translation and human translators; however, its importance is clearly restricted to supporting translators involved in the localization industry.

For developers, building translation tools that are compliant with these three language-industry standards is important. These standards allow interoperability between different tools that greatly benefit developers, translation companies and professional translators. Since the introduction of these standards, many translation tools have undergone certification that allows the logo of the specific standard to be used. Thus some translation tools, such as the SDLX 2004 translation memory system by SDL International, has been certified by TMX, while the Heartsome Translation Suite is fully compliant with all three standards.

Having focused on the three interchange standards in relation to the four translation types, we now turn our attention to the importance of data-interchange standards for the different groups who are involved in translation (Table 7.13).

End-users such as professional translators and those involved in the localization industry find data-interchange standards of considerable importance, as they enable a variety of tools to perform specific functions during the translation or localization process. A terminology database may be accessed, for example, to search for a suitable equivalent while using a translation memory system. Assuring a smooth flow of work from one tool to another, for example from using a translation memory system to update a terminology database to translating a text with the support of a terminology management system, is an added benefit for professional translators, translation companies and localizers and preferable to just working with one tool at a time.

Table 7.13 Translation groups and data interchange standards

	Translation standard (TMX)	Terminological standard (TBX)	Localization standard (XLIFF)
Professional translators	VI	VI	P
Translation companies	VI	VI	VI
Localization industry	VI	VI	VI
Researchers	I	I	I
Developers	I	I	I

VI = very important; I = important; P = possible

Two groups that are concerned with standards but not as end-users are researchers, who are involved in the development of standards before publication, and developers, for whom it is important to ensure compliance with these accepted standards in order for tools to be marketable. For example, some newer versions of translation memory systems must obtain certification for TMX before they are released onto the market. This is one strategy to boost sales since end-users want to ensure that the new tool they intend to buy is compatible with the tools they already own.

Evaluation

Our last topic in this section is the evaluation of translation tools, another area of importance to different groups involved in the translation industry, including translation companies, professional translators and developers. Evaluation procedures are designed to ensure that the tool developed performs as expected by developers and by users, that is translators. Tables 7.14 and 7.15 focus respectively on the level of system evaluation required as dictated by translation type, and the methods of evaluation for each level as previously discussed in Chapter 5.

We know from Chapter 5 that the evaluation of translation tools can be performed in two principal ways, namely by looking at particular components in a system or by evaluating the whole system. We can also recall that component evaluation means that either a single component or several components in a system are evaluated at any one time while a tool is in the developmental stage. A whole system evaluation, on the other hand, encompasses the performance of the whole tool, once development has been completed. Both types of evaluation are important to all translation types involving computer tools.

'Evaluation' is a term applied to the assessment of translation output from automated systems; so evaluation in this sense is not applicable to the work of human translators. There are other ways of trying to ensure

Table 7.14 Levels of evaluation

	MT		HAMT	CAT	HT
	Specific	General			
Components in system	I	I	I	I	n/a
Whole system	I	I	I	I	n/a

I = important; n/a = not applicable

that human translation meets certain quality standards and these are largely institutional, for example through translation courses and accreditation. In many countries, translation courses are offered at universities. Accreditation, on the other hand, is normally professionally certified based on qualifications, experience and/or direct assessment to confirm competence in translation and/or interpreting. Typically, accreditation obtained in one country would allow a translator to practise in that country in named language pairs and directions. For example, an individual who wants to work as a translator between English and Korean in Australia must obtain accreditation from the National Accreditation Authority for Translators and Interpreters Ltd (NAATI) for that language pair. In some countries, such as Australia, Canada and South Africa, accreditation is required before a translator can work in the translation industry, while in others, such as Malaysia, Singapore and Thailand, no accreditation requirement is needed for either translators or interpreters to practise.

Having considered the two levels of evaluation for automated and semi-automated tools, let us now consider how each level is evaluated (Table 7.15).

The aim in Table 7.15 is to provide a clearer perspective on which evaluation methods are better suited to test an individual component in a system or an entire system. Each method uses different variables or test material to perform the evaluation. Some test material consists of linguistic phenomena that have been artificially created to evaluate particular features of the system (test suite), while other test material is extracted from a corpus (test corpus). A variety of tests is used to evaluate a specific component of a tool during its developmental stage, whereas to evaluate an entire system, the most suitable methods are human judgement, automation and black-box.

Having reviewed our chosen topics in relation to the original four translation types proposed well over a decade ago, it is clear that since

Table 7.15   Methods of evaluation

	Components in a system	Whole system
Human	Y	Y
Automation	Y	Y
Test suite	Y	N
Test corpus	Y	N
Glass-box	Y	N
Black-box	N	Y

Y = yes; N = no

then technological developments have led to a need for reappraisal. We have attempted to do this by taking a multidimensional approach in which it has been shown that groupings and classifications of translation as an activity involving machines and/or humans shift according to the perspective assumed. It is a complex picture which changes with each new development.

In the last sections of this chapter, we focus on two particular types of translation, machine translation and computer-aided translation, in order to explore some perspectives in more depth.

Machine translation systems

This section is concerned with a number of topics related to machine translation systems discussed previously, in particular in Chapter 3. Tables 7.16 and 7.17 show the different approaches to machine translation such as direct translation, ruled-based and corpus-based approaches as they relate to particular design features and coverage of language pairs respectively. Rule-based and corpus-based approaches are further divided into their respective sub-types.

Table 7.16 Features in a machine translation system

	Direct translation	Rule-based		Corpus-based	
		Interlingua	Transfer	Statistical-based	Example-based
Algorithms	N	N	N	Y	Y
Examples	N	N	N	N	Y
Dictionaries	Y	Y	Y	N	N
SL analysis	M	Y	Y	N	N
TL synthesis	M	Y	Y	N	N
Abstract representations	N	Y	Y	N	N
Transfer module	N	N	Y	N	N
Language model	N	N	N	Y	Y
Translation model	N	N	N	Y	N
Modularity	N	Y	Y	Y	Y
Corpora	N	N	N	Y	Y

Y = yes; N = no; M = minimal

Algorithms and corpora are important features in the statistical- and example-based approaches. Clearly, corpora are critically important to corpus-based approaches, as they are needed to produce new translations either by prediction or selection. The statistical-based approach uses both language and translation models to generate new translations. The example-based approach, on the other hand, employs only a language model. As for rule-based approaches, while abstract representations of the source-language text and the target-language text are a common feature, only the transfer approach includes, as its name implies, a transfer module.

Two of the most important features for rule-based systems are the source-language analysis module and the target-language synthesis module. The earlier direct translation approach may also be said to include these two features, although the analysis and synthesis are not carried out by separate modules, meaning that this early approach has minimal analysis and synthesis capabilities. The main reason for this is that it is based on the word-for-word translation method, which in itself has limited linguistic analysis and synthesis capabilities (see also Chapters 2 and 3). The corpus-based approach does not require dictionaries or analysis and synthesis modules, since the corpora from which the new translations are derived provide all the information needed to select the best translation for a specific source-language segment.

Table 7.16 also shows that dictionaries (monolingual and bilingual) constitute a feature that direct and rule-based approaches share, even the toy system of the Georgetown University System, as we saw in Chapter 3. In current machine translation systems, the general dictionary can contain more than one million words, as for example the general dictionary in the @Promt Professional 7.0 system by PROMT Ltd for translating between German and Russian. More specialized dictionaries are available in some systems.

One feature found in nearly all machine translation systems from the second generation onwards (rule-based and corpus-based systems) is modularity, meaning that the components of the system are independent of each other so that a researcher can change or improve a particular module without this affecting the performance of other modules of a system (see also Chapter 3). Modularity is desirable in a machine translation system as it can reduce development and maintenance costs when new language pairs are added (Table 7.17). A feature that is also important to machine translation development is the reversibility property that enables a language pair working in one direction to be reversed.

Table 7.17 Language coverage in machine translation systems

	Direct translation	Rule-based		Corpus-based	
		Interlingua	Transfer	Statistical	Example
One language pair	Y	Y	Y	Y	Y
More than one language pair	N	Y	Y	Y	Y

Y = yes; N = no;

Unlike other translation tools, all machine translation systems are language-dependent (see Table 7.10) and contain minimally one language pair. As natural-language processing technology has improved, particularly with respect to the modular feature, most second-generation machine translation systems onwards have been able to offer more than one pair of languages. This is exemplified by online machine translation systems such as WorldLingo Free Online Translator, which offers translation of texts, web pages and e-mails in 13 languages (Simplified and Traditional Chinese are considered two languages owing to the different scripts used).

Computer-aided translation tools

In this section we return to the topics of text types, language dependency and language pair coverage (Tables 7.18, 7.19 and 7.20 respectively), but this time in relation to computer-aided translation tools, which are further sub-divided (see Chapter 4) into translation tools such as terminology management systems and translation memory, localization tools, and linguistic tools including concordancers, electronic lexical resources and spell-checkers.

The translation of semi-technical and highly technical texts can benefit from the support offered by all the types of tool shown (Table 7.18). In Chapter 4 it was shown that most of these tools have been developed mainly with the translation of technical texts in mind, and consequently translation tools such as translation memory are unlikely to be as useful for semi-creative and highly creative texts, as a high percentage of repeated words or phrases is not normally a characteristic feature. Instead, these types of texts are more likely to contain ambiguous words, phrases and sentences, possibly with idiosyncratic features according to the author and the genre.

Table 7.18   Texts and computer-aided translation tools

	Translation tools	Localization tools	Linguistic tools
Highly creative	U	NU	VU
Semi-creative	U	NU	VU
General	U	NU	VU
Semi-technical	VU	VU	VU
Highly technical	VU	VU	VU

VU = very useful; U = useful; NU = not useful

Localization tools are not designed for the translation of semi-creative, highly creative and general-purpose texts. As we have seen, they have been developed to deal with technical texts such as product specifications and instruction manuals. Whether translation or linguistic tools are useful in the translation of general-purpose texts may depend on the translator, the degree of ambiguity and the purpose of the translation. Linguistic tools such as electronic dictionaries and spell-checkers, for example, are useful for all types of text. Moreover, electronic dictionaries are available for both general-purpose and subject-specific texts, and spell-checkers can be 'trained' by users according to the particular vocabulary and terms required. Concordancers can indicate possible solutions for the translation of all types of text by revealing lexical patternings.

Unlike machine translation systems, translation and localization tools are rarely language-dependent, whereas some linguistic tools such as spell-checkers, grammar checkers and dictionaries can be language-dependent. Concordancers, on the other hand, tend to be language-independent, as shown in Table 7.19. Language-independency, a feature making the use of the tool less restrictive, is something that professional translators and translation companies find very attractive.

Translation and localization tools are similar to language-processing applications such as Word, whereby any language can be processed as

Table 7.19   Language dependency in computer-aided translation tools

	Translation tools	Localization tools	Linguistic tools
Language-dependency	L	L	H/L

H = high; L = low

long as the character sets for that language are supported digitally. For some translation and localization tools, the question of language-dependency only arises when part of, or the entire character set of a language is not digitally supported, as in Javanese, spoken mainly in Indonesia. Linguistic tools such as electronic dictionaries and thesauri, on the other hand, are highly language-dependent since they are content-based, whereas linguistic tools such as OCRs and concordancers are not dependent on any particular language (although they may be limited to the scripts they support).

In the discussion related to Table 7.19, translation and localization tools were shown to be language-independent. Looking at this in another way, it can also be said that these two types of tool can successfully be applied to many languages and are therefore potentially multilingual (Table 7.20).

Table 7.20 Number of languages in computer-aided translation tools

	Translation tools	Localization tools	Linguistic tools
Monolingual	n/a	n/a	H
Bilingual	n/a	n/a	H
Trilingual	n/a	n/a	L
Multilingual	H	H	L

H = high; L = low; n/a = not applicable

Linguistic tools such as monolingual electronic dictionaries, glossaries and thesauri are easily available online or on compact disks for a wide range of specific languages. Bilingual electronic dictionaries or glossaries are also widely available. As the number of languages increases to three or more, the harder it is to find linguistic tools, as indicated in Table 7.20.

Conclusion

This chapter has been written with the intention of providing a basic summary of each and every topic covered in the book. In some cases, what is presented is cutting-edge information and it is not unlikely that in the near future changes will occur as technology becomes increasingly sophisticated and new technologies are introduced. As we have seen in Chapter 6, it is also not an easy task to illustrate translation technology that, with each passing day, is becoming increasingly complex. For this reason, some of the tables presented above deal with overlapping topics. They contain similar criteria and touch on similar issues but each of them adopts a different perspective, indicating the complexity of the topics discussed and the high degree of interdependency between them. The overall picture becomes even more complex as a result of the existence of a number of sub-types of machine translation and computer-aided translation, as well as the involvement of a wide range of 'agents' from researchers and tool developers, through evaluators to various end-user groups including professional translators, trainers and translation companies. To present all this in one table has proven to be impracticable, evidence to show that the topics touched on in this book are multidimensional. The variety of 'sub-types' which have been distinguished – notably for machine translation systems and computer-aided translation (computer-aided translation tools) – have been presented separately, as they are governed by a number of factors which affect each sub-type in a different way.

Many issues need further investigation in order to discover how translation technology can or cannot support the increasingly diverse translation activities pursued by both computers and translators through the development of more and increasingly sophisticated translation tools. On the other hand, there is also considerable scope for research into the use of translation tools by translators, which may in turn lead to further improvements in the tools themselves, but can also be expected to contribute to our knowledge of the process of human translation in the modern idiom.

Appendices

The Language Key for all the following Appendices tables appear on p. 203.

A1 Examples of commercial machine translation systems

Name	Website	Language
Abc Thai	http://www.ablume.com	E/Th, G/Th
Alpha Works	http://www.alphaworks.ibm.com/ aw.nsf/html/mt?open&t=gr, p=Word2Word	E-(F, G, J, I, Cs, Ct, S, K) (F, G, S, I)-E
Intertran	http://www.tranexp.com/win/ itserver.htm	Al, Bo, E, Pb, B, Cr, Cz, Da, D, S, Fi, F, Fl, G, Gr, H, Hi, Ic, I, J, K, L, N, Ta, Po, P, R, S, Se, Sl, Swe, W, T, V
Ling98	http://www.ling98.com	E, U, G, R
Promt XT	http://www.e-promt.com/ technology.shtml	E, G, F, S, I, R
SDL	http://www.sdlintl.com/enterprise-systems/enterprise-translation-server/ ets-demo/ets-demo-text-translator.htm	(S, F, G)-E, E-(S, F, G, I, P)
Systran 4.0	http://www.systransoft.com/	E/(D, J, K, Cs, Ct, R, S, F, G, I, P), F/(P, D, S, F, P, I, G)

A2 Examples of online machine translation systems

Name	Language	Domain	Website
Ajeeb	E/A	Web, Text	http://tarjim.ajeeb. com/ajeeb/default. asp?lang=1
Bultra	E/B	Text	http://www.bultra. com/online_test_e.htm
Catalin Zaharia	Ro/E	Text	http://www. catalinzaharia. go.ro/ e_index.html

(Continued)

Name	Language	Domain	Website
Enterprise Translator Server (ETS)	E-(F, G, S, I, N, P), (S, G, F, I, P)-E	Text, Web	http://www.mezzofanti. org/translation/
e-Translation Server	G-(E, F), E-(G, F, I, S, J, C, Tai, K, P), F-(G, E), (I, S, J, C, Tai)-E	Text	http://www.linguatec. net/online/ptwebtext/index.shtml
EWtranslite	E-(Cs, Ct, M, In), (Cs, Ct, M, In)-E	Text	http://www.ewgate.com/ewtranslite.html
Finnish Trans	E/Fi	Word	http://finnishtrans.8bit.co.uk/testfintrans.html
Finnish Trans	E/Fi	Word	http://finnishtrans.8bit.co.uk/testfintrans.html
Foreignword. com	Af, B, C, Cr, Cz, Da, D, E, Fi, F, G, Gr, H, Ic, In, I, J, K, M, N, P, Pb, P, Ro, R, S, Se, Sl, Swa, Swe, Ts, U, W, Y	Word, Text	http://www.foreignword.com/Tools/transnow.htm
Free Translation	(S, F, G, I, P, D, R)-E, E-(S, G, F, I, N, P, D, Cs, Ct, R)	Text	http://www.freetranslation.com/
Itrans	Gu, Hi, Mar, San, Be, Tam, Ka, Te, Gur	Text	http://www.aczone.com/itrans/online/
Language Translator	E-(F, G, I, P, S), F-(G, E), G-(E, F), (I, S, P)-E	Text	http://www.freelanguagetranslator. com
Logomedia	E, U, S, F, G, I, J, K, Po, P, R, C	Text, Web	http://www.logomedia.net
LingvoBit	Po/E	Word, Sentence	http://www.poltran.com
Lycos Zone	E-(F, G, S, I, P), (F, G, S, I, P)-E F- (E, G, S, I, P), (G, S, I, P)-F	Text, Web	http://translate.lycoszone.com/
Mytranslate	E-(F, G, I, P, S), F-(E, G), G-(E, F), (I, S, P)-E	Text, Word	http://www.mytranslate.com
OCN	E/J, K/J	URL, Text	http://www.ocn.ne.jp/translation/
ParSit Thai Translator	E, Th	Text, Web	http://www.links.nectec.or.th/services/parsit/index2.html
Postchi.com	E/Pe	Email	http://www.postchi.com/email/index.cfm
Promt XT	(E, G, F, S, I)-R, E-(G, S)	Text, Web, Email	http://www.translate.ru/translator.asp?lang=en
Reverso	(E, G, S)-F, F-(E, G, S), (G, F, S)-E, E-(G, F, S)	Text, Web	http://www.reverso.net/textonly/default.asp

A3 Examples of online dictionaries

Monolingual

Name	Website	Language
Britannica	http://www.britannica.com/	E
Longman	http://www.longmanwebdict.com/	E
Merriam-webster	http://www.m-w.com/	E

Bilingual

Name	Website	Language
Al Misbar	http://195.217.167.3/dict_page.html http://www.almisbar.com/dict_page_a.html	E, A
Albi	http://www.argjiro.net/fjalor/	Al, E
Bhanot	http://dictionary.bhanot.net/	E, M
Capeller	. http://www.uni-koeln.de/phil-fak/indologie/ tamil/cap_search.html	San, E
Ceti	http://www.ceti.com.pl/~hajduk/	Bel, E
Danish-Jpn Dic	http://www.fys.ku.dk/~osada/djdict/djdict.html	J, Da
Darkstar	http://darkstar.sal.lv/vocab/index.php	Oj, E
E-Est Dic	http://www.ibs.ee/dict/	E, Est
E-Fi	http://foto.hut.fi/sanasto.html	E, Fi
E-H	http://consulting.medios.fi/dictionary/	F, H
En-Romanian	http://www.castingsnet.com/dictionaries/	E, Ro
Francenet	http://www.francenet.fr/~perrot/breizh/ dicoen.html	Bre, E
Galaxy	http://galaxy.uci.agh.edu.pl/~polak/slownik/	Po, E
Gr-E	http://users.otenet.gr/~vamvakos/alphabet.htm	Gr, E
Hebrew Dic	http://www.dictionary.co.il/	He, E
Islandes	http://www.fut.es/~mrr/islandes/islandes1.html	Ic, Ca
Kamus Jot	http://www.jot.de/kamus/	G, In
Kihon	http://kihon.aikido.org.hu/dict.html	H, J
Learning Media	http://www.learningmedia.co.nz/ngata/ index.html	Ma, E
Lexiconer	http://www.lexiconer.com/ecresult.php	E, C
Lexitron	http://lexitron.nectec.or.th/	Th, E
Lingresua	http://lingresua.tripod.com/cgi-bin/onlinedic.pl	E, U
Persian Online Dic	http://www.wdgco.com/dic/	Pe, E
Spanishdict	http://spanishdict.com/	S, E
TechDico	http://membres.lycos.fr/baobab/techdico.html	F, E
Potawatomi	http://www.ukans.edu/~kansite/pbp/books/ dicto/d_frame.html	Pot, E

Trilingual

Name	Website	Language
Cambridge	http://dictionary.cambridge.org/	E, F, S
Cari.com	http://search.cari.com.my/dictionary/	E, M, C
CSC	http://www.csc.fi/cgi-bin/math-words	E, Fi, Swe
FeM	http://www-clips.imag.fr/geta/services/dicoweb/dicoweb_en.html	F, E, M
Francenet	http://www.francenet.fr/~perrot/breizh/dico.html	Bre, E, F
Jim Breen	http://www.csse.monash.edu.au/cgi-bin/cgiwrap/jwb/wwwjdic?1C	E, J, F
Qaamuuska Xisaabta	http://www.dm.unipi.it/~jama/alif/qaamuus/qaamuus_en.html	So, I, E

Multilingual

Name	Website	Language
Ectaco	http://www.ectaco.com/online/?refid=577	E, Al, A, B, Cz, D, Est, F, G, Gr, H, I, K, La, Pe, Po, P, Ro, R, Se, Slo, S, Swe, T, Y
Foreign Word	http://www.foreignword.com/Tools/dictsrch.htm	Af, Al, B, Bel, Bre, Ca, Ce, Ch, C, Cr, Cz, Da, D, Esp, Est, Far, Fi, F, Fr, G, Ga, Gr, Ha, he, H, Il, In, Ir, I, J, Kh, K, L, La, Li, M, Ma, N, Pe, Po, P, R, Rot, San, Sar, Se, Slo, S, Swa, Swe, Ta, Tam, Th, Ti, T, U, V, W, Y
Free Dict	http://www.freedict.com/onldict/ita.html	Af, Da, D, Fi, F, H, In, I, J, L, N, P, R, S, Swa, Swe
Lexicool.com	http://www.lexicool.com/	Af, Al, A, Ar, Ba, Bo, Bre, B, Ca, Ch, Cher, C, Cre, Cr, Cz, Da, D, E, Esp, Est, Fi, F, Ga, G, Gr, He, Hi, H, Ic, In, I, J, K, L, La, M, N, Pe, Po, P, Ro, R, Se, Sl, Slo, So, S, Swa, Swe, Tam, Th, T, U, Ur, V, W, Wo, Y
Uwasa	http://www.uwasa.fi/comm/termino/collect/	Af, Alg, A, Ba, Bel, Be, Bra, Ca, Ch, Che, C, Cr, Cz, Da, D, Eg, E, Esp, Est, Far, Fi, F, Gae, G, Gr, Gua, Ha, He, H, Ic, In, Ir, I, J, K, Ku, L, La, Mand, Ma, N, Pah, Po, P, Ro, R, San, Se, Slo, Sl, S, Swa, Swe, Tam, Th, T, Ti, Ur, W, Wo

A4 Examples of online thesauri

Monolingual

Name	Website	Language
Britannica	http://www.britannica.com/	E
CLAD	http://www.eastendliteracy.on.ca/ ClearLanguageAndDesign/thesaurus/	E
Merriam-webster	http://www.m-w.com/home.htm	E
NASA	http://www.sti.nasa.gov/thesfrm1.htm	E
ROGET	http://humanities.uchicago.edu/ forms_unrest/ROGET.html	E
Signum	http://www.lenguaje.com/english/ herramientas/tesauro/default.htm	S
Thesaurus.com	http://thesaurus.reference.com/	E
Webster	http://www.citibay.com/citibay/subhome/ referencesearch/thesaurus/thesaurus.shtml	E

Multilingual

Name	Website	Language
Eurovoc	http://europa.eu.int/celex/eurovoc/ cgi/sga_doc?eurovoc_dif!SERVEUR/ menu!prod!MENU&langue=EN	S, Da, G, Gr, E, F, I, D, P, Fi and Swe

A5 Examples of online glossaries

Monolingual

Name	Website	Language
Biochemistry	http://www.fhsu.edu/chemistry/twiese/ glossary/biochemglossary.htm	E
BioTech	http://filebox.vt.edu/cals/cses/chagedor/ glossary.html	E
Classical mythology	http://www.classicalmythology.org/ glossaries/	E
Genome	http://www.ornl.gov/sci/techresources/ Human_Genome/glossary/	E
Medwebplus	http://www.medwebplus.com/obj/25888	E

Bilingual

Name	Website	Language
A.D. Miles	http://www.ctv.es/USERS/amiles/glossaryhome.htm	E, S
Actuaries	http://www.actuaries.ca/publications/lexicon/default.htm	E, F
Andersen	http://www.business.auc.dk/evolution/micro/ Glossary-alfa.html	E, Da
Dewsbery	http://www.dewsbery.de/	G, E
Trans-K	http://www.trans-k.co.uk/glossary.html	E, G

Trilingual

Name	Website	Language
Reiterin	http://www.reiterin.ch/l/lexikon.htm	E, F, G

Multilingual

Name	Website	Language
Glossary Agent	http://www. insurancetranslation. com/ Glossary Agent/index.htm	Mono-, bi-, multi-: E, S, Ic, G, D, I, P, R, Gr, F, Po, I, Swe
Microsoft	http://www.lai.com/ microsoft.html	A, Ca, C, Cz, Da, D, Fi, F, G, Gr, He, H, I, J, K, N, Po, P, R, Sl, Slo, Swe, T
Magus	http:// www.informatika.bf. uni-lj.si/magus.html	Cr, Cz, Po, Sl, Slo, Se, B, Mac, Se, Sor, Bel, R, U, Da, D, E, Far, Fr, G, Ic, N, Swe, Fri, I, Rom, Ro, Sar, Ca, F, Ga, O, P, S, La, Li, Est, Fi, H, Sam, T, Ba, Bre, Ir, Sc, W, Al, Esp, Gr, Malt, Ro, Y

A6   Examples of online encyclopaedia

Name	Website	Language
Americana	http://gi.grolier.com/presidents/ea/ea_ toc.html	E
Botany	http://www.botany.com/	E
Britannica	http://www.britannica.com/	E
Columbia	http://education.yahoo.com/reference/ encyclopedia/	E
Encarta	http://encarta.msn.com/artcenter_0/ Encyclopedia_Articles.html	E
Encyclopedia.com	http://www.encyclopedia.com/	E
Hyperhistory	http://www.hyperhistory.com/online_n2/ History_n2/a.html	E
Informationsphere	http://www.informationsphere.com/	E

(Continued)

Name	Website	Language
Medline	http://www.nlm.nih.gov/medlineplus/encyclopedia.html	E
Natureserve	http://www.natureserve.org/explorer/	E
Newadvent	http://www.newadvent.org/cathen/	E
Spartacus	http://www.spartacus.schoolnet.co.uk/	E
Stanford	http://plato.stanford.edu/	E
Techtarget	http://whatis.techtarget.com/	E

A7 Language key

A = Arabic
Af = Afrikaans
Al = Albanian
Alg – Algerian Darja
B = Bulgarian
Ba = Basque
Be = Bengali
Bel = Belarusan
Bo = Bosnian
Bra = Braille
Bre = Breton
C = Chinese
Ca = Catalan
Ce = Cebuano
Ch = Chechen
Che = Cheyenne
Cher = Cherokee
Cr = Croatian
Cre = Creole
Cs = Chinese Simplified
Ct = Chinese Traditional
Cz = Czech
D = Dutch
Da = Danish
E = English
Eg = Egyptian
Esp = Esperanto
Est = Estonian
F = French
Far = Faroese
Fi = Finnish
Fl = Flemish
Fr = Frisian
Fri = Friulian

G = German
Ga = Galician
Gae = Gaelic
Gr = Greek
Gu = Gujarati
Gua = Guarani
Gur = Gurmukhi
H = Hungarian
Ha = Hawaiian
He = Hebrew
Hi = Hindi
I = Italian
Ic = Icelandic
Il = Ilango
In = Indonesian
Ir = Irish
J = Japanese
K = Korean
Ka = Kannada
Kh = Khmer
Ku = Kurdish
L = Latin
La = Latvian
Li = Lithuanian
M = Malay
Ma = Maori
Mac = Macedonian
Malt = Maltese
Mand = Mandinka
Mar = Marathi
N = Norwegian
Oj = Ojibwe
P = Portuguese
Pah = Pahlavi

Pb = Portuguese (Brazillian)
Pe = Persian
Po = Polish
Pot = Potawatomi
R = Russian
Ro = Romanian
Rot = Rotuman
S = Spanish
San = Sanskrit
Sar = Sardinian
Sc = Scotish
Se = Serbian
Sl = Slovenian
Slo = Slovak
So = Somali
Sor = Sorbian
Swa = Swahili
Swe = Swedish
T – Turkish
Ta = Tagalog/Pilipino
Tai = Taiwanese
Tam = Tamil
Te = Telugu
Th = Thai
Ti = Tibetan
Ts = Tswana
U = Ukranian
Ur = Urdu
V = Vietnamese
W = Welsh
Wo = Wolof
Y = Yiddish

/ = bidirectional
- = unidirectional

References

Ahmad, K. and M. Rogers (2001) 'Corpus Linguistics and Terminology Extraction', in *Handbook of Terminology Management. Vol. 2: Application-Oriented Terminology Management*, S.E. Wright and G. Budin (eds). Amsterdam: John Benjamins: 725–60.

Alemu, A., L. Asker and M. Getachew (2003) 'Natural Language Processing for Amharic: Overview and Suggestions for a Way Forward', *TALN 2003 Workshop: Natural Language Processing of Minority Languages and Small Languages*, France, http://www.sciences.univ-nantes.fr/irin/taln2003/articles/alemu.pdf. August 2003.

Allen, J. (2000) 'Taking on the Critics: Giving the Machine Equal Time', *Language International*, 12(3): 24–5, 44–5.

——(2001a) 'Post-editing: An Integrated Part of a Translation Software Program', *Language International*, 13(2): 26–9.

——(2001b) 'Post-editing or No Post-editing', *International Journal for Language and Documentation*, 8: 41–2.

——(2003) 'Post-editing', in *Computers and Translation: A Translator's Guide*, H.L. Somers (ed.) (2003a). Amsterdam: John Benjamins: 297–317.

Allen, J. and C. Hogan (2000) 'Towards the Development of a Post-editing Module for Machine Translation Raw Output: A New Productivity Tool for Processing Controlled Language', *Proceedings of CLAW2000*, Washington, http://www.geocities/mtpostediting/allen-hogan-claw.doc. January 2004.

ALPAC (1966) 'Language and Machines: Computers in Translation and Linguistics', *A Report by the Automatic Language Processing Advisory Committee*, Division of Behavioral Sciences, National Academy of Sciences, National Research Council. Washington D.C.: National Academy of Sciences and National Research Council.

Altintas, K. and I. Cicekli (2002) 'A Machine Translation System between a Pair of Closely Related Languages', in *Proceedings of ISCIS2002*. Florida: CSC Press: 192–6.

Ananiadou, S. (1987) 'A Brief Survey of Some Current Operational Systems', in *Machine Translation Today: The State of the Art*, M. King (ed.). Edinburgh: Edinburgh University Press: 171–91.

Archer, J. (2002) 'Internationalisation, Technology and Translation', in *Perspectives: Studies in Translatology*, 10(2): 87–117.

Arnold, D. (2003) 'Why Translation is Difficult for Computers', in *Computers and Translation: A Translator's Guide*, H.L. Somers (ed.) (2003a). Amsterdam: John Benjamins: 119–42.

Arnold, D., L. Balkan, S. Meijer, R.L. Humphreys and L. Sadler (1994) *Machine Translation: An Introductory Guide*, Oxford: NCC Blackwell.

Austermühl, F. (2001) *Electronic Tools for Translators*. Manchester: St Jerome Publishing.

Baker, M. (2001) 'Investigating the Language of Translation: A Corpus-based Approach', in *Pathways of Translation Studies*, P. Fernández Nistal and J.M. Bravo Gozalo (eds). Spain: Centro Buendía, Universidad de Valladolid: 47–56.

Balkan, L. (1992) 'Translation Tools', *META*, 37(3): 408–20.

——(1996) 'Machine Translation and Translation Theory', in *The Knowledge of the Translator: From Literary Interpretation to Machine Classification*, M. Coulthard and P.A. Odber de Baubeta (eds). Lewiston, New York: The Edwin Mellen Press: 121–34.

Balkan, L., D. Arnold and S. Meijer (1994) 'Test Suites for Natural Language Processing', *Translation and the Computer: 16th Conference*, http://www.essex.ac.uk/linguistics/clmt/group/projects/tsnlp/papers/tsnlp-aslib.ps.gz. March 2004. ,

Bar-Hillel, Y. (1960/2003) 'The Present Status of Automatic Translation of Languages', in *Readings in Machine Translation*, S. Nirenburg, H.L. Somers and Y. Wilks (eds) (2003) Cambridge, Mass.: MIT Press: 45–76.

Bédard, C. (1993) 'Forum: Translators and MT – How Can Translators Contribute to MT Research?', in *Progress in Machine Translation*, S. Nirenburg (ed.). Oxford: IOS Press, 254–61.

Bel, N., B. Dorr, E. Hovy, K. Knight, H. Iida, C. Boitet, B. Maegaard and Y. Wilks (2001) 'Chapter 4: Machine Translation', *Multilingual Information Management: Current Levels and Future Abilities*, E. Hovy, N. Ide, R. Frederking, J. Mariani and A. Zampolli (eds), http://www-2.cs.cmu.edu/~ref/mlim/chapter4.html. February 2003.

Bell, R. (1991) *Translation and Translating: Theory and Practice*, London: Longman.

Benis, M. (1999) 'Unlocking Your Potential: Talking Yourself Out of Trouble', in *Bulletin of the Institute of Translation and Interpreting*. 12–16.

——(2003) 'Much More Than Memories', in *Bulletin of the Institute of Translation and Interpreting*. 25–9.

Bennett, P. (2003) 'The Relevance of Linguistics for Machine Translation', in *Computers and Translation: A Translator's Guide*, H.L. Somers (ed.) (2003a). Amsterdam: John Benjamins: 143–60.

Bennett, S. and L. Gerber (2003) 'Inside Commercial Machine Translation', in *Computers and Translation: A Translator's Guide*, H.L. Somers (ed.) (2003a). Amsterdam: John Benjamins: 175–90.

Berger, A.L., P.F. Brown, S.A. Della Pietra, V.J. Della Pietra, J.R. Gillett, J.D. Lafferty, R.L. Mercer, H. Printz and L. Ures (1994) 'The Candide System for Machine Translation', *Human Language Technology: Proceedings of a Workshop*, New Jersey, http://acl.ldc.upenn.edu/H/H94-1028.pdf.

Berment, V. (2002) 'Several Directions for Minority Languages Computerization', in *Proceedings of COLING2002*, Taiwan, http://acl.ldc.upenn.edu/coling2002/proceedings/data/area-17/co-276.pdf. August 2003.

Berners-Lee, T., J. Hendler and O. Lassila (2001) 'The Semantic Web', *American Scientific.com*, http://www.scientificamerican.com/print_version.cfm?articleID=00048144-10D2-1C70-84A9809EC588EF21. March 2005.

Berners-Lee, T. and E. Miller (2002) 'The Semantic Web lifts off', *ECRIM News*, Online edn. 51, http://www.ercim.org/publication/Ercim_News/enw51/berners-lee.html. March 2005.

Biguenet, J. and R. Schulte (eds) (1989) *The Craft of Translation*. Chicago: University Chicago Press.

Boltz, W.G. (1996) 'Early Chinese Writing', in *The World's Writing Systems*, P.T. Daniels and W. Bright (eds). Oxford: Oxford University Press. 191–99.

Bononno, R. (2000) 'Terminology for Translators: An Implementation of ISO 12620', *META*, 45(4): 646–69.

Bowker, L. (2002) *Computer-Aided Translation Technology: A Practical Introduction.* Ottawa: University of Ottawa Press.

Bowker, L. and M. Barlow (2004) 'Bilingual Concordancers and Translation Memories: A Comparative Evaluation', *Proceedings of LR4TransII at COLING2004*, Switzerland, http://www.ifi.unizh.ch/cl/yuste/lr4trans-2/WKS_ PAPERS/8.pdf. November 2004.

Branchadell, A. and L.M. West (2004) *Less Translated Languages*, Amsterdam: John Benjamins.

Brown, P.F., S.A. Della Pietra, V.J. Pietra and R.L. Mercer (1993) 'The Mathematics of Statistical Machine Translation: Parameter Estimation', *Computational Linguistics*, 19(2): 263–311.

Bruckner, C. and M. Plitt (2001) 'Evaluating the Operational Benefit of Using Machine Translation Output as Translation Memory Input', *Proceedings of MT Summit VIII*, Spain, http://www.eamt.org/summitVIII/papers/bruckner.pdf. November 2002.

Calzolari, N., J. McNaught, M. Palmer and A. Zampolli (eds) (2003) *International Standard for Language Engineering: D14.2 Final Report*, http://www.ilc.cnr.it/EAGLES96/isle/ISLE_D14.2.zip. November 2003.

Carl, M. (2000) 'A Model of Competence for Corpus-based Machine Translation', in *Proceedings of COLING2000*, Vol. 2, Germany, http://acl.upenn.edu/C/C00/C00-2145.pdf. February 2003.

Carl, M., C. Pease, L.L. Iomdin and O. Streiter (2000) 'Towards a Dynamic Linkage of Example-based and Rule-based Machine Translation', *Machine Translation*, 16: 223–557.

Carl, M. and A. Way (eds) (2003a) *Recent Advances in Example-based Machine Translation: Text, Speech and Language Technology*, Vol. 21. Dordrecht: Kluwer Academic.

——(2003b) 'Introduction', *Recent Advances in Example-based Machine Translation: Text, Speech and Language Technology*, Vol. 21, M. Carl and A. Way (eds) (2003a). Dordrecht: Kluwer Academic: xvii–xxxi.

Catford, J.C. (1965) *A Linguistic Theory of Translation*. London: Oxford University Press.

Chellamuthu, K.C. (2002) 'Russian to Tamil Machine Translation System at TAMIL University', *Proceedings of INFITT2002*, California, http://www.infitt.org/ti2002/papers/16CHELLA.PDF. May 2003.

Chesterman, A. (2000) 'What Constitutes "Progress" in Translation Studies?', *Översättning och tolkning: Rapport från ASLA:s höstsymposium*, B.E. Dimitrova, (ed.). Uppsala: ASLA, http://www.helsinki.fi/~chesterm/2000cProgress.html. March 2003.

——(2003) 'Does Translation Theory Exist?', *Käätäjä*, 6(4): Finland, http://helsinki.fi/~chesterm/2003c.exist.html. January 2004.

Chesterman, A. and E. Wagner (2002) *Can Theory help Translators?*. Manchester: St Jerome Publishing.

Chomsky, N. (1957) *Syntactic Structures*. The Hague: Mouton.

——(1965) *Aspects of the Theory of Syntax*. Cambridge, Mass.: The MIT Press.

Church, K.W. and E.H. Hovy (1993) 'Good Applications for Crummy Machine Translation', *Machine Translation*, 8: 239–58.

Coulombe, C. (2001) *Hybrid Approaches in Machine Translation: From Craft to Linguistic Engineering*, http://www.federation-nlp.uqam.ca/publications/01/coulombe.pdf. January 2003.

Cronin, M. (2003) *Translation and Globalization*. London: Routledge.

Crystal, D. (1993) 3rd edn. reprint. *A Dictionary of Linguistics and Phonetics*. Oxford: Blackwell Publishers.

Dabbadie, M., W. Mustafa El Hadi and I. Timimi (2004) 'CESTA: The European Evaluation Campaign', *Multilingual Computing and Technology*, 65(15.5). http://www.multingual.com/. January 2005.

Delisle, J. and J. Woodsworth (1995) *Translators through History*. Amsterdam: John Benjamins.

Diz Gamallo, I. (2001) 'The importance of MT for the Survival of Minority Languages: Spanish–Galician MT System', *Proceedings of MT Summit VIII*, Spain, http://www.eamt.org/summitVIII/papers/diz.pdf. November 2002.

Doan-Nguyen, H. (2001) 'Generation of Vietnamese for French-Vietnamese and English-Vietnamese Machine Translation', *Proceedings of ACL2001-EWNLG*, France, 64–73.

Dori, D. (2003) 'The Visual Semantic Web: Unifying Human and Machine Semantic Web Representations with Object-process Methodology', *Proceedings of 1st International Workshop on Semantic Web and Databases*, Germany, http://www.cs. uic.edu/~ifc/SWDB/papers/Dori.pdf. March 2005.

Drakos, N. and R. Moore (2001) *Machine Translation Techniques*, S.H.S. Konecna Wong (translator), http://www.fi.muni.cz/usr/wong/teaching/mt/notes/. February 2003.

EAGLES (1996) *Evaluation of National Language Processing Systems: Final Report*, http://issco-www.unige.ch/projects/ewg96/index.html. May 2002.

Eisele, A. and D. Ziegler-Eisele (2002) 'Towards a Road Map on Human Language Technology: Natural Language Processing', *Proceedings of the MT Road Map Workshop (TMI2002)*, Japan, http://www.eamt.org/archive/tmi2002/workshop/ws06_eisele.pdf. June 2002.

Elliott, D., A. Hartley and E. Atwell (2003) 'Rationale for a Multilingual Corpus for Machine Translation Evaluation', *Proceedings of CL2003*, UK, http://www.leedsac.uk/eric/cl2003/ElliottHartleyAtwell.doc. October 2003.

Esselink, B. (1998) *A Practical Guide to Software Localization*. Amsterdam: John Benjamins.

——(2000) *A Practical Guide to Localization*. Amsterdam: John Benjamins.

——(2002) *The Differences between Localization and Translation*, http://www.languagesnto.org.uk/business/localization.htm. January 2003.

——(2003) 'Localisation and Translation', in *Computers and Translation: A Translator's Guide*, H.L. Somers (ed.) (2003a). Amsterdam: John Benjamins: 67–86.

Fawcett, P. (1997) *Translation and Language: Linguistic Theories Explained*. Manchester: St Jerome Publishing.

Finch, G. (2000) *Linguistic Terms and Concepts*. London: Macmillan Press.

Freigang, K-H. (2001) 'Teaching Theory and Tools', *Language International*, 13(4): 20–3.

Frankenberg-Garcia, A. and D. Santos (2003) 'Introducing COMPARA, the Portuguese–English Parallel Translation Corpus', in *Corpora in Translation Education*, F. Zanettin, S. Bernardini and D. Stewart (eds). Manchester: St Jerome Publishing: 71–87.

Gajer, M. (2002) 'The Implementation of the Example-based Machine Translation Technique on German to Polish Automatic Translation System', *INFORMATICA*, 13(4): 417–40.

Galinski, C. and G. Budin (1997) 'Terminology', in *Survey of the State of the Art in the Human Language Technology*, R. Cole, J. Mariani, H. Uszkoreit, A. Zaenen and V. Zue (eds). Cambridge: Cambridge University Press. 395–9.

Gamper, J. and P. Dongilli (1999) 'Primary Data Encoding of a Bilingual Corpus', *Proceedings of GLDV*, Germany, http://www.inf.unibz.it/~dongilli/papers/gldv-99.pdf. November 2004.

Gambier, Y. (ed.) (2003) *Screen Translation*, Special Issue of the Translator: 9(2) Manchester: St Jerome Publishing.

Gao, J.F., A. Wu, M. Li, C-N. Huang, H.Q. Li, X.S. Xia and H.W. Qin (2004) 'Adaptive Chinese Word Segmentation', *Proceedings of ACL2004*, Spain, http://research.microsoft.com/~jfgao/paper/acws.acl04.pdf. November 2004.

Gaspari, F. (2001) 'Teaching Machine Translation to Trainee Translators: A Survey of Their Knowledge and Opinions', *Proceedings of MT Summit VIII*, Spain, http://www.eamt.org/summitVIII/papers/gaspari.pdf. January 2003.

Gazdar, G., E.H. Klein, G.K. Pullum and I.A. Sag (1985) *Generalized Phrase Structure Grammar*. Oxford: Blackwell.

Gentzler, E. (1993) *Contemporary Translation Theories*. London: Routledge.

——(1997) 'Foreword', in *What is Translation? Centrifugal Theories, Critical Interventions*, D. Robinson (1997). Ohio: The Kent State University Press: ix–xxiii.

Gerasimov, A. (2002) 'Trados: Is it a must?', *Translation Journal*, 6(4), http://accurapid.com/journal/22trados.htm. April 2003.

Godwin-Jones, B. (2001) 'Emerging Technologies: Tools and Trends in Corpora use for Teaching and Learning', *Language Learning and Technology*, 55(3): 7–12.

Gómez-Pérez, A., M. Fernández-López and Ó. Corcho (2002) *OntoWeb: Technical Roadmap D.1.1.2*. Amsterdam: OntoWeb Consortium.

Goshawke, W., I.D. Kelly and J.D. Wigg (1987) *Computer Translation of Natural Language*. England: John Wiley & Sons.

Gough, N., A. Way and M. Hearne (2002) 'Example-based Machine Translation Via the Web', *Proceedings of AMTA-2002*, S.D. Richardson (ed.). New York: Springer: 75–83.

Graddol, D. (1998) 'What is the Future for Languages?', *The Linguist*, 37(5): 144–6.

Gross, A. (1992) 'Limitations of Computers as Translation Tools', in *Computers in Translation: A Practical Appraisal*, J. Newton (ed.) (1992a). London: Routledge: 96–130.

Hajic, J., J. Hric and V. Kubon (2000) 'Machine Translation of Very Close Language', *Proceedings of ANLP2000*, Washington, http://acl.ldc.upenn.edu/A/A00/A00–1002.pdf. May 2005.

Halliday, M.A.K. (2001) 'Towards a Theory of Good Translation', in *Exploring Translation and Multilingual Text Production: Beyond Context*, E. Steiner and C. Yallop (eds). Berlin: Mouton de Gruyter: 13–8.

Hartley, A. and C. Paris (2001) 'Translation, Controlled Languages, Generation', in *Exploring Translation and Multilingual Text Production: Beyond Context*, E. Steiner and C. Yallop (eds). Berlin: Mouton de Gruyter: 307–25.

Hatim, B. and I. Mason (1990) *Discourse and the Translator*. London: Longman.

Haynes, C. (1998) *Breaking Down the Language Barriers*. London: Aslib.

Holmes, J.S. (1988/2000) 'The Name and Nature of Translation Studies', in *The Translation Studies Reader* , L. Venuti (ed.) (2000). London: Routledge: 172–85.

Hovy, E., M. King and A. Popescu-Belis (2002a) 'An Introduction to Machine Translation Evaluation', in *Workbook of the LREC2002 Workshop on Machine Translation Evaluation: Human Evaluators meet Automated Metrics*, M. King (ed.). Spain: 1–7.

——(2002b) 'Principles of Context-based Machine Translation Evaluation', *Machine Translation*, 17: 43–75.

——(2002c) 'Computer-aided Specification of Quality Models for Machine Translation Evaluation', *Proceedings of LREC2002*, Spain, http://andreipb. free.fr/ textes/eh-mk-apb-lrec-02.pdf. November 2004.

Hunt, T. (2002) 'Translation Technology Failures and Future', *LISA Newsletter*, XI(4.6), At http://www.lisa.org/archive_domain/newsletters/2002/4.6/ring.html. January 2003.

Hutchins, W.J. (1979) 'Linguistic Models in Machine Translation', *UAE Papers in Linguistic*, 9: 29–52.

——(1994) 'Research Methods and System Designs in Machine Translation: A Ten-year Review, 1984–1994', *International Conference: Machine Translation: Ten Years On*, UK, http://ourworld.compuserve.com/homepages/WJHutchins/ Cranfld.htm. November 2002.

——(1995) 'Machine Translation: A Brief History', in *Concise History of the Language Sciences: From the Sumerians to the Cognitivists*, E.F.K. Koerner and R.E. Asher (eds). Oxford: Pergamon Press: 431–445.

——(2000a) 'The IAMT Certification Initiative and Defining Translation System Categories', *Proceedings of 5th EAMT Workshop*, Slovenia, http://ourworld. compuserve.com/hompages/WJHutchins/IAMTcert.html. April 2002.

——(ed.) (2000b) *Early Years in Machine Translation: Memoirs and Biographies of Pioneers*. Amsterdam: John Benjamins.

——(2003) 'Commercial Systems: The State of the Art', in *Computers and Translation: A Translator's Guide*, H.L. Somers (ed.) (2003a). Amsterdam: John Benjamins: 161–74.

Hutchins, W.J. and H.L. Somers (1992) *An Introduction to Machine Translation*. London: Academic Press Limited.

Hutchins, W.J., W. Hartmann and E. Ito (2004) *Compendium of Translation Software*, 8th edn, http://ourworld.compuserve.com/homepages/WJHutchins/. January 2004.

Internet World Stats (2004) *Internet Usage Statistics*, http://www.internetworldstats.com/ stats.htm. December 2004.

Jakobson, R. (1959/2000) 'On Linguistic Aspects of Translation', in *The Translation Studies Reader*, L. Venuti (ed.) (2000). London: Routledge: 113–18.

Janowski, W. (1998) 'CL14: Controlled languages: Risk and Side Effects', *TC-Forum*, 2–98, http://www.tc-forum.org/topiccl/cl14cont.htm. April 2003.

Jewtushenko, T. and P. Reynolds (2002) 'XLIFF: An XML Standard for Localization', *Proceedings of LREC2002*, Ireland, http://lrc.csis.ul.ie/publications/presenta- tions/2002/Conf/Presentations/xliff-lrc2002.ppt. July 2003.

Jones, D.A. and G.M. Rusk (2000) 'Towards a Scoring Function for Quality-driven Machine Translation', *Proceedings of COLING2000*, Vol. 1, Germany, http://acl/ upenn.edu/C/C00/C00-1055.pdf. February 2003.

Joshi, A.K., L. Levy and M. Takahashi (1975) 'Tree Adjunct Grammar', *Journal of Computer Systems and Sciences*, 136–63.

Jurafsky, D. and J.H. Martin (2000) *Speech and Language Processing: An Introduction to Natural Language Processing, Computational Linguistics and Speech Recognitions*, New Jersey: Prentice-Hall.

Kaji, H. (1999) 'Controlled Languages for Machine Translation: State of the Art', *Proceedings of MT Summit VII*, Singapore: 37–9.

Kaplan, R.M. and J. Bresnan (1982) 'Lexical-functional Grammar: A Formal System for Grammatical Representation', in *The Mental Representation of Grammatical Relations*, Cambridge, MA: The MIT Press: 173–281.

Kay, M. (1984) 'Functional Unification Grammar: A Formalism for Machine Translation', *Proceedings of COLING1984*, California, http://acl.ldc.upenn.edu/P/P84/P84-1018.pdf. February 2005.

Kenny, D. (1998) 'Corpora in Translation Studies', in *Routledge Encyclopedia of Translation Studies*, M. Baker (ed.). London: Routledge: 50–3.

King, M., A. Popescu-Belis and E. Hovy (2003) 'FEMTI: Creating and Using a Framework for MT Evaluation', *Proceedings of MT Summit IX*, Louisiana, http://www.amtaweb.org/summit/MTSummit/FinalPapers/37-King-final.pdf. November 2003.

Kit, C., H. Pan and J.J. Webster (2002) 'Example-based Machine Translation: A New Paradigm', in *Translation and Information Technology*, S.W. Chan (ed.). Hong Kong: Chinese University of Hong Kong: 57–78.

Koby, G.S. (2001) 'Editor's Introduction – Post-editing of Machine Translation Output: Who, What, Why, and How (much)', in *Repairing Texts: Empirical Investigations of Machine Translation Post-editing Processes*, H.P. Krings (2001) G.S. Koby, G.M. Shreve, K. Mischerikow and S. Litzer (translators). Ohio: The Kent State University Press: vii–x, 1–23.

Kosavisutte, K. (1996/2001) *Basic Concept of the Thai Language*, http://www.fedu.uec.ac.jp/ZzzThai/thailang/. May 2003.

Környei, T. (2000) 'Wordfisher for MS Word', *Translation Journal*, 4(1), http://accurapid.com/journal/11wf.htm. April 2003.

Krings, H.P. (2001) *Repairing Texts: Empirical Investigations of Machine Translation Post-editing Processes*, G.S. Koby, G.M. Shreve, K. Mischerikow and S. Litzer (translators). Ohio: The Kent State University Press.

Laurian, A-M. (1984) 'Machine Translation: What Type of Post-editing on What Type of Documents for What Type of Users', *Proceedings of COLING1984*, California, http://acl.ldc.upenn.edu/P/P84-1051pdf. January 2003.

Lefevere, A. (1996) 'Translation: Who is Doing What For/against Whom and Why?', *Translation Perspectives IX 1996: Translation Horizons Beyond the Boundaries of Translation Spectrum*, M.G. Rose (ed.). USA: State University of New York at Binghamton. 45–55.

Lehrberger, J. and L. Bourbeau (1988) *Machine Translation: Linguistic Characteristics of MT Systems and General Methodology of Evaluation*. Amsterdam: John Benjamins.

Lewis, D. (1992) 'Computers and Translation', in *Computers and Written Texts*, C.S. Butler (ed.). Oxford: Blackwell. 75–113.

Lin, C-Y. (1999) 'Machine Translation Information Access Across Language Barrier: The MuST System', *Proceedings of MT Summit VII*, Singapore: 308–16.

LISA (2002) *TBX: TermBase eXchange (TBX) Format: TBX Specification Draft 1j*, Oscar Group.

——(2003) *The Localisation Industry Primer*, 2nd edn. LISA.

Macklovitch, E. (1999) 'Regional Survey: M(A)T in North America', *Proceedings of MT Summit VII*, Singapore: 73–9.

——(2001) 'The New Paradigm in NLP and its Impact on Translation Automation', *Proceedings of the Symposium: The Impact of New Technology on Terminology Management, Canada*, http://www.onterm.gov.on.ca/ISO/docs/textMacklovitch. html. August 2003.

Macklovitch, E. and A.S. Valderrábanos (2001) 'Rethinking Interaction: The Solution for High-quality MT?', *Proceedings of MT Summit VIII*, Spain, http:// www.eamt.org/summitVIII/papers/valderrabanos.pdf. November 2002.

Mahsut, M., Y. Ogawa, K. Sugino and Y. Inagaki (2001) 'Utilizing Agglutinative Features Japanese-Uighur Machine Translation', *Proceedings of MT Summit VIII*, Spain, http://www.eamt.org/summitVIII/papers/mahsut.pdf. November 2002.

Malone, J.L. (1988) *The Science of Linguistics in the Art of Translation*, Albany. New York: State University of New York Press.

Mason, I. (1998) 'Communicative/Functional Approaches', in *Routledge Encyclopedia of Translation Studies*, M. Baker (ed.). London: Routledge: 30–3.

Mason, M. and J. Allen (2000) 'Human Language Technology Issues for Haitian Creole: A Minority Language', *ELSNEWS*, 10.1, http://www.geocities/ mtpostediting/elsnews101.htm. January 2004.

Matthiessen, C.M.I.M. (2001) 'The Environments of Translation', in *Exploring Translation and Multilingual Text Production: Beyond Context*, E. Steiner and C. Yallop (eds). Berlin: Mouton de Gruyter: 41–124.

McEnery, T., P. Baker and L. Burnard (2000) 'Corpus Resources and Minority Language Engineering', *Proceedings of LREC2000*, Greece, http://www. emille.lancs.ac.uk/reports/lrec2000.pdf. November 2004.

McKinsey, K. (2001) 'The Mother of All Tongues', *Far Eastern Economic Review*, http://pgoh.free.fr/mt.html. April 2002.

Melby, A. and C.T. Warner (1995) *The Possibility of Language: A Discussion of the Nature of Language with Implications for Human and Machine Translation*, Amsterdam: John Benjamins.

Moore, S. (2002) *Private Communication*, November 2002, Singapore.

Mossop, B. (2000) 'The Workplace Procedures of Professional Translators', in *Translation in Context: Selected Contributions from the EST Congress, Granada 1998*, A. Chesterman, N. Gallardo San Salvador and Y. Gambier (eds). Amsterdam: John Benjamins: 39–48.

Munday, J. (2001) *Introducing Translation Studies: Theories and Applications*. London: Routledge.

Mustafa El Hadi, W., M. Dabbadie, I. Timimi, M. Rajman, P. Langlais, A. Hartley and A. Popescu-Belis (2004) 'Work-in-progress Project Report: CESTA – Machine Translation Evaluation Campaign', *Proceedings of COLING2004*, Switzerland, http://www.ifi.unizh.ch/cl/yuste/lr4trans-2/WKS_PAPERS/2.pdf. December 2004.

Nagao, M. (1989) *Machine Translation: How Far Can It Go?*, N.D. Cook (translator), Oxford: Oxford University Press.

Neubert, A. (1996) 'Textlinguistics of Translation: The Textual Approach to Translation', in *Translation Perspectives IX 1996: Translation Horizons Beyond the Boundaries of Translation Spectrum*, M.G. Rose (ed.). USA: State University of New York at Binghamton: 87–106.

Newmark, P. (1981) *Approaches to Translation*, Oxford: Pergamon Press.
——(1988) *A Textbook of Translation*, London: Prentice-Hall.
——(1996) 'Looking at English Words in Translation', in *Words, Words, Words. The Translator and the Language Learner*, G. Anderman and M. Rogers (eds). Clevedon: Multilingual Matters. 56–62.
Newton, J. (ed.) (1992a) *Computers in Translation: A Practical Appraisal*. London: Routledge.
——(1992b) 'Introduction and Overview', in *Computers in Translation: A Practical Appraisal*, J. Newton (ed.), (1992a). London: Routledge: 1–13.
Nida, E.A. (1964) *Towards a Science of Translation*, Leiden: E.J. Brill.
——(1969) 'Science of Translation', *Language*, 45(3): 483–98.
——(1975) *Language Structure and Translation: Essays by Eugene A. Nida*, Selected and introduced by A.S. Dil. Stanford, California: Stanford University Press.
Nie, J-Y. (2003) 'Cross-language Information Retrieval', *IEEE Computational Intelligence Bulletin*, 2(1): 19–24.
Nirenburg, S. (1996) 'Bar-Hillel and Machine Translation: Then and Now', at http://crl.nmsu.edu/Publications/nirenburg/bar-hillel.html. August 2002.
Nirenburg, S., J. Carbonell, M. Tomita and K. Goodman (1992) *Machine Translation: A Knowledge-Based Approach*, San Mateo. California: Morgan Kaufmann Publishers.
Nirenburg, S., H.L. Somers and Y. Wilks (eds) (2003) *Readings in Machine Translation*. Cambridge, Mass.: MIT Press.
Noguiera, D. (2002) 'Translation Tools Today: A Personal View', *Translation Journal*, 6(1): http://accurapid.com/journal/19tm.htm. January 2003.
Nunberg, G. (1996) 'E-Babel', *Languages in Cyberspace*, http://infoweb.magi.com/~mfettes/es7.html#anchor%20babel. November 2002.
Nyberg, E., T. Mitamura and W-O. Huijsen (2003) 'Controlled Language for Authoring and Translation', in *Computers and Translation: A Translator's Guide*, H.L. Somers (ed.) (2003a). Amsterdam: John Benjamins: 245–81.
OASIS (2003) *XLIFF 1.1: A White Paper on Version 1.1 of the XML Localisation Interchange File Format*.
O'Hagan, M. and D. Ashworth (2002) *Translation-Mediated Communication in A Digital World: Facing the Challenges of Globalization and Localization*. Cleveden: Multilingual Matters.
Palmer, M. and T. Finin (1990) 'Workshop on the Evaluation of Natural Language Processing Systems', *Computational Linguistics*, 16(3): 175–81.
Papineni, K., S. Roukos, T. Ward and W-J. Zhu (2002) 'BLUE: A Method for Automatic Evaluation of Machine Translation', *Proceedings of ACL2002*. Pennsylvania, http://acl.ldc.upenn.edu/P/P02/P02-1040/pdf. September 2003.
Petrits, A. (2001) *EC Systran: The Commission's Machine Translation System*, European Commission Translation Service, http://europa.eu.int/comm/translation/reading/articles/pdf/2001_mt_mtfullen.pdf. September 2002.
Piperidis, S., H. Papageorgiou and S. Boutsis (2000) 'From Sentence to Words and Clauses', in *Parallel Text Processing: Alignment and Use of Translation Corpora*, J. Véronis (ed.) (2000a). Dordrecht: Kluwer Academic: 117–38.
Pollard, C. and I.A. Sag (1987). *Information-based Syntax and Semantics*. Stanford: CSLI.
Prasad, R. and A. Sarkar (2000) 'Comparing Test-suite Based Evaluation and Corpus-based Evaluation of a Wide-coverage Grammar for English', *Proceedings*

of LREC 2000 Satellite Workshop: Using Evaluation with HLT Programs: Result and Trends, Greece, http://www.sfu.ca/~anoop/papers/pdf/hlt-eval.pdf. November 2003.

Pugh, J. (1992) 'The Story so Far: An Evaluation of Machine Translation in the World Today', in *Computers in Translation: A Practical Appraisal*, J. Newton (ed.) (1992a). London: Routledge: 14–31.

Puntikov, N. (1999) 'MT and TM Technologies in Localization Industry: The Challenge of Integration', *Proceedings of MT Summit VII*. Singapore: 63–70.

Pym, A. (2004) *The Moving Text: Localization, Translation and Distribution.* Amsterdam: John Benjamins.

Quah, C.K., F. Bond and T. Yamazaki (2001) 'Design and Construction of a Machine-tractable Malay-English Lexicon', *Proceedings of ASIALEX2001*, Korea: 200–5.

Rajapurohit, B.B. (1994) 'Automatic Translation: Then and Now', in *Automatic Translation: Seminar Proceedings*, H. Basi (ed.). Thiruvananthapuram: DLA Publications.

Reeder, F. (2000) 'ISA or not ISA: The Interlingual Dilemma for Machine Translation', in *MITRE Technical Papers*: http://www.mitre.org/work/tech papers/tech_papers_00/reeder_isa/reeder_isa.pdf. January 2004.

Reiss. K. (1977/1989) 'Text Types, Translation Types and Translation Assessment', in *Readings in Translation Theory*, A. Chesterman (ed.) (1989). Helsinki: Finn Lectura: 105–15.

Riccardi, A. (ed.) (2002a) *Translation Studies: Perspectives on an Emerging Disciplines.* Cambridge: Cambridge University Press.

——(2002b) 'Introduction', in *Translation Studies: Perspectives on an Emerging Disciplines*, A. Riccardi (ed.) (2002a). Cambridge: Cambridge University Press: 1–9.

Rinsche, A. (1997) 'Terminology Systems and Translation Workbenches', *Proceedings Language Toolkit for Engineers in Business.* UK: 1–9.

Robichaud, B. and M-C. L'Homme (2003) 'Teaching the Automation of the Translation Process to Future Translators', *MT Summit IX: Proceedings of Workshop on Teaching Translation Technologies and Tools*, Louisiana, http://www.dlsi.ua.es/~mlf/t4/docum/proceedings.pdf. November 2003.

Robinson, D. (1997) *What is Translation? Centrifugal Theories, Critical Interventions*, Ohio: The Kent State University Press.

——(2003) *Performative Linguistics: Speaking and Translating as Doing Things with Words.* London: Routledge.

Rogers, M. (2005) 'Terminology, Term Banks and Termbases for Translation', in *Encyclopedia of Language and Linguistics*, 2nd edn. K. Brown (ed.). Oxford: Elsevier.

Sager, J.C. (1994) *Language Engineering and Translation: Consequences of Automation.* Amsterdam: John Benjamins.

Sato, S. and M. Nagao (1990) 'Toward Memory-based Translation', *Proceedings of COLING1990*, Finland. http://acl.ldc.upenn.edu/C/C90/C90-3044.pdf. November 2003.

Savory, T. (1968) *The Art of Translation.* London: Jonathan Cape Ltd.

Schadek, S. and T. Moses (2001) 'Machine Translation: An Introduction and Some History', *Language and Computers Seminar*, Germany: http:/www.uni-gessen. de/~ga1007/Language_and_Computers/machine_translation/machine_translation. ppt. March 2002.

Schäffner, C. (ed.) (2000) *Translation in the Global Village.* Clevedon: Multilingual Matters.

Schäler, R., A. Way and M. Carl (2003) 'EBMT in a Controlled Environment', in *Recent Advances in Example-based Machine Translation: Text, Speech and Language Technology,* Vol. 21, M. Carl and A. Way (eds) (2003a). Dordrecht: Kluwer Academic: 83–114.

Schmitz, K-D. (2001) 'Data Management Methods: Criteria for Evaluating Terminology Database Management Programs', in *Handbook of Terminology Management. Vol. 2: Application-Oriented Terminology Management,* S.E. Wright and G. Budin (eds). Amsterdam: John Benjamins: 536–50.

Schwarzl, A. (2001) *The (Im)possibility of Machine Translation.* Frankfurt am Main: Peter Lang.

Shreve, G.M. (2002) 'Translation Expertise and Expertise Studies', in *Translation Studies: Perspectives on an Emerging Disciplines,* A. Riccardi (ed.) (2002a). Cambridge: Cambridge University Press: 150–71.

Shuttleworth, M. and M. Cowie (1999) reprint. *Dictionary of Translation Studies.* Manchester: St Jerome Publishing.

Slocum, J. (1988) 'A Survey of Machine Translation: Its History, Current Status, and Future Prospects', in *Machine Translation Systems,* J. Slocum (ed.). Cambridge: Cambridge University Press: 1–40.

Smart Communications, Inc. (2005a) in *Demonstration of the MAXit Checker and Simplified English.* New York: Smart Communications, Inc.

——(2005b) *Controlled English for Global Documentation,* A White Paper. New York: Smart Communications, Inc.

——(2005c) 'Example of a Maintenance Procedure in Controlled English and Simplified Arabic'. New York: Smart Communications, Inc.

Snell-Hornby, M. (2000) 'Communicating in the Global Village: On Language, Translation and Cultural Identity', in *Translation in the Global Village,* C. Schäffner (ed.). Clevedon: Multilingual Matters: 103–20.

Somers, H.L. (1997) 'A Practical Approach Using Machine Translation Software: "Post-editing" the Source Text', *The Translator,* 3(2): 193–212.

——(1998a) 'Machine Translation: History', in *Routledge Encyclopedia of Translation Studies,* M. Baker (ed.). London: Routledge: 140–3.

——(1998b) 'Machine Translation: Methodology', in *Routledge Encyclopedia of Translation Studies,* M. Baker (ed.). London: Routledge: 143–9.

——(1998c) 'Language Resources and Minority Languages', *Language Today,* 5: 20–24.

——(ed.) (2003a) *Computers and Translation: A Translator's Guide.* Amsterdam: John Benjamins.

——(2003b) 'Introduction', in *Computers and Translation: A Translator's Guide,* H.L. Somers (ed.) (2003a). Amsterdam: John Benjamins: 1–11.

——(2003c) 'The Translator's Workstation', in *Computers and Translation: A Translator's Guide,* H.L. Somers (ed.) (2003a). Amsterdam: John Benjamins: 13–30.

——(2003d) 'Translation Technologies and Minority Languages', in *Computers and Translation: A Translator's Guide,* H.L. Somers (ed.) (2003a). Amsterdam: John Benjamins: 87–103.

——(2003e) 'Sublanguage', in *Computers and Translation: A Translator's Guide,* H.L. Somers (ed.) (2003a). Amsterdam: John Benjamins: 283–295.

——(2003f) 'An Overview of EBMT', in *Recent Advances in Example-based Machine Translation: Text, Speech and Language Technology*, Vol. 21, M. Carl and A. Way (eds) (2003a). Dordrecht: Kluwer Academic: 1–57.

——(2003g) 'Machine Translation', *Proceedings of ALTSS/ALTW*, Australia. http://alta.asn.au/events/altss_w2003 proc/courses/somers/somers.html. February 2005.

Sornleitlamvanich, V. (2002) *A Report of Workshop: Survey on Research and Development of Machine Translation in Asian Countries*, Thailand, http://www.jp.apan.net/meetings/020722-asia-broadband/REPORT-OF-MT_editeddoc. February 2003.

Sparck Jones, K. and J.R. Galliers (1996) *Evaluating Natural Language Processing: An Analysis and Review*. Berlin: Springer-Verlag.

Sprung, R.C. and A. Vourvoulias-Bush (2000) 'Adapting TIME Magazine for Latin America', in *Translating into Success: Cutting-edge Strategies for Going Multilingual in a Global Age*, R.C. Sprung (ed.). Amsterdam: John Benjamins: 13–27.

Steiner, E. and C. Yallop (eds) (2001) *Exploring Translation and Multilingual Text Production: Beyond Context*. Berlin: Mouton de Gruyter.

Streiter, O., M. Carl and L.L. Iomdin (2000) 'A Virtual Translation Machine for Hybrid Machine Translation', *Proceedings of the DIALOGUE2000: International Seminar in Computational Linguistics and Application*, Russia: http://www.iai.uni-sb.de/docs/sci00.pdf. February 2003.

Streiter, O. and E.W. De Luca (2003) 'Example-based NLP for Minority Languages: Tasks, Resources and Tools', in *TALN 2003 Workshop: Natural Language Processing of Minority Languages and Small Languages*, France, http://www.sciences.univ-nantes.fr/irin/taln2003/articles/streiter1.pdf. August 2003.

Sumita, E. and K. Imamura (2002) 'EBMT Tutorial', *Proceedings of TMI2002*. Japan: 1–50.

Swartz, A. and J. Hendler (2001) 'The Semantic Web: A Network of Content for the Digital City', *Proceedings of 2nd Annual Digital Cities Workshop*, Japan. http://blogspace.com/rdf/SwartzHendler. March 2005.

Tomás, J. and F. Casacuberta (2001) 'Monotone Statistical Translation Using Word Groups', *Proceedings of MT Summit VIII*, Spain, at http://www.eamt.org/summitVIII/papers/tomas.pdf. January 2003.

Tomás, J., J. Àngel Mas and F. Casacuberta (2003) 'A Qualitative Method for Machine Translation Evaluation', *Proceedings of EACL2003*, Hungary, http://www. dcs.shef.ac.uk/~katerina/EACL03-eval/eacl-doc/Tomas.pdf. February 2005.

Tong, L.C. (1994) 'Translation: Machine-aided', in *The Encyclopedia of Language and Linguistics*, Vol. 9, R.E. Asher and J.M.Y. Simpson (eds). Oxford: Pergamon Press: 4730–7.

Tribble, C. and G. Jones (1997) *Concordances in the Classroom: A Resource Guide for Teachers*, 2nd edn. Houston, Texas: Athelstan.

Trujillo, A. (1999) *Translation Engines: Techniques for Machine Translation*. London: Springer-Verlag.

Tsujii, J. (1991) 'Machine Translation and Machine-Aided Translation: What's Going On', in *Translating and the Computer 12*, C. Picken (ed.). London: Aslib: 3–24.

Turcato, D. and F. Popowich (2003) 'What is Example-based Machine Translation', in *Recent Advances in Example-based Machine Translation: Text, Speech and Language Technology*, Vol. 21, M. Carl and A. Way (eds) (2003a). Dordrecht: Kluwer Academic: 59–81.

Ulrych, M. (2002) 'An Evidence-based Approach to Translation', in *Translation Studies: Perspectives on an Emerging Disciplines*, A. Riccardi (ed.) (2002a). Cambridge: Cambridge University Press: 198–213.

Van Slype, G. (1979) *Critical Study of Methods for Evaluating the Quality of Machine Translation: Final Report*, http://www.issco.unige.ch/projects/isle/vanslype.pdf. November 2003.

Vasconcellos, M. (1995) 'Languages and Application Domains', in *Advanced Software Application in Japan*, E. Feigenbaum, M. Harrison, E. Rich and G. Wierhold (eds). New York: William Andrew Publishing: 371–6.

Vasconcellos, M. and D.A. Bostad (1992) 'Machine Translation in a High-Volume Translation Environment', in *Computers in Translation: A Practical Appraisal*, J. Newton (ed.) (1992a). London: Routledge: 58–77.

Venuti, L. (ed.) (2000) *The Translation Studies Reader*, London: Routledge.

Vermeer, H. (1996) *A Skopos Theory of Translation: Some Arguments For and Against*, Heidelberg: TEXTconTEXT – Verlag.

Vertan, C. (2004) 'Language Resources for the Semantic Web: Perspectives for Machine Translation', *Proceedings of LR4TransII at COLING2004*, Switzerland, http://www.ifi.unizh.ch/cl/yuste/lr4trans-2/WKS_PAPERS/4.pdf: March 2005.

Vertan, C. and W.V. Hahn (2003) 'Specifications and Evaluation of Machine Translation Toy System: Criteria for Laboratory Experiment', *MT Summit IX: Proceedings of Workshop on Teaching Translation Technologies and Tools*, Louisiana: http://www.dlsi.ua.es/~mlf/t4/docum/proceedings.pdf. May 2004.

Véronis, J. (ed.) (2000) in *Parallel Text Processing: Alignment and Use of Translation Corpora* Dordrecht: Kluwer Academic.

Vinay, J-P. and J. Darbelnet (1995) *Comparative Stylistics of French and English: A Methodology for Translation*, J.C. Sager and M-J. Hamel (translators). Amsterdam: John Benjamins.

Wassmer, T. (2000) 'Comparative Review of Four Localization Tools: Déjà Vu, Multilizer, MultiTrans and TRANS Suite 2000 and their Various Capabilities', in *Multilingual Computing and Technology*, 55(14.3), http://www.multingual.com/. April 2003.

——(2004) 'Review of Trados 6.5: New Version is More Than a Minor Update', *Multilingual Computing and Technology*, 61(15.1), http://www.multingual.com/. January 2005.

White, J.S. (2003) 'How to Evaluate Machine Translation', in *Computers and Translation: A Translator's Guide*, H.L. Somers (ed.) (2003a). Amsterdam: John Benjamins: 211–44.

Whitelock, P. and K. Kilby (1995) *Linguistic and Computational Techniques in Machine Translation System Design*, 2nd edn. London: University College London Press.

Whyman, E.K. and H.L. Somers (1999) 'Evaluation Metrics for a Translation Memory System', *Software-Practice and Experience*, 29(14): 1265–84.

Wilss, W. (1996) *Knowledge and Skills in Translator Behavior*. Amsterdam: John Benjamins.

——(1999) 'Interdisciplinarity in Translation Studies', *Target*, 11(1): 131–44.

Wojcik, R.H. and J.E. Hoard (1997) 'Controlled Languages in Industry', in *Survey of the State of the Art in the Human Language Technology*, R. Cole, J. Mariani, H. Uszkoreit, A. Zaenen and V. Zue (eds). Cambridge: Cambridge University Press: 238–9.

Wright, S.E. and G. Budin (compiler) (1997) *Handbook of Terminology Management.* Vol. 1, *Basic Aspects of Terminology Management.* Amsterdam: John Benjamins.
——(2001) *Handbook of Terminology Management.* Vol. 2, *Application-Oriented Terminology Management.* Amsterdam: John Benjamins.

Wu, J-C., K.C. Yeh, T.C. Chuang, W-C. Shei and J.S. Chang (2003) 'TotalRecall: A Bilingual Concordance for Computer-aided Translation and Language Learning', *The Companion Volume to the Proceedings of ACL2003*, Japan, http://acl.ldc.upenn.edu/P/P03/P03-2040.pdf. November 2004.

Yuste-Rodrigo, E. (2001) 'Making MT Commonplace in Translation Training Curricula – Too Many Misconceptions, so much Potential!' *Proceedings of MT Summit VIII*, Spain, http://www.eamt.org/summitVIII/papers/yuste-2.pdf. January 2003.

Yuste-Rodrigo, E. and F. Braun-Chen (2001) 'Comparative Evaluation of the Linguistic Output of MT Systems for Translation and Information Purposes', *Proceedings of MT Summit VIII*, Spain, http://www.eamt.org/summitVIII/papers/yuste-1.pdf. January 2003.

Zaharin Yusuf (1989) 'On Formalisms and Analysis, Generation and Synthesis in Machine Translation', *Proceedings of EACL1989*, UK, http://ucrel.lancs.ac.uk/acl/E/E89/E89-1042.pdf. February 2005.

Zerfass, A. (2002) 'Evaluation Translation Memory Systems', *Proceedings of LREC2002*, Spain, http://ifi.unizh.ch/cl/yuste/postworkshop/repository/azerfass.pdf. November 2003.

Zhang, Y., R.D. Brown and R.E. Frederking (2001) *Adapting an Example-based Translation System to Chinese*, http://hlt2001.org/papers/hlt2001-02.pdf. February 2003.

Zhou, Y., J. Qin, H. Chen and J.F. Nunamaker (2005) 'Multilingual Web Retrieval: An Experiment on a Multilingual Business International Portal', *Proceedings of HICSS'05*, Hawaii, http://csdl2.computer.org/comp/proceedings/hicss/2005/2268/01/22680043a.pdf. May 2005.

Index

abstract representations, 63, 71, 192
adequacy, 131, 141
algorithms, 78–9, 81, 83, 96, 100, 127,
   136, 138, 146, 173, 177, 186
aligned bilingual corpus, 77, 81, 83
aligned bilingual texts, 64
alignment, 93, 95, 100–1, 110–11, 184
ALPAC, 60–1, 129–30, 135–6
Applied Translation Studies, 37, 41–3

Bayes' rule, 78
Bayes' theorem, 76–7
black-box, 138–9, 142, 190
body, 29, 47, 121, 124, 126, 183

CESTA, 149–50
commercial machine translation
   systems, 3, 10–11, 19, 58, 62–3,
   87–9, 150, 153, 155, 157
commercial translation tools, 4, 13,
   101, 117–19, 157
computational linguistics, 57, 60, 63,
   107, 165
computer-aided translation, 1–4, 6–8,
   14, 18–19, 21, 36, 42, 63, 65, 83,
   9–4, 97, 113, 117, 120, 128–9,
   131–2, 140, 151–2, 156–8,
   172–6, 179–82, 184–8, 191,
   193, 196
computer science, 32, 37, 57, 63
concordancers, 42, 93, 106–7, 112–13,
   128, 174, 184–5, 194–5
constraint-based grammar, 32–4, 62
Controlled English, 49, 52–3
controlled language, 3, 11, 22, 26, 43,
   45–6, 48–9, 50, 52–3, 55, 89, 155,
   178–9, 181, 186
corpora, 38, 41, 64, 77, 80, 83, 91,
   107–8, 160, 163, 167–8,
   187, 192
corpus-based approaches, 62, 64, 66,
   76, 85, 91, 149, 156, 166, 177,
   191–2
corpus-based architectures, 66, 87
corpus-based machine translation
   systems, 69, 76, 84, 156, 187, 192
corpus linguistics, 111, 165

creative texts, 28, 66, 93, 183–4, 194
cryptographic techniques, 59
c-structure, 33–4

description, 26–7, 30, 32
Descriptive Translation Studies, 37–8
developers, 1, 19, 85–6, 89, 129–33,
   137–8, 140, 145–8, 188–9, 196
dictionaries, 5, 10, 13–14, 18, 32, 40,
   42, 66–7, 69–71, 74, 93, 105–7,
   123, 128, 149, 160, 163–4, 174,
   179, 183–5, 187, 192, 194–5
direct translation approach, 32, 39, 70,
   177, 192
direct translation systems, 69–70
dynamic equivalence, 24

EAGLES, 94, 132, 135, 142–4, 146, 149
evaluation, 2, 4, 41, 43, 129–51, 173,
   189–90
evaluation methodology, 130, 145–6
evaluation methods, 129–30, 135–7,
   140, 151, 173, 190
evaluators, 4, 135–7, 140, 146, 150, 196
example-based approaches, 62, 76, 81,
   83, 91, 177, 192
example-based machine translation
   systems, 81, 83–4, 167–9
experimental machine translation
   systems, 2–3, 11, 62, 85, 88, 133,
   150, 153, 160, 162
expressive texts, 40, 182

FEMTI, 142, 146–7, 149
fidelity, 130–1, 135–6, 139
filter, 93, 95, 98–9, 126
first-generation machine translation
   systems, 39, 69
formal approach, 31
formal grammars, 32, 177
formal linguistics, 31
formal versus dynamic, 24
formalisms, 3, 32, 35, 55
f-structure, 33–4
functional approaches, 25, 31
fuzzy matching, 95, 96, 97, 100,
   127, 132